TRIBAL PANORAMA OF NORTH EAST INDIA

TRIBAL PANORAMA OF NORTH EAST INDIA

Edited by

SARTHAK SENGUPTA

GYAN

Tribal Panorama of North East India

ISBN: 978-81-212-1153-6

Published in 2013 in India by
Gyan Publishing House
23, Main Ansari Road
New Delhi-110002
Phones : 23282060, 23261060
Fax : 011-23285914
E-mail: books@gyanbooks.com
Website: www.gyanbooks.com

Laser Typesetting : Quick Media, Delhi
Printed at : Chawla Offset Printers, Delhi

Dedicated
to the
sacred memory of
my eldest sister
Sandhya Sengupta

Contents

Preface

North East India, the erstwhile greater Assam, presently the rainbow land of seven sister states covers geo-political units namely the states of Arunachal Pradesh, Assam, Manipur, Meghalaya, Mizoram, Nagaland and Tripura and is located between latitude 22° and 29.5° North and longitude 89°46′ and 97°50′ East. The indigenous inhabitants of this region, who are mostly tribes who came from different directions at different historical times, are bewildering in their variety, ethnicity, culture and folklore. The area is endowed with rich resources of land, water, forests and minerals etc. and perched at the confluence of countries like Bhutan, China and Tibet in the north, Myanmar in the east and north and Bangladesh in the west. This region is connected with the rest of India by a narrow corridor towards west between Nepal and Bangladesh. Because of its geographical features, historical background, cultural heritage and ethnic composition North East India is regarded as a distinct geo-ethnic setting. In that sense states like Sikkim and the northern extreme of West Bengal can also be included in this region.

The northeast region of India together with Sikkim has an area of 2, 62,179 sq. km. having a hilly and wild topography and comprises about 7.90% landmass of India and is a biodiversity hotspot because of its floral and faunal diversity. It is also a cultural hotspot because of its astounding cultural and ethnic diversity. The whole of North East India consists of parts of five river basins – Brahmaputra, Barak-Surma-Meghna, Tizu, Manipur and Kaladan. The mighty river Brahmaputra flows from north east of this region to the west. The two sides of the Brahmaputra valley are covered by hills of varying altitudes except the Barak valley in the south western part and the Imphal valley of Manipur. The long and narrow Brahmaputra valley, which is about 500 km in length and 60 km in breadth, is the most expansive plain area which may conveniently be divided into three zones called Upper, Middle and Lower Assam.

The hills of the region are formed mainly by the ranges derived from the Eastern Himalayas. These hills are sparsely populated in comparison to the valleys. The average population density of the region is 150 (approx), which is much lower than the all-India average of 313. The literacy rate of the region is 68.50 percent and the urban population stands at 15.45 percent of the total population.

The North East India and more particularly the Brahmaputra valley is considered to be a meeting place of representatives of two major races of mankind—the Caucasoid and the Mongoloid. In many parts of this region people belonging to these two major races are living side by side since long back. At present, major part of the region has been occupied by different streams of the Mongoloid people who came from north and the east at different periods. The Australoids came to this region before the coming of the Mongoloids who partially or fully absorbed the Australoid strains. At present all the tribes of North East India are Mongoloid in origin, while the Caucasoid (Indid) group is formed by the Hindu castes and the Muslims. However, there are few populations belonging to the Mongoloid stock, which has not been recognized as tribes. The Koch, a populous detribalized caste population in Assam is also believed to be of Mongoloid origin. In recent years Australoid elements once again freshly penetrated to the composition of the people of North East India by various tribal groups who mainly migrated to Assam to work in the Tea Gardens as indentured labourers.

There is a rich assembly of cultures and communities in this rugged expanse of the eastern Himalayas. As told, there are upwards of 130 major tribal groups in North Eastern India, including the few inhabiting the plains areas. In other words, one third of the total number of listed tribes for the whole of India is to be found in this region.

It is estimated that out of approximately 38.8 million (precisely 38,875,769 persons) people living in North East India (including Sikkim), about 10.4 million (10,465,898 persons) of them are made up of tribal people of the hills and plains. The percentage of tribal population of this region is 26.93 as per 2001 census. The distribution of the tribals among the units of the region is not uniform. At present, in four of the seven states in North East India, the tribals are in majority.

Arunachal Pradesh which covers an area of about 83,600 sq. km. attained statehood from Union Territory status only in 1984, alone accounts for some twenty-five major tribal groups (Adi, Aka, Apatani, Bangni, Khamba, Khampti, Khowa, Memba, Miji, Hill Miri, Mishing, Monpa, Na, Nishi, Nishi, Nocte, Shedukpen, Sulung, Singpho, Tagin, Tangsa, Wancho, Yobin, Zakhring) and these constitute about 64.20% (705,158 persons) out of the total population of 1,097,968 persons. Arunachal Pradesh has recorded more females in the population with sex ratio of 1003.

Assam covers an area of about 78,000 sq. km and comprises of three distinct geographical regions, *viz.*, the Brahmaputra valley, the Barak valley and the hilly regions formed by the Mikir hills and North Cachar hills. The total population of Assam in 2001 Census has been 26,655,528 persons. Of them, 3,308,570 persons are Scheduled Tribe. Tribes living in the states of Assam are categorized into fourteen hill tribes (Chakma, Dimasa, Garo, Hajong, Hmar, Khasi, Kuki, Lakher, Man, Mizo, Mikir, Naga, Pawi, Synteng) and nine plains tribes (Barman, Boro, Deori, Hojai, Sonowal, Lalung, Mech, Mishing, Rabha) and the state accounted for merely 12.40% tribal population.

Manipur covers an area of about 22,350 sq. km and is the abode of twenty-nine tribal groups (Aimol, Anal, Angami, Chiru, Chothe, Gangte, Hmar, Kabui, Kacha Naga, Koirao, Koireng, Kom, Lamgang, Mao, Maram, Maring, Mizo, Monsang, Moyon, Paite, Ralte, Sema, Simte, Sahte, Tangkhul, Thadou, Vaiphei, Zou) which makes up approximately 34.20% (741,141 persons) out of the total population 2,166,788 persons.

Meghalaya covers an area of about 22,500 sq. km., came into being in 1972, is a tribal dominated (1,992,862 persons or 85.90% to the total population of 2,318,822 persons) state and noted for its three matriarchal tribal groups (Khasi, Garo and Jaintia) besides seventeen other notified Scheduled Tribes (Hajong, Rabha, Koch, Mikir, Kuki, Mizo/Lushai, Naga, Boro Kachari, Hmar, Man, Dimasa, Chakma, Pawi, Lakher etc).

Mizoram, the land of the Mizos which covers an area of about 21,000 sq. km was also born in 1972, is again dominated (94.50%

out of total population 888,573 persons) by the fourteen notified tribal communities (Chakma, Dimasa, Garo, Hajong, Hmar, Khasi, Kuki, Lakher, Man, Mizo, Karbi, Naga, Pawi).

Nagaland, which was made a separate state in 1963 covers an area of about 16, 572 sq. km where tribal population constitute more than 89.10% (out of the total population of 1,990,036 individuals) . As the name of the state implies, the Nagas are the dominating people of Nagaland. The word Naga is some sort of generic name for the sixteen distinctly recognized tribal groups (Ao, Angami, Chakhesang, Chang, Chiru, Khiemnungan, Konyak, Lotha, Makwari, Phom, Rengma, Sangtam, Sema, Tikhir, Yimchungre, Zeliang). Some other tribes like the Garo, Kachari, Kuki and Karbi in small numbers also live in Nagaland.

In Sikkim, the proportion of Scheduled Tribe is only 20.60% out of total population of 540,851 persons and Bhutia and Lepcha are two notified Scheduled Tribe.

Of all the states in North East India, Tripura is the smallest in size and covers an area of about 10, 500 sq. km, where Scheduled Tribe (993,426 individuals) constituted 31.10% of the total population of 3,199,203 persons. The state is the home of nineteen different Scheduled Tribes (Bhil, Bhutia, Chaimal, Chakma, Garo, Halam, Jamatia, Khasi, Kuki, Lepcha, Lushai, Magh, Munda, Noatia, Oraon, Riang, Santal, Tippera, Uchai).

In North East India, the tribal communities living in the valleys are predominantly depending on agriculture. Rice is the main crop cultivated by the people. Tribal people living in the hill areas of the region mainly practice *jhum* (shifting cultivation). A few small tribal communities living in the extremes of the north eastern parts of Arunachal Pradesh and eastern boundary of Nagaland carry on non-monetized exchange system.

The fair and festivals celebrated in the region have their roots in a varied number of faiths and beliefs, majority of which are celebrated with the flavor of brotherhood and harmony. Most of the festivals celebrated are springtime festivals, related to the cultivation or harvest. Fairs or the *melas* like *Junbeel mela, Ambubachi mela, Daranga mela* also have a theme of brotherhood and harmony among various communities and tribes.

Several languages belonging to different language families are spoken in North East India. More than 200 languages or mother tongues are spoken in the region. But some of these languages have less than 10,000 speakers and hence are not listed in the 114 Indian languages classified by the 1991 Census of India. Of the classified languages in the region, five languages, *viz,* Assamese, Bengali, Nepali, Manipuri (Meitei) and Bodo are scheduled languages. The first three belong to the Indo-Aryan and the last two belong to the Tibeto-Burmese linguistic family. Assamese is the mother tongue of the Assamese people and it is mainly confined to the Brahmaputra valley. The Mongoloid people of this region speak languages of different divisions and sub-divisions of the Sino-Tibetan linguistic family, which has been divided into two major branches, namely, Tibeto-Burman and Siamese-Chinese. The original language of the Ahom, Khampti, Tai-Phake, Khamiyang etc., of Assam belongs to the Tai sub-division. The Khasi groups of Meghalaya are affiliated to the Austro-Asiatic (Mon-Khmer) language family. The Khasi language has similarities on one hand with certain languages spoken in South East Asia and on the other with Munda language of central India. The Arunachal Tribes speak languages which belong to the North-Assam group of Tibeto-Burman linguistic division. Before the advent of the British, the Nagas belonging to different communities used to communicate with one another in *Nagamese* or broken Assamese which still in practice. We also find *Nefamese* as link language in Arunachal Pradesh. Similarly, among the tea garden workers in Assam, *Sadani* (*Cha Bagichar Asomiya*) has come up as the *lingua franca* between different groups.

The overwhelmingly majority of the people living in North East India are Hindus and constitute dominant population in Tripura, Assam and in Manipur. The Hindus account for 67.13 percent in Assam, 86.51 percent in Tripura, 68.47 percent in Sikkim, 57.65 percent in Manipur and 36.99 percent in Arunachal Pradesh. The second largest religious group is the Muslim which forms a sizable section mainly in Assam. The Muslims in Assam constitute 28.43 percent, in Tripura 7.29 percent and in Manipur 7.11 percent of the population. The Christian accounts for 87.44 percent in Nagaland, 85.65 percent in Mizoram, 64.56 percent in Meghalaya; and 34.14 percent in Manipur. A significant concentration of Buddhist is found in Arunachal Pradesh and Sikkim; in the former the Buddhists constitute 12.83 percent and in the latter 27.09 percent. The tribes of the region have their own traditional religious faith and are mainly concentrated in Arunachal Pradesh. Many tribal people of the plain region of Assam and also in Arunachal Pradesh have accepted Hinduism. Many others are Hinduised.

One of the conspicuous developments among many contemporary tribal population groups in North East India is ethnicity, which has its roots in the past and continuing throughout the history of North East India. The north eastern region, in fact, is too diverse a region and each state in the grip of insurgent politics has a distinct history and culture of its own. Apart from socio-economic and political factors, socio-historical and cultural factors have also been acting as strong propellants for these movements. While some of the movements have aimed at the creation of autonomous states within the Indian Union, some are aspiring to be included under VI Schedule; others have been demanding separation from the country. In most cases the Indian states have succeeded in accommodating the peoples' demands within the ambit of the Constitution. But, there are still certain organizations which have been able to solicit a large measure of support from the people, for their separatist agenda. Recently, several numerically small and politically weaker tribal communities in North East India have shown a predilection for identity shifts and creating new alliances or strengthening olden ties. There is considerable fluidity in the situation. In most of the cases efforts of changing identity depend upon the prevailing ethno-political situation. In Manipur, with regard to ethnic alignment, there are several cases of shift from the Kuki to the Naga axis in recent years. Thus, the discourse of ethnicity is at the moment triumphant in this remote part of our country.

This concise compilation contains a collection of fifteen thought-provoking scholarly articles contributed by a cross-section of eminent anthropologists and other social scientists having first-hand involvement with the study of the north eastern region of India and offer discrete metaphors of the economy, polity, social organization, demographic features, time-honoured institutions, bio-anthropological perspectives and several other aspects of the tribes of north eastern India, including Sikkim. The articles included in the treatise seek to break new ground in showing the colourful life-style of the tribal people of the region. Obviously, the present volume in no way can claim to have projected a thorough perspective of the multifarious tribal people of the region within its limited space. It touches upon only some important segments of the vast and varied area of the canvass.

My endeavor will be well rewarded if this compilation proves to be informative, stimulus and useful to anthropologists besides other social scientists; planners, policy makers and indeed anyone with a concern about the tribal people of north eastern India.

July, 2012 Sarthak Sengupta

Acknowledgements

Many individuals extended their cooperation and shared information for which I would like to express my utmost gratitude. I owe a deep debt of gratitude to all the contributors to this volume. Without their kind academic cooperation, it was impossible for me even to take up this project. I am really indebted to all of them. I also feel obliged to Prof. Sekh Rahim Mondal of North Bengal University for taking keen interest in the publication of this volume.

It has been possible for me to continue my academic pursuit because of the infrastructural facilities provided by the authorities of Dibrugarh University. I avail of this opportunity to express my thanks. I also wish to express my sincere thanks to Mrs. Neelanjana Barua who neatly typed the manuscript for press, to Dr. Mohendra Nath Dutta for his timely academic support and to all others who directly or indirectly helped me to finalise this volume.

I have no words to thank my wife Kaveeta, and sons – Sushruta and Samrat for their tolerance, encouragement and keeping my spirit high during weaker moments.

Finally, I would like to express my appreciation to Gyan Publishing House, New Delhi for honouring my proposal to publish the manuscript.

Sarthak Sengupta

List of Contributors

Dr Upala Barua, Department of Anthropology, Cotton College, Guwahati, Assam, 781 001

Dr Sarit Kumar Choudhuri, Department of Anthropology, Faculty of Tribal Studies, Rajib Gandhi University, Rono Hills, Doimukh, Itanagar, Arunachal Pradesh, 791 111

Dr Palash Chandra Coomar, Directorate of Census Operation, Kolkata, West Bengal

Dr Girindra Nath Das, District Research Officer, Diphu, Karbi Anglong, Assam

Dr Ksh.Vedmani Devi, Department of Anthropology, Manipur University, Canchipur, Imphal, Manipur, 795 003

Dr Gitimallika Gogoi, Department of Anthropology, N.L.B. City College, Dibrugarh, Assam, 786 003

Dr Rip Roshina Gowloog, Anthropological Survey of India, North East Regional Centre Mawblei, Shillong, Meghalaya, 793 021

Sultana Hazarika, Department of Zoology, D.H.S.K. College, Dibrugarh, Assam, 786 001

Prof. Romendra Khongsdier, Department of Anthropology, North Eastern Hill University, Umshing, Shillong, Meghalaya, 793 022

Dr Mayanglambam Mani Babu, Department of Anthropology, Manipur University, Canchipur, Imphal, Manipur, 795 003

Prof. Birinchi Kumar Medhi, Department of Anthropology, Gauhati University, Gopinath Bordoloi Nagar, Jalukbari, Guwahati, Assam, 781 014

Dr A.K. Nongkynrih, Department of Sociology, North Eastern Hill University, Umshing, Shillong, Meghalaya, 793 022

Dr M.K. Raha, Revati F/1, Neelachal Abasan, 98 Rajdanga Gold Park, Kolkata, West Bengal, 700 107

Dr Sankar Kumar Roy, Department of Anthropology, Gauhati University, Gopinath Bordoloi Nagar, Jalukbari, Guwahati, Assam, 781 014

Dr M. Sasi Kumar, Anthropological Survey of India, North East Regional Centre, Mawblei, Shillong, Meghalaya, 793 021

Dr S. Jibon Kumar Singh, Department of Anthropology, Manipur University, Canchipur, Imphal, Manipur, 795 003

Prof. K. Saratchandra Singh, Department of Anthropology, Manipur University, Canchipur, Imphal, Manipur, 795 003

Dr Arifur Zaman, Department of Anthropology, Dibrugarh University, Dibrugarh, Assam, 786 004

1

Mijis of Arunachal Pradesh—A Small Tribe in Transition

—*Sarit Kumar Chaudhuri*

The Mijis live in the valleys of the Pakesa and Bichom rivers which are placed in the middle belt of East and West Kameng districts of Arunachal Pradesh. The early records are silent about the existence of the Mijis either during the Ahom rule or the early period of British administration. They appeared for the first time in the administrative report of 1882-83 where they were described as Mijis, living to the north of the Akas. Mackenzie in his book, 'The North-East Frontier of Bengal' published in 1884, mentioned this tribe as 'a fierce and cognate race in the interior'.

The Mijis called themselves as Dhamai in Nafra Circle of West Kameng and Natmai in Lada Circle of East Kameng and at present more commonly known as Sajolang as such. In fact, there is no word as 'Miji' in their dialect. According to a legend, the name 'Miji' was first given to designate them by the Akas, their southern neighbours. In the remote past, the Akas exchanged their land for the habitation of the Sajolangs with fire and since then they used to call them as the Miji (Jha, 1994).

They are one of the small tribe of Arunachal Pradesh and according to 2001 Census, their population was only 5,721. The entire Miji belt is mountainous with deep gorge and covered with quite dense sub-tropical forest. The hilly area rendered inaccessibility and still remains one of the most backward area in terms of the indicators of development.

The only road, stretched 60 km., which connect Bomdila with Nafra Circle Headquarter, is mostly non-metalled and still this area remains completely isolated during rainy season. Even different villages of Nafra Circle as well as Lada Circle are yet to have any proper road. During fair weather a small Govt. bus occasionally runs between Bomdila and Nafra Headquarter. This is one of the vital hindrances blocking towards the progress of this Miji belt. Under Nafra Circle, at present 27 Miji villages are viz.: Janching, Challan, Karallang, Lapusa, Nizung, Khellong, Sanchipam, Upper Dzong, Lower Dzong, Nachingland, Saddle, Rurng, Ditchik, Dibbgin, Mathow, Bulu, Chinglang, Dishing, Dillung, Wathung, Dibrick, Silikpudung, Kabyang, Nazang, Nakhu, Nachibon and Nafra. Whereas, 20 Miji villages are there under Lada Circle viz.: Lada, Salang, Wabang-lang Nabolang, Orangjang, Wakke, Droksi, Rojo, Kojo, Jarkam, Sekong, Kampao, Ramda, Pio, Dongko, Sachung, Nissangjang, Wado, Pipiang and Besai.

This entire area is bounded by the Dafla hills to the East, Monpa area to the West, Tibet to the North and Aka hills to the South. They speak a language of their own which has a certain amount of similarity to that of the Akas though there is a slight dialectical variation between the Mijis staying in Nafra Circle and Lada Circle. Till date, there is no comprehensive work available portraying this small community as such except a few scrappy articles reflecting some of their traditional socio-cultural institutions.

Conceptual Framework

It is a well known fact that over a century, the tribal people of India are coming in contact with a large number of forces which have brought a series of changes in their overall socio-cultural life. Such forces may be perceived in terms of modernisation, industrialisation, communication, education, welfare programmes, new legislation and various reformative movements etc. It is true that forces of such change are working in a different mode and at different scales in Arunachal Pradesh due to its strategic location as well as politico-historical happenings which this State has experienced during its life span.

Unlike other backward areas of the country, Arunachal Pradesh which, till 1972, was known as NEFA has lately been integrated to the national economy. The economic backwardness of this State cannot be ascertained to have occurred due to market imperfections. Rather, it has been the cost of its long isolation from the network of market economy. As this State is the abode of numerous tribal communities, the tribal socio-economic basis has been continued even after independence. In fact, it is the State which has superimposed the forces of modernity upon the traditional socio-economic structure in Arunachal Pradesh. Moreover, the objective and the strategy of development in Arunachal Pradesh have greatly been influenced by a number of socio-economic factors, e.g., the strategic location of the State, peculiarities of tribal population, experience of the incidents of other areas of North East India etc. (Das, 1994).

As a result of the above drives, we find that in Arunachal Pradesh, the tribal people have been compelled to cast aside many of their traditional cultural traits and accepted many new elements through the various process of acculturation assimilation. Naturally, these has resulted modification at different magnitude and at the different levels of their lives depending on their proximity to above mentioned forces of changes. Eventually, within such a crucial transition phase, most of them are also retained or trying to retain various elements of their culture.

Considering the above scenario in the present chapter a preliminary attempt has been made to ascertain the nature of continuity and change in the socio-economic life of the Mijis placed in a comparatively backward and difficult terrain of Arunachal Pradesh.

Contemporary Scenario

Undoubtedly, land is their most valuable economic resource as agriculture constitutes the mainstay of this community though it is largely restricted to shifting hill cultivation depending upon the geomorphologic nature of land under their possession. Surrounding hilly forest is also playing a crucial multiple roles not only in their economic or material life but also in their sacred life. In brief, still their whole life is inseparable from forest. Whereas, water in the form of river or rivulets as an economic resource plays trivial role as they practice fishing in a limited scale.

As per their traditional notion, land can be classified into three categories. Village land, individual land and clan land. In fact the village land which is used for shifting cultivation is further sub-divided as per the various clans residing in a single village. Of course, this does not ensure that each and every clan will have their own land within the specified *jhum* land which comes under a specific village. However, they do not have any specific word to designate clan land as it is evident in case of village land (*Tsoubangnah*) or individual land (*Tsongdangnah)*. Generally demarcation of clan land is done on the basis of available huge pebbles, big tress or small streams etc. Whereas, in case of individual land it is done by constructing walls made of locally available stone flakes of different sizes. The hilly forest land which is absolutely kept for hunting along with collection of the fire woods comes under the possession of a village without any further division of clan or individual land. Any Miji of a particular village has a right to hunt in the forest which belongs to his village. Permanent individual land is not a common phenomena and it can be perceived as an extension of our concept of homestead land available in a close proximity of a particular household demarcated clearly from another such a piece of land. Naturally, communities as such do not have any proper or accurate idea regarding the total amount of land possessed by a Miji family.

Traditional norms for the land inheritance are strictly followed without any significant change. Females generally do not inherit landed property. Cases of land disputes involving different villages or clans or individuals are not rare. Obviously, it is the land coupled with cattle, mainly *Mithun,* which determine the economic strata as well as power structure of a Miji village. Some of the earlier writings mentioned that the Miji society is stratified into two groups. Within such a ladder of hierarchy, the group which is at the top is called *Nyubbu* and which is at the bottom are called *Nyullu.* But the present work reveals that there is another strata placed between these two recognised lairs which is known as *Kianlin.* In fact the third group *Nyullu* can be further sub-divided into two almost synonymous categories *Glaiw* and *Sulung.* If we look towards the material condition of the productive forces, then perhaps these groups or strata can be perceived in terms of the Marxian concept of 'Class' rather than Hinduised model of 'Caste' which depicts a different arrangement of socio-economic reality. More interestingly, each such class is represented by some specific clans, most of which are identified in the present study. It is clearly evident that the upper class (*Nyubbu*) holds the dominant share of the economic resources. Especially in terms of cultivable land, the lowest class (*Nyullu*) which includes *Glaiw / Sulung,* hardly posses anything. In fact, traditionally they were operating within the institutional framework of 'Slavery' and naturally dependent solely on their masters, mostly belonging to upper class and to some extent from the middle class also. So the incorporation of the Sulung which is a completely separate ethnic group within the wider canvas of Miji society is nothing unique as it was a common practice in some other major tribal groups of Arunachal Pradesh. Prevalence of such an institution in Arunachal Pradesh has its root within the history of evolution of social system of this region. However, like other areas, such institutional practice is gradually toning down though not effaced due to the imposition of legislative measures along with other exogenous forces of change penetrated within the Miji belt. Occupational mobility is just initiated but not in a very significant way as most of them is still dependent on shifting cultivation without any technological change towards the direction of 'Scientific

Jhuming'. Extremely poor literacy rate as an extension of implicit flaws which existing educational structure provides, not helped them in a meaningful way to unlock the doors of new economic opportunities. However, the involvement of monetary economy transformed their mode of economic transactions, through *Mithun* and other cattle or crops are still used in a very limited scale as a symbol of their traditional notion of barter transaction/economy. This is evident especially in a situation of economic hardship of a particular family.

Concept of 'hired labourer' is introduced though it is largely restricted within the village members only and the usual mode of payment to such hired labourers is Rs. 15.00 only irrespective of sexes. This rate is not strictly followed and varies depending on the nature of contract with the land owners and the labourers. The concept of 'share cropping' is not yet traced within the studied villages. Sulungs who take care of their master's land do not get any direct share of what they produce though a master remains responsible to look after his Sulung or *Glaiw* families including the whole expenditure required for the marriage of their offsprings.

Besides *Nyullu* class, sometimes a member of a middle class (*Kianlin*) also stays under the patronage of upper class mostly as an instrument of agricultural operation but they are not considered within the category of *Nyullu* as they remain free of any bondage and not handed down through trans-generational process.

Such a well defined social stratification had a great bearing on their value system which exemplified in the form of taboos, which prevented marriage between two different classes especially between upper and lower classes. But such a coercive cognition is gradually faded out and at present many cases are traceable to supplement such a statement. Even there are instances where marriage is taking place between the upper class Mijis and Sulungs. Besides marriage with the Akas which historically sanctioned, there are some examples of inter-community marriages for which the Miji society is not showing a great apathy rather they are expressing arguments which rationalises such an act of inter-community marriage. Similarly, traditional preference for marriage by negotiation is replaced to a great extent by marriage by mutual consent though other forms of marriage viz., marriage by elopement or marriage by exchange etc., are not totally wiped out. These are related with the poor economic status of the majority of Miji society as marriage by mutual consent can be settled or negotiated at the lowest level of bride price. It may be noteworthy to mention here that the whole concept of bride price are distinctly categorised depending upon the number of *Mithuns* along with some other socially valued items. More interestingly each such category are aptly equated or fixed with number of items consisting of different types of ornaments which should come from girls' side. Each such typical ornament has distinct nomenclature with high economic value and rotating within the Miji society through trans-generational process. And it becomes more difficult for girl's party to arrange or accumulate those different items of traditional pieces of ornaments rather than arranging bride price mostly comprises of cattle.

Polygamy is still in practice, but in a lower scale among the members of new generation. A Miji belongs to Upper Dzong village married for the six times out of which three wives are already divorced by him as per their socially sanctioned law. As per this law if a man seeks to divorce, then he has to return all the ornaments and other related articles received from girl's side whereas in just reverse situation bride price has to be returned. Such practice generally was limited within the economically better placed people. For example, quite aged *Gaonbura* of Lower Dzong village is still having two wives from Aka community though another wife had died long ago.

Rules of inheritance of movable property, mainly the ornaments rotate through female line. Status of unmarried women remained unchanged and as they are assumed as a burden of a Miji family and most of the time they had to find their way to eke out their subsistence.

The traditional notion of joint family system is gradually breaking down with the increasing trend towards the formation of neo-local families as it is evident in Lower Dzong village. As a sequel to it the son who is taking care of parents is getting slightly better share of his parental properties. In case of a sudden death of a man who was having more than one son, it is the responsibility of the *Gaonbura* to share property among the sons in consultation with the clan elders of that particular clan.

There is no significant departure from the various life cycle rituals which are associated, since the birth of a child, to the death of an individual in Miji society. These rituals are still performed at the house-hold level with the active association of their various priests. Still any unnatural death causes a great fear psychosis within the family which follows a different and elaborate process of burial rites performed by the priests, where family members of the deceased person hardly participate. However, the rituals associated with the death rites reveal that they are the strong believer of the concept of 'soul' and its rebirth.

In fact, religion still plays a very crucial role in their society. A careful observation of various elements, associated with their traditional house, symbolises how strongly the Mijis are associated with their indigenous religious beliefs and practices. However, due to their long historical contact with the surrounding Buddhist communities, some of the Miji villages under Nafra Circle are imbibing Buddhist religious elements, though they are practising their traditional religious beliefs and practices which can be conceived of within the category of 'Animism'. Christianity is yet to make its root into Nafra Circle but already penetrated through the Mijis of Lada Circle under East Kameng district. Symbolic celebration of *Loser*, one of the most famous festivals of the Monpas, and typical long flags with scripts are some of the imprints of the emerging Buddhist influence. Within the close proximity of Circle Office, two temples for Hindu God and Goddesses (*Shiva* and *Durga*) are constructed by the people those who came in order to serve various development agencies. Since the last five years, celebration of Durga worship started and the Mijis are also started enjoying it.

Apparently, there is no strong movement which can be termed as revivalist or reformative movement to put a check on the newly emerging religious terrain. But newly devised method of celebration of *Chindang* Festival, on community basis which is gradually assuming greater importance in Nafra Circle, may be conceived of as a significant and conscious move by some of the Miji elites to organise the mass for maintaining their cultural boundary. Basically, this is a village festival performed by different villages on different dates after the period of harvesting between 8th to 16th October of each year. But since last few years, people of Nafra Circle decided that 15th October would be the sacred day for this festival to be celebrated on community basis, though it is still celebrated in different villages as per their convenient days.

Another important festival of the Mijis is *Khan* Festival. For the long past this *Khan* was their most important festival and was being organised by the community as a whole. But now-a-days it has lost its importance, and is being celebrated by a few rich families of higher class, as it is too expensive to be performed by the poor families. During the festival, besides merry making, people used to perform sacrificial rites and offer prayer to various gods and goddesses for bumper harvest in the next harvesting season. They also used to apologies before *Jang Lang Noi* for killing various creatures in course of preparation of their fields for shifting cultivation, and pray for prosperity of the community. Performing *Khan* Worship at family level involves an elaborate ritual. In this ritual they pray to their family god *Sishangui* to ward-off evil spirits as well as to increase their cattle wealth which in turn will bring prosperity for that particular family.

So far as the traditional mechanism of social control is concerned, it has experienced a significant transformation on both the structural as well as functional level. Introduction of *Panchayat Raj* system erased their traditional notion of village chief (*Nanukhok*), who is replaced by *Gaonbura* (G.B), whose number depends upon the total population strength of a particular village. Usually one post of *Gaonbura* is fixed for 100 populations. And as a result of that there are some Miji villages within Nafra Circle, where 5 to 6 *Gaonburas* are acting on behalf of that particular village. This new administrative structure or approach is well defined with various stratified positions between a *Gaonbura* and Commissioner of a particular district. *Gram Panchayat* members are generally selected by the Mijis by raising hands, but in case of *Anchal Samity* members (A.S.M.) or other higher post up to *Zilla Parishad*, members (Z.P.M.) are elected by secret ballots. It is evident that most of such representatives, starting from *Gaonbura*, came from the upper class, including the present Member of the Legislative Assembly, who is also a Minister of the present State Government. In fact, traditional cognition of a leader along with emerging network of election mechanism hardly provide any scope for the Mijis who belong to the lowest strata of their social structure. Large numbers of villagers including both male and female Mijis are practising adult franchise in favour of an individual without much concern about the political party which that candidate represents. This is precisely due to the fact that the very notion of democratic political ideology is yet to strike significantly at the level of mass consciousness.

In case of solving inter village or intra village disputes, their customary law still plays the dominant role. Codification of such customary laws not yet took place, but in most of the cases, villages are now in favour of keeping written agreement as a valid document involving administrative head of a Circle, *Gaonbura* and some other important members who take part for an amicable solution. In order to trace or identify guilty person, they follow their age-old ordeal system involving their priests to take care of their supernatural devices. If both the parties involved in any disputes are failed to come out with an amicable solution as per their customary laws, then Circle Officer is empowered to refer that case to higher authority viz., Deputy Commissioner of West Kameng District, Bomdila. Settlement of such disputes at local level sometimes take even fifteen days depending on the nature of disputes or the nature of arguments in that. During final settlement of disputes, cash transaction in the form of fine is becoming the usual mode of payment rather than cattle which was prevalent earlier. Of course in some cases options are placed before a convicted person or a party to choose between the two modes of payment.

At present at least 10 Government agencies are working within the Nafra Circle with an aim to bring economic upliftment of the Mijis. Moreover, establishment of a privately owned chemical factory, to extract pine oil out of huge pine forest, helped a few villagers to earn a good amount of cash money as royalty. For instance, each and every household of Lower Dzong village received about 10,000 rupees in 1996 as a royalty from the Nafra Chemical Factory. Unfortunately, introduction of such easy cash money failed to bring any positive benefits. Except a few Mijis, most of the families were unable to make judicious use of that amount. And at the same time most of the villagers does not have any concept of savings. Naturally, whole amount is spent within a very limited period, not even a month in many cases, simply with food and modern drinks available in local market area. In a process, people are becoming less industrious with a greater inclination towards branded alcohols instead of indigenously prepared liquor and also creating a sense of apathy towards the shifting cultivation which involves hard labour.

Conclusions

Even though the Mijis or Sajolangs of Nafra Circle have remained partially isolated from the 'mainstream' due to its typical geographic terrain coupled with improper, communicable earth ways. They have, as a matter of fact, been exposed to the forces of 'development' and 'modernisation'. This exposure came about with greater post colonial administrative penetration and their long interaction with the neighbouring communities in the areas of trade and commerce. All these have collectively precipitated a process of gradual social change uneven and diffuse in character, which is taking place at various levels of their socio-economic structure as well as value-system.

Nevertheless, the important question is to understand the nature of the synthesis taking place between tradition and modernity in Miji society. Is it confliction or complementary?

Analysis of ethnographic reality does not speak of a very optimistic tread. Undoubtedly, traditionally stratified classes are uniquely operating within the existing model of change and the major share is taken by the people belonging to upper class (*Nyubbu*). As an extension of the same process, a powerful elite section is emerging where the lowest class (*Nyullu*) hardly finds any place. But at the same time it has resulted in a flexible social system by generating possibilities of mobility at socio-economic level. So the people belonging to the lowest class in some cases are having comparatively better ways of livelihood and even they are choosing their partner from superior classes which were strictly forbidden in earlier days.

Introduction of statutory *Panchayat* system or the formal administrative machinery enhanced their community solidarity by replacing frequent inter-community and intra-community feuds and bloodsheds. Though mechanism of social control still pivoted round the customary laws which are passing on though the trans generational process but gradually villagers are more inclined to keep a written document of a final agreement while settling a dispute at local level. Perhaps this may be an area where intermingling is going on in a comparatively balancing way. Even in the field of religion new horizon is cropping up instead of their dependence on traditional beliefs and practices.

It is true that through IRDP, ICDS and other schemes, some of the Mijis received some benefits, but as such induced development schemes are yet to make any significant impact on their life.

It may be noteworthy to mention here that in response to the existing backwardness as well as negligence, some of the Miji youths launched a movement for the creation of a separate 'Bichom district' which will benefit both Mijis and Akas (Chaudhuri, 2003). Even both these tribes are planning a common identity taking cue from their mythical common ancestry – may be termed as a quest for expansive identity. They organised many rallies and submitted memorandum to the Chief Minister of Arunachal Pradesh for the same.

Social change, whatever its degree is inevitable as the policy of isolation, is no more a viable proposition to address the tribal question in Arunachal Pradesh. Naturally the Mijis are also passing through a transitional phase which has resulted in both positive as well as negative impacts on their social structure and cultural system.

REFERENCES

Chakravarty, L.N., 1989, *Glimpses of the Early History of Arunachal Pradesh*, Directorate of Research, Itanagar.

Chaudhuri, S.K., 2002, "Marginalised in Our Own Homeland: Bichom Movement in Arunachal Pradesh". In Indira Barua, Sarthak Sengupta and D. Dutta Das (Eds): *Ethnic Groups, Cultural Continuities and Social Change in North East India*. Mittal Publications, New Delhi.

Das, G., 1994, "The Strategy of Development Planning in Arunachal Pradesh Since Independence". *Resarun*, 20, pp. 1 - 2: 1

Jha, B.N., 1994, "The Religion and Festivals of the Sajolangs: Continuity and Change". *Resarun*, 20, pp. 1 - 2: 61

Mackenzie, A., 1884, *History of the Relations of the Government with the Hill Tribes of North East Frontier of Bengal*, Calcutta.

2

The Sherpa of Sikkim and Their Land

—Palash Chandra Coomar and *M.K. Raha*

Every human society, particularly those which have agro-based economy, considers land as the most important immovable asset. Their economy depends on land. All their socio-cultural activities revolve round their land. All their customs, manners, world view, folklore etc. are intimately inter-woven with their agricultural activities. Their social ceremonies and religious worships and festivities, have some concern with their land and agricultural activities. Even those who do not have land to cultivate or marginal landowners directly or indirectly depend on land and agriculture like the share-croppers or agricultural labourers, also have their socio-cultural life connected with land. The Sherpa of Sikkim is not an exception. They have very intimate relation with their land, though no doubt they have other occupations too. Their life revolves round the land. They mainly maintain themselves and their families by means of their agricultural productions. As they survive mainly on their agricultural productions, so obviously they have a very soft corner for their land.

The Eastern Himalayan State of Sikkim, according to 2001 Census, has a total population of 5, 40,851 of which 2, 88,484 are males and 2, 52,376 females. The sex-ratio of this State is only 875 females per 1000 males. The literacy rate is 69.68% for the population in general, the males having 76.73% and the female 61.46% literacy. Here in this State 49.91% of the total populations are cultivators, 6.43% are agricultural labourers, 1.23% is household industry workers and 42.42%

are 'other workers'. As cultivators and as agricultural labourers, the females (62.93% and 8.55% respectively) surpass male cultivators and agricultural labourers (42.27% and 5.19% respectively). On the other hand, as household industry workers and as 'other workers', the males (1.38% and 51.16% respectively) have overshadowed the female household industry workers and 'other workers' (0.99% and 27.53% respectively).

The total population of Sikkim (5, 40,851) also includes a total of 1, 11,405 Scheduled Tribe population according to 2001 Census. Of these Scheduled Tribe populations, 56,940 are males and 54,465 females. This Himalayan State also has a Scheduled Caste population of 27,165 with 13,807 males and 13,358 females (Census of India 2001; India, Final Population Totals, Series-I).

In Sikkim, the Sherpas are considered as a Scheduled Tribes. They are included in the broad category, 'The Bhotia'. In fact, the Bhotia is a generic term for a group of tribes (Raha, 2005). The tribes which are included under the Bhotia, along with the Sherpas are the Dukpa and the Kagatay, and of course the Bhotia.

The Sherpas are mostly found in Sikkim and Darjeeling District of West Bengal. But their main concentration is in Nepal. As the Sherpa, Kagatay and the Dukpa are included in the Bhotia category, so the Census authority did not enumerate these tribes separately but they have enumerated with the Bhotia in general. So, separate figures of the Sherpa population are not available. However according to 1991 Census the Bhotias population in Sikkim were 59,449. According to 1981 Census, there were 48,664 Bhotias in Sikkim. In this case also the Bhotia population covered the Sherpas, Dukpas and the Kagatays. Of these populations, 25,373 (52.14%) were males and 23,292 (47.86%) females. Most of the Bhotia population (81.81%) according to 1981 Census used to live in the rural areas. The remaining 18.69% only lived in urban centers. The Bhotias were according to the same Census, mostly illiterate

(69.72%). In rural areas 59.04% Bhotia males and 81.29% Bhotia females were illiterate. Though the literacy rate of the Bhotias dwelling in the urban centers was a little higher than that of the Bhotias of the rural areas, still it is not that significantly high. Only 42.63% Bhotia, inhabiting urban centers, were literates. Of these literate Bhotia population 45.19% males and 40.35% females were literates according to 1981 Census.

In Sikkim the Sherpas as also all other tribes of the Bhotia groups, are Mongoloid and speak Sherpali language with their own community people (Coomar and Raha, 1997). But often they use Nepali language as the medium of communication with the Nepali people and also use Nepali script while writing (Raha and Coomar, 2001). They use Hindi when they talk to non-Bhotia, non-Nepali people. Some of them also know Bhotia and a few of them can speak English.

In Sikkim the Sherpa live in an endogamous society. According to the rule of endogamy, they are not supposed to marry outside their community. They used to follow this rule strictly in the past. But some relaxation of this rule of endogamy is noticed in recent years. Due to their close contact with the members of other neighbouring communities, the Sherpas have now started entering into marital alliance with the non-Sherpas also (Coomar and Raha. 1999).

In Sikkim the Sherpa society is divided into a number of exogamous clans, called *thar* or *ru*. Marriage within ones own *thar* or *ru* is strictly prohibited. Such marriage is considered as incestuous and heinous sin. The *thar* or *ru* do not have any status differentiation. The Sharpas consider all *thar* or *ru* as having equal status. The families of the Sharpas are patrilineal and patri-kin oriented. Residence after marriage is either patrilocal or neolocal. Monogamy is the societal norm.

Basically, as the Sherpas of Sikkim are agriculturists and also horticulturists. Generally, the landless and the marginal land-owners work as agricultural labourers (Commar and Raha, 1999). But some of the Sherpas, particularly those who live in urban centers, remain engaged with other jobs such as service, business, teachings, or act as professionals etc.

In Sikkim almost all Sherpas are Buddhists. According to 1981 Census, 98.21% of the Bhotia who also include the Sherpa along with the Kagatay and the Dukpa, were Buddhists. They perform various rituals, religious festivals, worship etc. besides meditation and prayer. Turning of prayer wheels and circumambulation of *gompa* and *chorten* etc. are also part of their religious functions (Raha and Coomar, 2001).

The land tenure system which Sherpas follow is somewhat different from the land tenure system prevalent among the other groups of other areas. The Sherpa land-owners often lease out whole or part of their cultivable lands to the tenants for the cultivation of different types of crops on different terms and conditions. The different systems which they follow are as follows:

Adhiya : In this type of land tenure system, the Sherpa land-owners let out part or whole of their cultivable land to one or more tenants on the condition that tiller of the soil will give 50.00% share of the yields of the land-owner's cultivable land to the land-owner after the harvest is over. The entire expenditure for the cultivation of the crop will be incurred by the share-cropper(s). The expenditure includes the procurement of the seeds of the crop, manure, insecticides, etc. For the purpose of different types of agricultural operations i.e., ploughing, manuring, harrowing, weeding, spray of insecticide and finally harvest, share-cropper has to arrange different agricultural implements, cattle for agriculture and also the agricultural labourers if required. The land-owner pays only the land revenue to the Government. The *Adhiya* type of land tenure system is generally applicable for the cultivation of crops like maize, millet, and potato.

If the cultivable land has low fertility and the production of the crop is comparatively less, the share-cropper pays only 25.00% share of the cultivated crops to the land-owner after harvest. It is a mutual arrangement between the land-owner and the share-cropper as the expenditure for the cultivation is borne by the share-cropper. The share-cropper keeps 75.00%

cultivated crop for own consumption. Generally, in the initial year of harvest of large cardamom (3rd year or 4th year) they follow this type of share-cropping system. In the initial year, the production of the large cardamom is comparatively less, but the expenditure for the cultivation remains the same.

Kud: In this type of tenure system, the land-owner makes a contract with the share-cropper, known as *Kudhiya*. Under this contract, the *Kudhiya* pays a certain amount of cultivated crop or equivalent money to the land-owner. The amount depends on the fertility of the soil and the location of the land. But parties (land-owner and share-cropper) mutually decide the amount of the crop or the money to be given to the land-owner. In case of *Kud*, the *Kudhiya* incurs the entire expenditure of the cultivation. The land-owner pays only the land revenue to the Government.

For all the above-mentioned share-cropping systems, the land-owner and the share-cropper make fresh contact every year.

Owner-Cultivator: In this type of land tenure system, the owner of the agricultural land himself cultivates his/her own land. For the smooth completion of different types of agricultural operations, the land-owner either engages his/her own family members or hires *Khethala* (agricultural labour). For the purpose of cultivation, the land-owner also arranges seeds, manure, agricultural implements, bullocks etc.

In Sikkim there are two types of land, hilly land and plain land. In this state the entire area of land has been classified into three broad categories *viz*. Circle-A, Circle-B and Circle-C. In Circle-A category the entire land is the plain land and is situated in the valley area between two hills. Circle-B type land includes the mixture of plain and the hilly land. But Circle-C covers that area of land, the maximum of which, is situated in the hilly areas. Land covered by Circle-A category is normally double crop land. Twice production in a year is also possible in the other two types of land. As the fertility of these two types of land is less, so they do not utilise these types of land for double crop. The quality of different categories of land differs and so does the fertility of land. Each of these three types of land is again sub-divided into three sub-categories according to the altitude of the land. Lands situated in the altitude up to 2500 feet above mean sea level, are categorised as No. I, lands situated between 2501 and 3500 feet above mean sea level are categorised as No. II. The category of No. III lands are situated between the altitude of 3501 feet and above. Fertility of the lands varies according to the altitude of the lands. Lands in the category No. I are more fertile than the lands of the category No. II or No. III. As the production of large cardamom depends on the fertility of the different categories of lands so the yield varies as follows:

Different Types of lands	Fertility
Lands of category No. I	13 Munds per Hectare
Lands of category No. II	8 Munds per Hectare
Lands of category No. III	5 Munds per Hectare
Lands of category No. IV	2 Munds per Hectare

Besides these above-mentioned types of lands, in Sikkim land has also been classified on the basis of the availability of irrigation facility and composition of the soil. Accordingly, land here is classified into four types, viz. (1) Wet field, (2) Dry field (3) *Banjo* field and (4) Large cardamom field.

Wet Field: In this type of land, irrigational facility is available with the help of small canals. As irrigational facility exists in this type of land; therefore two crops a year are possible in this type of land. Generally, this type of land is utilised for paddy cultivation.

Dry field: In this type of land, irrigational facility is not available. The land-owner of this type of land depends entirely on rain water for the cultivation. Maize, millet, potato etc. are produced in this type of land. Production of different types of crops is comparatively less in the dry field than that of the wet field.

Cardamom field: The land which is utilised for large cardamom cultivation is classified as cardamom field. Irrigational facility is not available in this type of field. Cardamom field is not classified on the basis of Circle class. Cardamom field is categorised into four types according to the altitude and fertility of the land. *i.e:* No. I., No. II., No. III., and No. IV.

Banjo field: The rocky land is considered as the *Banjo* field. Cultivation of all kinds of crop is not possible in the *Banjo* field. This type of land is mainly utilised for the growth of fuel wood and cattle fodder, bamboo grove etc.

Khas Mahal: Khas Mahal is Government owned land. All the reserve forests are situated in this type of land. In the reserve forests, different types of trees for the purpose of furniture, house building, fuel wood, bamboo groves, *pareng* groves etc. are grown. *Mane* (grave yard) is also situated in this type of land.

Different types of lands have different rates. Of the different types of lands, cardamom field has the highest economic value, as the large cardamom is the main cash crop of the people of Sikkim State. Likewise, as no crop is produced in the *Banjo* field, so the people can not earn any profit from this type of field. For this reason, the *Banjo* field has the lowest economic value. Government rates of different types of land are given below:

Kind of Land	*Circle – A*	*Circle – B*	*Circle – C*
Cardamom Field	*75,000/-*	*70,000/-*	*62,500/-*

Kind of Lands	*Class of Lands*	*Different Circles of Lands*		
		Circle – A	*Circle – B*	*Circle – C*
1	2	3	4	5
Paddy Field	I	Rs. 69,160/- per Hectare	Rs. 64,220/-	Rs. 59,280/- per Hectare
		Rs. 28,000/- per Hectare	Rs. 26,000/-	Rs. 24,000/- per Hectare

1	2	3	4	5
	II	Rs. 63,232/- per Hectare	Rs. 59,280/-	Rs. 54,340/- per Hectare
		Rs. 25,600/- per Hectare	Rs. 24,000/-	Rs. 22,000/- per Hectare
	III	Rs. 54,340/- per Hectare	Rs. 51,870/-	Rs. 49,400/- per Hectare
		Rs. 22,000/- per Hectare	Rs. 21,000/-	Rs. 20,000/- per Hectare
Wet Land	I	Rs. 48,906/- per Hectare	Rs. 44,460/-	Rs. 39,520/- per Hectare
Dry Field		Rs. 19,800/- per Hectare	Rs. 18,000/-	Rs. 16,000/- per Hectare
	II	Rs. 44,460/- per Hectare	Rs. 39,520/-	Rs. 37,050/- per Hectare
		Rs. 18,000/- per Hectare	Rs. 16,000/-	Rs. 15,000/- per Hectare
	III	Rs. 39,520/- per Hectare	Rs. 37,050/-	Rs. 29,640/- per Hectare
		Rs. 16,800/- per Hectare	Rs. 15,000/-	Rs. 12,000/- per Hectare
Banjo Field		Rs. 34,580/- per Hectare	Rs. 32,110/-	Rs. 29,640/- per Hectare
(No. Class)		Rs. 14,000/- per Hectare	Rs. 13,000/-	Rs. 12,000/- per Hectare
Cardamom Field	I	Rs. 74,100/- per Hectare		
		Rs. 30,000/- per Hectare		
(No. Circle Class)	II	Rs. 69,160/- per Hectare		
		Rs. 28,000/- per Hectare		
	III	Rs. 61,750/- per Hectare		
		Rs. 25,000/- per Hectare		
	IV	Rs. 51,870/- per Hectare		
		Rs. 21,000/- per Hectare		

Source: Land Revenue Department, Govt. of Sikkim, vide Notification No. 22/LR(S), dated 20.11.1990.

This rate is applicable to Government purchase. But in case of a person or a private body i.e. Monastery Committee, the rate depends on the negotiation between the seller and the buyer. The rates varies according to the location of the land, whether the land is situated near road side, or near the market place, the lands which have good communication facility etc. generally have the higher rate than other lands. The lands which have big trees also have a higher rate due to the economic value of the trees. The lands where big boulders are lying obviously have lower rate because of the presence of big boulders in fields. These create difficulty in the agricultural operations. The rate of the land also varies according to the altitude of the land. The lands situated in higher altitude have comparatively lower rate than the lower altitude land. In the high altitude land snowfall causes the damage of crops during winter season. As the lower attitude lands do not experience snowfall so these have a higher rate of production.

The entire Bakim block, our studied area, falls under the category of Circle-C of No.-III class. People here acquire land, mainly by two ways i.e. either through inheritance or by self acquisition. Generally, the sons inherit the land of their father. All the sons get the equal share of their father's land. If a person has no son, in that case the daughter/daughters inherit her/their father's land. In certain cases, father during his life time, may distribute part or whole of his landed property equally among his sons. But in case, a person during his life time does not part with his land, then after his death his sons divide their father's landed property equally, and each son takes a part of the land. Now-a-days, all the offsprings apply for succession certificate to the Sub-Divisional Magistrate mentioning that they are the only legal successors of their father. After verification by the Government officials, succession certificate is given. On receipt of the succession certificate, all the legal owners hand-over the deed of the land along with the succession certificate to the office of Sub-Divisional Magistrate for the transfer of ownership of land from their late father's name to their names. Sometimes without proper registration of the land in their names, they cultivate their father's land. When an individual distributes his landed property, during his life time, among his offsprings, he demarcates the portion of his land in the name of each of his sons and daughters. Then he applies to the sub-Registrar of the Sub-Divisional Magistrate for the transfer of ownership of a particular plot of land in the name of a particular son or daughter. In case of self-acquisition of land, they purchase the land from others. The rate of the land is mutually decided by both the seller and the buyer depending on the location and the quality of the land. The owner of the land requires to apply to the Sub-Divisional Magistrate mentioning that he/she wants to sell his/her land to the buyer. After getting the application, the office of the Sub-Divisional Magistrate sends the case to the *Gram Panchayat* and V.L.O. for proper verification. The *Gram Panchayat* and V.L.O. verify whether the land in question is under mortgage, or whether the land has any litigation. The ownership of land is verified by the owner of land, situated on the boundary of that particular land. So to sell a plot of land, signature of boundary land owners is necessary. If the verification reports of *Gram Panchayat* and VLO are satisfactory, then the Sub-Divisional Magistrate gives the permission for the transfer of ownership of the land. Both parties make a sale-deed mentioning the sale value, area of land, boundary of the land, etc. Signature of both parties is required in the sale deed. At the time of preparing any sale deed, they pay stamp duty to the Government, which is Rs. 5/- per Rs. 1000/- of sale value. So if a person purchases a plot of land say, at a valuation of Rs. 50,000/-, he/she has to pay a stamp duty of Rs. 250/-. Those who are landless, they can apply to the Government for the allotment of land. The Government after proper investigation and verification allots the vested land to the landless after getting the recommendation of *Gram Panchayat*.

Large cardamom is the main crop among the Sherpas of Sikkim. Apart from large cardamom, they also cultivate potato, maize, millet, and different other types of vegetables. For the cultivation of these crops, they depend on the local varieties of seeds. To increase the fertility, they use organic manure and to protect the crops from any type of diseases they also use pesticides. For the investment in cultivation, the Sherpa of Sikkim take cash loan under different schemes, either from the Bank or from Government. In case of Bank loan they pay interest, but if it is from Government, it is, in certain cases, interest free. The loans/credits are given through different schemes. For the re-plantation of large cardamom and cultivation of large cardamom, they take 'Agricultural Term Loan—Long term loan'. If the scheme is sponsored by the Government, they get 50.00% subsidy of the loan amount. But if the scheme is sponsored by the Bank, there is no subsidy. In both cases they repay the loan amount after three years but within the six years from the date of taking the loan.

The Sherpas of Sikkim generally do not employ any modern know-how in the cultivation of different types of crops. For the purpose of cultivation, they follow their age-old plough cultivation and use their traditional agricultural implements. They do not use tractor, mechanised tilling machine or husking machine. Even for the purpose of bumper production, majority of them do not use any chemical fertiliser. Only a very few Sherpas of Darjeeling district, particularly, those who are economically well off and well informed, use chemical fertiliser like urea, at the time of potato cultivation. For higher production of the crops, majority of them depend on organic manure like cow dung, ash of fuel wood etc. If the crops affected by any kind of diseases, they use different types of pesticides according to the needs. On enquiry about how long they were using these chemical pesticides, the informants told that they started using these pesticides since thirty to forty years.

For ginger cultivation, they avail themselves of the facility of 'Agricultural Cash Credit – Short term loan'. Like the Agricultural Term loan, if it is the Government scheme, then they get 50.00% subsidy on the loan amount but in case it is the Bank Scheme, they do not get any subsidy. The rate of interest and the eligibility condition of the loan receiver is also the same like that of the 'Agricultural Term Loan'. In this scheme they will repay the amount within one year from the date of the receipt of the loan amount.

Besides these schemes, they also avail themselves of the loan facility for the cultivation of large cardamom, ginger, establishment of piggery and goat firm, purchase of bullock for the purpose of cultivation under the 'Integrated Rural Development Project' (I.R.D.P.). These schemes have been prepared either by the Sikkim Rural Development Agency (S.R.D.A.) or by the District Rural Development Agency. From the I.R.D.P. Scheme as sponsored by the Sikkim State Government, they get 30.00% subsidy on the loan amount. But if the scheme is sponsored by the Central Government, they get 50.00% subsidy. In case of the Central Government sponsored schemes of the total subsidy amount, 50.00% subsidy is borne by the Sikkim Government and the rest 50.00% is borne by the Central Government. In this Scheme the entire amount is financed by the State Bank of India. The National Agricultural and Rural Development Bank financed 60.00% amount (except subsidy) to the State Bank of India for this scheme. Up to Rs. 10,000/- loan, no security is required in priority sector i.e., agriculture, animal husbandry etc. An individual can get loan maximum three times under this scheme, if he/she clears his/her previous loan amount. If an individual takes loan for the purpose of large cardamom cultivation, he/she has to repay the loan in three equal installments after three years but within six years from the date of receipt of the loan. For ginger cultivation they repay the loan amount within one year. In case of establishment of piggery or for the purchase of bullock, the loan receiver has to repay the loan amount after one year but within the three years from the date of receipt of the loan. Through *Gram Panchayat,* the Sikkim Rural Development Agency selects the persons who are to get loan under this scheme. After the selection of the candidates, the Sikkim Rural Development

Agency recommends the names of the selected persons to the State Bank of India, and Bank finances those candidates on loan basis. The loan receivers pay interest at the rate of 12.50% per year.

The Sherpas of Sikkim often sell their surplus agricultural and kitchen garden products in the local market (weekly and regular). In some cases these markets are about 2 km. to 3 km. away from their village. They take the pain of going to the market in order to earn cash. Moreover, they have to purchase their daily necessities from these markets.

It is thus seen that the Sherpas of Sikkim depend basically on land for their livelihood. They are agriculturists and horticulturists, and their lands supply their much needed income. Therefore, their connection with their land is very deep-rooted.

REFERENCES

Coomar, P.C. and M.K. Raha, 1997, "Family among the Sherpas of West Bengal", In K.C. Mahanta (Ed.): *People of the Himalayas: Ecology, Culture, Development and Change*, Kamala Raj Enterprises, Delhi.

Coomar, P.C. and M.K Raha., 1999, "Women in the Sherpa Society in the Himalayas", In R. Indira and Deepak Kumar Behara (Eds.): *Gender and Change*, Manak Publications (P) Ltd., New Delhi.

Raha, M.K., 2004. "Buddhism (Lamaism) among the Sherpa of Sikkim". (unpublished).

Raha, M.K. and P.C. Coomar., 2001, "Some Aspects of the Sherpa Religion", In Sarthak Sengupta (Ed.): *Tribes of the Eastern Himalayas*, Mittal Publications, New Delhi.

3

Traditional Religious Beliefs and Practices of the Lepchas—A Study on Change and Continuity

—*Rip Roshina Gowloog*

Of the three main communities living in Darjeeling–Sikkim Himalayas – the Lepcha, Bhutia, and the Nepali – the first is the autochthonous community. The Bhutias came from Tibet, especially after the consecration of Phuntsog Namgyal as the first 'King of Righteousness' in 1641. Whereas the Limbus and Magars, who are counted among the Nepalis in this region are also original inhabitants whereas, rest of the Nepalis have come from across the border with Nepal but are numerically predominant. The Lepchas are a Scheduled Tribe, but they are not as well protected as the tribes under the Sixth Schedule of the Constitution of India. They are one of the backward and numerically insignificant communities of the region.

The Lepchas are referred to as 'Rong', 'Meri', 'Monpa', etc. but the word Lepcha is most widely known in the region as well as outside it. The term 'Lepcha' is supposed to be an anglicised form of the term *'Lapche'*, but according to some Lepcha scholars like Tshering (1971) and Foning (1987), it is a corrupt form of the Lepcha word *'lap-chyo'*, which means an elevated place for rest by travellers, which are quite common in the hill areas of this region. There are several instances from the North East India where the name of a community simply means a hill or mountain. The name Monpa or Memba is apparently given by the high-altitude dwelling Tibetans, to refer to the lowlanders as Lepchas to the Tibetans. Their eastern neighbours - the Bhutanese - used the name Meri for them. They came in close contact with the Bhutanese after Kalimpong went under the rule of Bhutan in 1706, following a war, between Sikkim and Bhutan, in which the Lepchas fought valiantly on the side of Sikkim but lost the war. The Lepchas refer to themselves as 'Rong' when they speak in their own language, and it is common for them to use clan names like Karthak, Namchu, Simick, and Gowloog as their surnames.

Traditional Religious Beliefs and Practices

Many anthropologists have studied the traditional religious beliefs and practices of simple societies in many parts of the world. The interest of native scholars in this subject has been rather limited not only because many of them were converted into organised religions, by the time they were educated, but also because they often looked at their own traditional religions as vestiges of the past and nothing to feel proud of. As a matter of fact, the educated native scholars often questioned the very premises on which their traditional religions were based. As a result, most of the knowledge on the subject is generated by the curiosity of the western scholars about the strange religious practices of others.

Of the very few attempts to explain the intricacies of the Lepcha traditional religion, Gorer's (1938) is perhaps one of the most exhaustive of all. He is aware of his limitations but the insight, which he shares with Morris (1938) who did his fieldwork in the same village called Lingthem together with Gorer, is valuable. It is quite natural that one often encounters traces of their bias towards the Lepcha religion but these do not belittle the value of their observations on this subject.

Gorer (1938) writes that "the discussion on the Lepchas' religion is rendered extremely difficult by the fact that they practice simultaneously and without any feeling of theoretical discomfort, two (or probably three) mutually contradictory religions". Actually, there are no contradictions from the Lepcha point of view but the same may appear so, when an anthropologist like Gorer looks at it. True to the European system of looking at things, he first delineates the fundamental characteristics of various religions and compares one religion with another on the basis of them. The Lepcha view of religion is, on the other hand, more holistic, to say the least. To a Lepcha, the characteristic features of his/her religion are not important for he/she is not an analyst but a practitioner.

This is not to indicate that they follow their religion instinctively, as it may often appear to a scholar studying their traditional religious beliefs and practices. Like all communities they have their share of traditional religions and practices, which cannot always be explained in rationalist terms. In fact, they worship many gods and goddesses without being able to explain why they do so. They, of course, never needed to explain to anyone why they worshipped certain gods and goddesses until they began to be asked by researchers from outside or the educated among themselves. It is often difficult for them to explain their complex beliefs and practices because of their lack of command in languages other than their own. It is also possible that some of them hesitated to say anything about their gods and goddesses lest they make a mistake and incur the wrath of the supernatural powers or lest they are made fun of. Hence, they often give a highly utilitarian explanation of their traditional religious practices, saying that they do so to please so and so deity, or to avoid the wrath of so and so deity.

Gorer has discussed the Lepcha religion under Lamaism, Mun-Bongthingism (Lepcha priest and priestesses) and as the worship of the "people of *Mayel*" (Lepcha ancestors). Lamaism, which is a kind of mixture between pre-Buddhist and Buddhist religious practices, was added to their traditional religious order after they came under the Lamaist theocratic rulers from Tibet. Although, almost every Lepcha family sent the youngest son to the nearby monastery for monk-hood, they apparently could never identify themselves fully with Lamaism or Buddhism for a number of reasons. One such reason was that all Buddhist scriptures were written in Tibetan script and not in their own Lepcha script. The other reason was that Buddhism or Lamaism was identified with the Bhutias who had originally migrated from Tibet, which was called Bhot, hence 'Bhote', which is now considered derogatory compared to the more civilised word 'Bhutia' after the name of their country. Until the consecration of the first Tibetan king in Sikkim in 1641, the influence of Buddhism was, if any, insignificant. They were Animists in the sense that they worshipped a plethora of gods and goddesses, the most important of which were their ancestors from the land of "*Mayel*" or their imagined place of origin. The Mun and Bongthing were their sacred specialists, who mediated between the common Lepcha people and the supernatural beings.

The Lepchas believe that their ancestors were seven brothers, each being the guardian deity of one of the crops. They lived in seven separate huts in heaven, a belief that takes them very close to the Khasis and Jaintias, who have similar beliefs and with whom the Lepchas share a good deal of linguistic similarity as well. The seven brothers were immortal; they would be babies in the morning, youths during the day and old in the evening. They had each a huge goiter, wore traditional Lepcha clothes made of nettle fiber and hats made of bamboo stripes. The Lepchas believed that on the way to *Mayel*, there lived three brothers who were their guardian spirits. Their names were Yookrum (or Pongrum to the hunters), Mitik and Tomtik. The younger two brothers were cruel deities.

The dry paddy, maize, and millet are believed to have originated from the land of *Mayel*. Birds called *Mayelfo* were sent to them on the earth by their ancestors in *Mayel* to indicate the seasons for various agricultural works.

The people of *Mayel* had no wives except the eldest two. Their wives were two sisters called Talyou Nimu and Sangvo Nimu. These two women were worshipped as spirits of the earth because their bellies were taken as cultivable lands on which the seeds of paddy, millet and maize were sown.

There are many Lepchas who still believe that *Mayel*, the habitat of their ancestors, is located somewhere near Mount Kanchanjangha in Sikkim. The people of *Mayel'* were worshipped exclusively in connection with dry paddy, millet and maize, on two occasions, after sowing and after harvesting of the dry rice. On the first occasion, sacrifice consisted of food arranged in three lines, the central being for the 'people of *Mayel'*, the right for men's patron gods and the left one for women's patron gods. The *lafet* or the sacrificial offer contained the flesh of a tiny bird killed by a virgin boy. If the bird was big or the boy not virgin, the gods would refuse the food and there would be bad harvest the next year. Before the ceremony began, a song was sung in honour of the *Mayel* people and then a Mun, or a Bongthing offered *sakyou faat*, another offering, to them. A virgin girl would stand by, to constantly fill the buttered cup with *chi,* which was finally drunk by the Mun or Bongthing in honour of the *Mayel* people.

The harvest ceremony was more complicated. It was necessary to keep the spleen (the *tafoot*) of a pig, smoked and ready along with *chi* made of ripe new dry rice. These were taken to the field on the day of harvesting and placed where the crop was heaped or at *zolam*. Then an old and experienced man, but not related to the owner of the crop, would be chosen to represent a man of *Mayel*. A woman not directly related to the owner of the land would be chosen to represent *Talyeu Nimu* who helped the *Mayel-bu* or the man chosen to represent a man of *Mayel* in carrying out the rest of the ceremony, which included dancing around the *zolam*, opening the baskets of rice, etc. After the ceremony was over the charcoal and *tafoot* would be taken away and measuring of the harvest would start.

From the above account, it is difficult to understand why they worshipped the people of *Mayel*. Did they worship them because of their tradition of ancestor worship? Was it the uncertainty of harvest that made them do it? Or was it because they really believed in the power of their ancestors to help or ruin them? There can probably be no single answer or no answer at all to these questions. The most reasonable answer is because it was impossible to acquire food from outside they depended entirely on what they could harvest, and harvest was contingent upon the whims of the supernatural beings. When there was no market for distribution of food, they were entirely dependent on their environmental resources. Under such circumstances they would be ready to propitiate any god or goddess to ensure a steady harvest. But they also had a strong belief in their "living" ancestors. Thus it was only natural that their ancestors received the veneration of their descendants.

The earliest religion of the Lepchas may be termed as Animism, in which the Mun or the priestess and the Bongthing or the priest held central positions in the society, not only as sacred specialists but also as diviners and healers. There is practically no difference between Mun and Bongthing as far as roles and functions are concerned and the two words are often used interchangeably.

The institutions of Mun and Bongthing

Let me now briefly describe the institutions of Mun and Bongthing. Such a person was considered very important in the past, as they were indispensable under their traditional religion which revolved round the spirits and deities that only such a specialist could control. When a Mun or Bongthing died, the spirit would not necessarily choose another person immediately; it often waited for a number of years to re-emerge in the person appropriate for the job.

The chief function of the Mun or Bongthing was to ward off the misfortunes and illness caused by evil spirits, which is done partly by making sacrifices and partly by directly communicating with the supernatural beings responsible for a misfortune or sickness. On certain occasions, the Mun or Bongthing would be possessed by his/her guardian spirit and start to make divinations and prophesy. At death ceremonies, he/she would summon the spirit of the dead person to know his/her last wishes through such a specialist. Their reputation depended on people's experiences about what the specialists had predicted, who they had treated, etc. and a few who had good reputation would always be in high demand. It was believed that under the expert guidance of a Mun or Bongthing, the spirit of the dead person would leave for the *rum-lyang* – the place of gods – where it would be reborn as an infant, and live an eternal life (Hermanns, 1954).

Gorer has made a commendable attempt to delineate three major functions, of Mun (or Bongthing) in the Lepcha society as enumerated below, which also indicate the kinds of major diseases from which the Lepchas suffered in the past and often died:

> "To get rid of *sor moong* (violent death) or *apang moong* (genito-urinary diseases)";
>
> "To drive away the ghost of a dead child, called *numeen moong,* which kills young children by infantile diarrhoea"; and
>
> "To get rid of *chyom moong,* that is the devil who causes people to die by falling from a tree or cliff; or *rot moong,* that is the devil who causes people to commit suicide" (Gorer, 1938).

Today, there is almost complete disappearance of Muns and Bongthings, which is a matter of concern to the Animist Lepchas, who are extremely few and far between, probably because they lost their clientele. It is only recently that some young and educated Lepchas have begun to speak nostalgically of what they term as "our own priests". But they know it well that one cannot just choose to become a Mun or Bongthing: one has to be born with such destiny. In other words, one must show signs of becoming so, such as trembling vigorously, behaving in rather abnormal ways, not eating meat, etc. And not all persons, who show such signs, succeed in graduating as Muns or Bongthings; the persons showing such signs must find a competent *guru* either in a serving Mun or Bongthing or be lifted away by the `abominable man' living in the forest for such training.

According to the lay Lepchas, the explanations for the disappearance of Muns and Bongthings are as follows. These specialists were basically required for driving away the evil spirits who mostly lived in dense forests but due to denudation of forests and increase of human population, the forests have vanished and along with forests such spirits have vanished too. Although diseases related to stomach or urinary organs continue to afflict the Lepchas, as they did in the past, there are alternative sources of medical help in modern doctors to whom they go even from the remotest areas where they live.

Roughly speaking, the Lepchas began to be converted into Christianity, soon after they came in contact with the British, which started in the Darjeeling hills in the early nineteenth century whereas in Sikkim, the Buddhist theocratic rulers did not permit the spread of Christianity there, until they lost their political control over Sikkim in 1975. Under their rule, the Lepchas had all been converted into Buddhism, although they continued to practise Animism because the spread of Buddhism was horizontal rather than vertical and it was tolerant of the Animistic practices. This is perhaps why there are not many Christians in Sikkim even today.

Thus the Lepchas have come a long way from Animism to Buddhism and from Buddhism to Christianity, especially in the Darjeeling hills and elsewhere. Even culturally and linguistically, they have been considerably influenced by the majority Nepalis to the extent that many of them are not able to speak in their own language properly or not at all. Thus, there is a reason to think that the Lepcha religious and cultural traditions need to be preserved before they are totally extinct. The idea of establishing a Lepcha museum at Bongbusty in Kalimpong, and having Lepcha artifacts in some other museums in the country is also driven by a similar concern for the preservation of their traditions.

There is no denying the fact that the Lepchas have changed considerably. The inability, of the younger generation Lepchas, to speak in their own language, particularly in Darjeeling, is indeed an important loss, although in Sikkim their linguistic situation is not bad. The Lepcha language is taught in Sikkim today upto the college level. Further regeneration of their language is very much possible, if it is strategically linked with employment and self-esteem. The other loss is their land. Once owners of most, if not all, of the land in present Darjeeling and Sikkim, they have lost a lot of their land to the Tibetans from the north and the Nepalis from the west. This would certainly not happen if the British did not so desire or if they had made laws to prevent the same from happening. But even when laws were made by independent India to protect their land, there were many loopholes in those laws, which were exploited by the richer tribes from the hills like the Bhutias.

However, some Lepchas, either Buddhists or Christians, have been able to continue their traditional religious beliefs and practices. One, of the most living examples of this, is the belief in a host of supernatural beings. Although many Christians in a normal state of health do not propitiate such beings nor make any sacrifices in their names, there are occasions when they are known to have succumbed themselves to such practices in the weakest of their moments. That they did so, without the knowledge of their Christian brethren only, shows their concern for not losing their face in the church or an awareness of the fact that such *'pagan'* activities would not be approved by the church authority. While the number of such Christians or Buddhists is extremely few and far between, almost every Lepcha believes in the supernatural beings of all kinds. Similarly, in the celebration of their festivals and their calendar, a linkage with the past is clearly maintained.

Conclusion

One of the most unfortunate developments, in the Lepcha society over the past one hundred years or so, is the sense of divide within themselves between the Buddhists and the Christians. The latter Lepchas are often alleged by the former that they do not follow the true Lepcha culture, whereas the latter claim that Buddhism is not their original religion either. There was a time when a Christian Lepcha was clearly identifiable by his/her cleanliness or education but that is no longer the case now. The difference, between the Buddhist and the Christian Lepchas, has actually blurred beyond any recognition, and the bitterness, that might have once developed between the two religious sections of this tribe is not always carried in the modern race for secular education and employment. What matters more today is his/her identity as a Lepcha than his/her identity as a Buddhist or Christian.

REFERENCES

Foning, A., 1987, *Lepcha: My Vanishing Tribe*. Sterling Publications, New Delhi

Gorer, G., 1938, *The Lepchas of Sikkim*. (Reprint 1984), Cultural Publishing House, Delhi.

Gowloog, R. R., 1995, *Lingthem Revisited*. Har-Anand Publications, New Delhi.

Hermanns, Fr. M., 1954, *The Indo-Tibetans: The Tibetan and Mongoloid Problem in the Southern Himalayan and North-East India*. K.L. Fernandes, Bombay.

Morris, Col. J., 1938, *Living with the Lepchas: A Book about the Sikkim Himalayas*. William Heinemann Ltd., London.

Subba, T.B., 1985, "The Lepchas: From Legends to the Present Day". *Religion and Society*, 32, pp. 2: 61-70.

Tshering, G., 1971, *Lepcha Jatiko Ṣanchipta Parichay* (in Nepali) Shyam Brothers. Darjeeling.

4

Polygyny and Status of Tribal Women in Manipur—Tradition and Change

— Mayanglambam Mani Babu

Polygyny, a social institution of great bio-social importance, is typically defined anthropologically, as a marital relationship involving multiple wives (Kottak, 1978). The study of this social system, in the light of the socio-political and culture-environment perspectives in the contemporary societies where this institution prevails, is of common interest of discussion to the anthropologists. The root of polygyny among the Homo sapiens, as proposed by Linton (1936), is from the general private urge to collect females. Among the 19th century evolutionary theorists, Engel (1985) comprehended that it occurred mainly in the middle ranges of the three societal complexities, that is, group marriage, polygynous marriage and monogamy. Engel's notion is however, corroborated by the subsequent cross-culture researches (Osmond, 1965; Blumberg and Winch, 1972; Martin and Voorhees, 1976; Hartung, 1982; Alvard, 1986; and others), viewed ploygyny as a reproductive strategy (known as, r-strategy) by which men maximise the number of their offsprings but minimise investment in each child which obviously suggests that polygyny has more reproductive benefits for men than for women. Hartung (1982), among others, also favours this male-centered notion of polygyny.

The prevalence of polygyny in many societies is seen to be related with many factors, such as economical, social-cultural, political, environmental, etc. Two kinds of the economic explanations for polygyny – one is based on household economics, and a second is based on the degree of agricultural intensifications – are known (Boserup, 1970; Goody, 1976; Burton and Reitz, 1981). An economic model of polygyny, summarised by Grossband (1976, 1980), includes several postulations: (1) As the value of women's subsistence contributions increases, polygyny becomes more likely, since the income that men gain from marriage increases; (2) As women's wage opportunities outside the domestic domain increase, polygyny decreases; (3) As inequality among men increases, polygyny increases, since women will choose and marry wealthy man who already has several wives. Further, wealthier men will be more likely to choose polygynous marriage; (4) Homogamy decreases the incidence of polygyny by limiting the possibilities for polygynous marriages; (5) As the sex ratio decreases, polygyny will increase; (6) If there are economics of the scale of polygynous households, polygyny is more likely.

A number of workers (Murdock, 1949; Heath, 1958; Osmond, 1965; Lee, 1979; Burton and Reitz, 1981; etc.) find positive relationship between polygyny and female economic contribution discerned at different subsistence levels. However, Goody (1973), rejecting the female contribution hypothesis, maintained that the reasons behind polygyny are sexual and reproductive rather than economic and productive. He further contended that men marry polygynously to maximise their fertility and to obtain large households containing many young dependent males. White and Burton (1988) flatly rejected this view of the relationship between the satisfaction of male sexual appetites and polygyny. The disparity in the adult sex ratio caused by the external and internal factors – such as, male mortality from disease, warfare, dangerous occupation, male labour migration, and so on – has significant relations to the prevalence of polygyny in a society (Dorjahn, 1959; Whiting, 1964; Lee, 1979; Dow, 1983; Ember, 1974, 1984-85; etc.). Ember (1974), postulated that polygyny is a consequence of high male mortality in warfare, which reduces the sex ratio. An ethnographic example, of adult sex ratio imbalances, outlined by Beals *et.al.* (1977 : 393) among the autocratic and monarchial Baganda of Uganda (East Africa), shows yet another unusual exogenous and endogenous factors of demographic processes which led the people to take up polygynous marriage.

The wide dispersal of polygyny among the Baganda was made possible by the high mortality rate among the Baganda males. In families chiefly, male children were often killed at birth; the prince of the royal house, once the successor to the throne had been chosen, were put to death; the king arbitrarily killed off male retainers and servants who displease him; males, never females, had to be sacrificed in great numbers to the gods at appropriate ceremonies, and great numbers of men were killed in the animal wars, the Baganda collected with their neighbours. As a result of these factors, plus the fact that large numbers of women, were taken as booty in war expeditions, the women outnumbered the men by three to one. It was this disparity in the relative numbers of men and women that made polygyny on so wide a scale possible.

Yet another explanation, of the causes of polygyny, which bears similar notion of sex ratio interpretation, is that of the higher age at marriage of men than women (Ember, 1984-85). The argument, here, is that delaying the age of marriage for men would produce an artificial, though not actual, excess of marriageable women – thereby causing adult sex ratio disparity. The cultural norms of having long postpartum sex taboos in some societies, for the reasons of baby's and mother's health, also tend to be polygynous (Whiting, 1964). It is seen that societies with low-protein staples (those whose principal foods are root and tree crops such as taro, sweet potato, banana and breadfruit) tend to have a long postpartum sex taboo (Ember and Ember, 1994), and a man's having more than one wife, perhaps, is a cultural adjustment to the taboo (*ibid*). Environmental bearings of polygyny were contended by, Boserup (1970) and Verdon (1983) who saw general differences in the rates of polygyny between the forest and savannah adaptations.

The rule of polygyny, obviously, exerts myriad impacts on the relative statuses of the females, the co-wives of polygynist man – manifesting varied sub statuses and sub roles in consonance with the respective socio-cultural settings. Here lies the special pursuit of deliberation among the social scientists since this aspect, rather, deviates from the general outlook of the relative status of women to gender disparity. Here the problem is not primarily between males and females but between the principal wife and co-wives, and amongst the co-wives of a polygynist on how much power and authority the first wife or the other wives have relatively to each other and their respective roles in a polygynous plural family. In this context, one needs to look for a relevancy of White's (1978) notion of female 'status' that it cannot be talked about as a single concept but with different spheres of her life. The term 'status', which was made popular by Linton (1936), is often used synonymously with the term 'role' and also interchangeably. Linton (*ibid*) defined status as the 'polar position......in patterns of reciprocal behaviour and role as a dynamic aspect of statuses'. 'Status, which is conveniently used for all the rights and obligations which attach to an individual or a group, according to the customs of the society' (Redfield, 1972) is 'a person's position relatively to that of others with whom he is in social relationships' (Mair, 1975). In essence, status refers to who a person is, and role defines what such a person is expected to do. And, as the two terms are interrelated, these cannot be viewed independently. When we are talking about the status of women, it seems to be determined by various taboos attached to the women, and their 'child-bearing and child-rearing functions' (Majumdar and Madan ,1977); and also by the four determinants – actual treatment, legal status, opportunity for social participation, and the character and extent of work (Lowie, 1920). In this cross-cultural research, White (1978) rated fifty-two different items that might be used to define the relative status of sexes

– which includes such parameters as : which sex can inherit property, who has final authority over disciplining unmarried children, whether the gods in the society are male, female, or both, etc. The present chapter is a brief account of the traditional aspect of polygyny and women's status among the tribal societies of Manipur, with a quick look into the significant changes in the system.

II

Manipur is a land of over two and half dozen different tribes who inhabit, sporadically in the centrally located valley, and thickly in the surrounding hilly terrains. The tribes are either affiliated to one of the three linguistic groups (Naga Bodo, Eastern Naga and Kuki Chin) of the Tibeto-Burman Family. For instance, under the Naga Bodo group, among others, Kabui and Khoirao are included. Maram, Tangkhul, Maring, etc. are within the Eastern Naga group. Aimol, Anal, Chiru, Hmar, Kom, Purum, Vaiphei, etc. are the tribal groups who belong to the Old Kuki sub-group of the larger Kuki-Chin. Likewise, Paite, Thadou, etc. are included under the Northern Chin sub-group of the Kuki-Chin. The tribes have a more or less similar socio-cultural set-ups. The traditional social system is strongly male-oriented, where the principle of organisation, fundamentally is to the agnation of who governed residence, descent, access to economic resources, political affiliation and linkages through marriage. Within the strong framework of clan exogamy[1] and tribe endogamy, the rule of bilateral cross-cousin (Mo Br Da) marriage[2] is the most preferred and ideal one. The practice of sororate is prevalent more commonly than levirate, the later being reported at least, among the Kabui Nagas. Polygyny is permissible among the tribes, though monogamy is the general rule. The prevalence of polygyny in most of the tribal societies was known to be more prominent among the chieftains, clan heads, kings, great warriors and rich men. The motive behind the rule was varied – the primary objective being economic manifestation as social prestige of the polygynic men and the sexual privilege. Among the Lusheis, it is simply a matter of money and consequently it is almost entirely confined to the chief, for few others can afford to keep up two establishments (Shakespear, 1975). Stewart (1855) described the privileges of the Kooki Kings, for cohabiting with any of the married or single women in their villages, who may have as many wives as he likes or can keep (c.f. *loc.cit.*, 194). The Meitei Kings, in the valley also had the same privilege of marrying any of the married or single women like his Kooki counterparts. However, the Tangkhul Nagas have a restricted norm to the rule of polygyny. Only persons who have no child to his first wife are sometimes allowed to marry a second wife with the approval of the first wife, and immovable properties for such a woman were apportioned by the family (Shimray, 1976). But in many instances, a good number of wives are married by the Tangkhul chiefs like those of his Konyak and Sema counterparts, who visited their wives by turn in their separate houses. In general, Naga warriors and wealthy persons married three wives and the village chief, five wives; however, Konyak chiefs could marry as many as fifty wives. The system of two wives norm was known practice among the Purum (Das, 1945), Maring (Das, 1988), Zomi[3] (Gougin, 1986) and Quoireng (Hodson, 1984). The practice, though allowed in the Purum society, was not usual one, and if practised, it is limited to two wives only and not more (Das, 1945). A Zomi chief also could acquire two wives at a time 'as a sign of despotism' and 'not as a customary practice' (Gougin, 1986). Polygyny is also known to the people of Anal and Lamgang who possessed at least three wives at a time (Shakespear, 1975). The autocratic and arbitrary motive of Zomi chiefs to the rule of polygyny, however, differs from the concepts of social necessity, philanthropic idea and sexual urge of the Nagas (Shimray, 1985) that led to the occurrence of polygyny in their society.

Socially, the chief and the persons in the public service should have enough manpower to manage the family and to maintain the status of the man. More males could not increase population and serve the public in feasts, and in field work only more wives could produce more.

The system of polygyny in Manipur is partly in consonance with the r-strategy described above. Also the female contribution, here, relates to an indirect subsistence extent, likely to be benefited by more manpower of the offspring's. Male sexual appetite and male status augmentation factors formed other explanations; but sex-ratio disparity was out of the scene.

Though it functioned as an accepted institution, the mode of occurrence is not homogeneously distributed probably due to many socio-economic factors. To the plain Meiteis, Chaki-Sirkar (1984) observed its more prevalence in urban areas than in the rural areas where the system is the exception rather than the rule. She further observed that the stronger hold of polygyny among the urban elite 'is probably a result of the adoption of sanskritised values by women, which inculcate the indissolubility of the marital bond' (*ibid:* 202). Among the Naga Tribes of Manipur, Hodson (1984) noticed that 'polygamy (here refers to polygyny, as no system of polyandry is known in Manipur) is the weakest in those groups in which the bachelors' hall is not definitely preserved'. The prevalence of concubine serves as one factor for the low occurrence of polygyny in the Maring society (Das, 1988). 'The Marings discourage polygamy by insisting upon the payment to the parents of the first wife of gifts of substantial value' (Brown, 1870, c.f., Hodson, *op.cit.*: 94).

Under the system of polygyny, all wives are not given equal share of socio-sexual privileges and treatments. The ambivalence of man's perception of the co-wives' socio-sexual role or privilege is, by and large, controlled by the cultural values and norms of the society concerned. As such, the first or the principal Maring wife has the highest position among the other wives and they are under the control of the major wife (Das, 1988). The non-major wives are also not entitled to maintain any separate house, unlike those of the Tangkhul

Nagas and Meiteis. Moreover, legalisation of a second wife to a Maring husband can be done only after the imposition of a fine on the second wife by the clan leaders (*ibid*). The first Konyak wife of, a village chief or rich or influential person of Nagaland, who could have as many as 50 wives like the Thangkul counterparts in Manipur – has the privilege of advising her husband and suggesting the girls who were likely to co-operate with her in family managements, which he (the husband) usually accepted (Shimray, 1985). Other than one major wife, a Meitei King unlike his Naga or Kuki counterparts may have three principal wives, with as many as one hundred and eight subsidiary partners The titles of the Raja's wives in order of precedence are – 1) *Maharani,* 2) *Apanbi* (which may mean either the preferred one or the one who rules) 3) *Leimakhubi* (Hodson, 1908).

Regarding the sexual right of the co-wives of a polygynous husband, either the principal wife or the most attractive one got more privilege than that of the others. But it was not always true in some cases. The first wife of the Anal and Lamgang men were entitled to the company of her husband for five nights, the second for four, and the third for three (Shakespear, 1975). The Tangkhul chiefs, like those of his Sema Naga counterparts of Nagaland, visited their wives by turn who have separate houses and establishment, though the most attractive one has the privilege with the highest number of the chief's visit (Shimray, *op.cit.,*:178). The husband's attention, to the several wives according to precedence, was strictly regulated among the Meiteis, - 'the eldest getting twice the nominal share of the wife next below her' (Hodson, 1908). Very often, owing to the unequal distribution of sexual privilege between the co-wives, - husband-wives confrontation, and bitterness or jealousy between co-wives cropped up – thereby resulting in tension and unhappiness in the polygynous homes. When a husband procures another wife, or gives more sexual privileges to the new wife – a deep sense of anguish, loss of honour and mental disturbances of being humiliated etc., are felt by the older wife/wives. And it is a general phenomenon in many polygynyous societies[4]. To obliterate such abhorrent state of affairs different envisages are made, such as categorisation of planned rotational period of sexual contact with the husband, maintenance and establishment of separate house for each wifes, and so on. Among the plain Meitics, such bitter situations are less recognised between the sororal co-wives who almost always live together – though this type of union is quite rare (ManiBabu, 1991a). Generally, in such circumstances 'a wife may seek to extra – marital liaisons' (Epstein, 1979). Such is the Meitei case where most marriages split up after the husband marries another women, or general encouragement in setting up a matrifocal family by the polygynous wives with separate hearths (*loc.cit.*). Singh (1972) also found a high percentage of separation among the Thanga Meities because of the husband's second marriage (cf. Chaki-Sircar *op.cit.* (87-88). Frequently, a Meitei woman who left her husband because of his second marriage, may settle for the role of second wife to another man (*ibid,* 223).

The concubine factor has posed as yet another domain in the network of polygyny. In a general sense, the tradition of concubine is a pseudo-polygynous norm that seems to stem out mistakably from monogamous rule, since the concubines are not treated as co-wives of a man on the one hand, and they are generally not entitled to live in the same house with the principal wife and cannot be assigned to a family without ambiguity on the other. In a deeper sense, however, a concubine is also a sexual partner of a man who takes the place of secondary wife even though she usually has lesser relative status and prestige than that of the other co-wife/ wives. In China and Japan, a man can have a concubine by way of purchasing, can bring her into his household, and since various Chinese laws and legal rulings defined their statuses, scholars think of these women as "secondary wives" and their children as members of the family (Goode, 1975). In fact, the literal meaning of concubine is the state of being cohabitation of a man and a woman who are not formally married to each other. Goody (1973) serves concubinage 'an attribute of monogamy rather than polygyny' (c.f. Das, 1988). Since it only involves sexual rights and not reproductive rights (*ibid*), there are a limited socio-sexual role in relation to other co-wives. Among the Meities, Singh (1963) took a woman's later marriage as concubinage. The female slaves of the Kukis of Lushei and Chin Hills (particularly the southern tribes) are treated as concubines with respect to their masters (Shakespear, 1975; Carey and Tuck, 1976). The lack of legal status, of the concubines and other lesser[5] illegitimate wives, often has disgrace impact on their children in regards to the inheritance of the father's property. More often, the legitimisation of concubine is intimately connected with the social placement of her children in the respective kinship network. In general, the children of the true wife (the principal wife) are only considered as the legitimate heirs. In some instances, the children of concubines may be legitimised, in case, there are no lawful descendants. Among the Siyin tribe of Chin Hills, the children of concubines and lesser wives have no claim to any estate, and in the event of there being no issue by the chief, the brother of the deceased seizes property, but will feed and keep the wives and children of his brother (Carey and Tuck, *op.cit.* :209). A Maring Naga way is that the sons of the secondary wives may claim if there is no son by the major wife, and the criteria of inheritance right is on the basis of seniority (Das, 1988).

The socially approved system of marriage of the deceased brother's widow in some tribal groups of Manipur also escalates the prescribed rule of polygyny. Though social sanction of such a union prevails – the option, however, rests either on the widow or the deceased's brother to accept the union, which led to a system of what may be termed as 'conditional levirate'. Among the Tangkhul Nagas such a marriage was entirely of inclination and not compulsion (Hodson, 1984). Hodson *(ibid)* also happened to see, among many of the tribes in Manipur (which had been subject probably to the Kuki influence), the prevalence of the rule of junior levirate and not the senior one probably with the objectives, one, 'to save the younger brother, if unmarried, the cost of a wife, and two, to make some use of a person, who would otherwise be a burden on the property of the deceased'. It is now clear that widows, whose natal households are not economically sound to pay back her bride wealth, in case, they want to come back to her family of procreation after a premature dissolution of marriage – are but to accept yet the another affinal ties their deceased husband's family as a levirate spouse, an inherited widow. The excellence of such a tie is, however, not for the widows and her natal members only, but is for the family of the deceased husband also, because the bride wealth likely to be paid out at the time of their younger son's marriage is saved from being expended. Thus the system of levirate has its economic manifestation within the larger social value and contents. If a widow agrees to marry her deceased husband's brother, she retains the rights of a formally-married wife among the Maring (Das, 1988). However her recognition as a legal wife is done through an imposition of a fine on her (called *ratukna*) which symbolises the recovery of the bride price from the second wife. It is also seen among some tribes that if in cases where such marriages are compulsory, the younger brother refuses to marry the widow, he has to pay a fine, *meithi*. If the woman refuses to marry her husband's brother, her price (*mangkat*) is refunded, and she is returned to her people ...(*loc.cit.*). The concept of buying and selling, however, may be inconceivable because a father may not always force his daughter into a marriage against her wishes on the fact that bride wealth cattle, etc. would have to be returned in the event of a divorce. 'The principle that a marriage made legal by bride wealth is not dissolved even by the return of the marriage cattle' (Mair, 1975) is widely seen among the tribal societies in Manipur.

The polygynic bearing upon bride wealth at the cost of the women's economic asset is perceived by Goody and Tambiah (1973) as follows:

It has been argued that polygyny is found where women make a substantial contribution to productive activity, specially the cultivation. And that a measure of their contribution is the bride wealth that is paid for them at marriage (Goody, 1973)

Bride wealth can neatly tie in with polygyny, with concubinage, with men of high status or great wealth 'acquiring' women of low status or in poor circumstances. When such propensities are carried to extremes, there is a distinct flavour of 'purchasing' women, of maintaining *'harems'* and the like (Goody and Tambiah, 1973).

However, it is pertinent to refer here that the system of bride wealth[6] being a socially accepted norm among the tribes in Manipur, such as Paite, is never in the sense of buying or selling a human being, but it means several ideals and values like compensating the family or parting a daughter, symbolising a new relationship between the two families and perpetuating relationship already in existence between the two families (Khothang and Khenthang, 1976). But among the tribes of Chin Hills, Carrey and Tuck (1976) foresaw girls as the very precious possession to a father or a brother, 'whom he sells to be wives at a very great profit'. And, the underlying motives of taking bride price in their societies are only to compensate the girls' parents for the loss of their daughter who was a great helper to them both in cultivation and household works (*ibid.*: 189). The refund of bride price by virtue of divorce or separation of a widow from her deceased husband's family, due to the refusal of levirate proposal, the system of taking fine from the younger brother who refuses to marry his deceased brother's widow, etc. among the Nagas (Brown, 1870, c.f. Hodson, 1984: 207), may be seen as cultural manifestations to the balanced position of the females within the social crux of patriarchy. In the light of the polygynous rule, bride wealth bears socio-economic footing of a woman, the attachment of the ideal value, etc., which are being manifested through the (social) status of a polygynous husband who could afford heavy bride price for more than one wife.

Hence, Sachchidananda's (1979) view of the bride price provision as an indication of higher status of tribal women is, however, justified by looking into the perpetuating rule practised in Manipur.

III

The present discussion on the female status in view of the rule of polygyny is no longer on the men-women controversy but between the principal wife and secondary wives, and between co-wives of a polygynous man. In a polygynous marriage, the hierarchy of wives is unequivocal and the inferiority of the secondary wives is beyond dispute. The social backgrounds of the secondary wives are always inferior to the standing of the first wife, and the right and authority of the latter are unquestionable in the hierarchy of secondary wives within the household. Though a principal wife exclusively enjoys a social privilege over her fellow co-wives, it is not the case in the sexual domain. The advantages of a principal wife include a superior authority image over the secondary wives within the polygynous infrastructure, involvement of both sexual and reproductive rights, the right of the principal wife's children in inheritance with a legal status, etc. The aggressiveness of the first wife – who, in no case, would not like a compromise to her full privilege of socio-sexual share – has a psycho-social stance of the male-centered system of polygyny. This social institution, being a cultural manifestation of patri-oriented society, is frequently susceptible by the husband's illegitimate sexual behaviour outside homes. The husbands are quite innocent of an analogical situation that if his wife happens to engage in it. Her husband's unbridled behaviour is likely to make the sole wife unhappy, and she is still not happy enough even when she gets the status of being a principal wife/first wife in the polygynous family. Her refusal to take that responsibility, of course, would not be viewed as unnatural, and is of more serious violations of role obligations than the refusal on the part of the secondary wives. A contrasting feature of cultural significances is the encouraging essence and spirit of the

Tangkhul and Konyak principal wives to the arrangement of subsequent marital alliances – who, at the cost of their husbands' pivoted status (owing to it) can raise their heads high with pride as the principal wives in a polygynous or plural family. The statuses of co-wives in respect to their head wife and amongst themselves, thus, exist when they acknowledged acceptance of the social alliance that cropped up in the system, and indicates the roles they hope to play in it. Hence, a woman in a polygynous family does not enjoy the normal ascribed status and role expectations of an ideal proud wife (as does by her counterpart in a monogamous family) but burdened with a number of sub-statuses with roles that carry.

The socio-sexual privileges of a principal wife and her proclamation over the role as major wife are not only influenced but affected by her child-producing functions. The mothers of only daughters have a shaky position and could not have the social privilege of a principal wife (in the family). In such situations, social privilege and prestige of the principal wife seems to have transferred to another wife who could produce a son. Though sons of the co-wives have no inheritance right over the property, they may have a claim, as in the Maring Naga society, if there is no son to the major wife. As prevalent among the tribal societies in Manipur, a Meitei wife's prestigious sex role is related to her child-bearing activity, and a childless and barren woman never reaches full status within the family as well as beyond (Mani Babu, 1991a). Naturally, the rights in *genetricem* by the husband over barren/ issueless wife gives way to a loose tie over the rights in *uxorem*, that gives rise to divorce or to polygyny (*ibid*). It is also seen that to bear children, especially sons, is important to a woman who establishes her position and prestige in her family of orientation and as more secure as that of the marriage rites. This is all the more important for the secondary wives whose marriage is, very often, not marked by rites of any kind. Additional descendants prove irresistible to grandparents and, whatever the background of the mother, she usually established herself in the family because of the children, who are thus an invaluable adjunct to her, rather, doubtful status as wife. A woman's loss of privileges occurs not because of her sex but because of her bargaining position. If the senior wife in traditional society gained prestige from her role in the plural family, the vestiges of this have been won rather than in today's tribal society in Manipur, and it is generally assumed that any woman would prefer to be a sole wife, other things being equal.

The practice of polygyny in Manipur witnessed marked changes or decline due to education, economic hardships, impact of Christianity, etc. Christianity and education are the two important components, among others, of modernisation and westernisation which act as the powerful forces of social change. Here, social change refers to a process in which is discernible significant alteration in the structure and functioning of a particular social system. Various trends in social relationships and changes in values are included in the concept of modernisation, in which a transformation of social, political and economic organisation is involved. Concept of modernisation is quite related with that of westernisation, which includes technology, institutions, knowledge, beliefs and values – in addition to the changes in dress, diet, and style of eating, manners and introduction of western education (Srinivas, 1966). Both the impacts of modernisation and westernisation to the system of polygyny are discernible to its change. Introduction of western education and Christianity in Manipur by the British colonialists was at the middle of 1890. Conflicts between the tribal animists and the Christian preachers were common occurrences in the hill areas (ManiBabu, 1991b; Singh, 1991). The two newly introduced systems are the most powerful agencies in making changes of the indigenous cultures and social values of the tribes. Obviously, these are responsible for the banishment of the traditional systems of slavery, head hunting, feasts of merit, bachelor's dormitory and so on. Moreover, a similar impact is also on polygyny. The system of polygyny – which can be viewed as man's freedom of sex at the cost of his wealth and status, have been heavily influenced by the divine Commandment of the religious faith of Christianity such as one, 'Thou shall not commit adultery' (Exo. 20:14, c.f., Shimray, 1985); two, 'if a man looks at a woman lustfully, he has already committed adultery with her in his heart' (Matt. 5:27. 28; c.f., *ibid*). These concepts on sexuality of Christian religion make significant changes on the tradition of concubinage and of having more than one wife to a husband – thereby monogamy got a strong footing in the tribal society. Chaki-Sirkar (1984) finds lower incidence of polygyny among the plain Meitei owing to the emotional ties between the spouses, duly encouraged by the social environment of modern education economic hardship, and so on. The educated and Christianised tribes are, now-a-days, quite aware of the negative effects of the institution in the society. The pious Zomi Christians, 'strictly adhere to monogamy on the plea that polygamy is not conducive to a healthy family and creates misunderstanding and discord' (Gougin, 1986). Owing to the impact of Western education – man's status, and prestige of being a husband of many wives have no place in the modern egalitarianism; and within the household man's energies are somewhat diverted into household tasks which are meant ideally for the females. This has a meaning, rather, to the female status within the patriarchal framework of the tribal society.

NOTES

1. Exogamous character of clan is remarkably absent in some tribes of Manipur, such as Paite, Thadou, Hmar etc., and also in some tribes of Indo-Myanmar border such as the Lakher, Lushai etc. (Goswami and Kamkhenthang, 1975). Among the Paite society, clans neither observe exogamy nor endogamy, and 'a man can marry any women within the clan except his begetters, his sister or daughter' (*ibid*: 48). It is pertinent to note that 'incest prohibition is limited to the nuclear or joint family only' (*ibid*: 50).
2. Paite follows the Fa Br Da marriage.
3. A generic name of the Kuki, Chin, and Mizo people (Gougin, 1986).

4. Exceptionally among the Arapesh tribe of New Guinea, such a situation is reported to be out of the scene, and the married life in the polygynous marriages 'is so even and centered that there is nothing to relate of it at all' (Mead, 1950).

5. Women who become sexual partners without a formal social recognition ceremony may also be included under such a group. A woman who becomes a mistress without a *Chenba* among the Meitei, is called *Oktabi* i.e. lustful or *Kasubi* i.e. prostitute (Chaki-Sirkar, 1984).

6. Bride wealth transaction, in the tribal societies of Manipur which consist mainly of livestock, - varies from tribe to tribe. Karong (1976) reported that the Kom bride price consists of five *mithuns,* one gong of eight palms and another gong of seven palms at the first instance; - and one number of each of *mithun* and pig of five palms, and several jars of *zu* (local rice beer) as the *manpui* (principal bride wealth). The bride price offered by a Tangkhul consists of two dogs and two *daos.* It is a pig and spear for Mao; a pig and a hoe for the Anals and the Purums. The price of a Vaiphei girl varies from two to ten *mithuns.* A Hmar fixes it within three to seven *mithuns,* one hoe, a pair of cloth and a jar of rice beer. The price of a Lamgang girl is fixed for the pigs or buffaloes or cattle, a necklace of conch-shells, one bracelet and a black or blue cloth. The price of the Thadou girl is generally fixed between two and ten *mithuns* or pigs, two large gongs, two sets of ordinary gongs and two beads. The price of a Chiru girl is only a gong (Ansari, 1991).

REFERENCES

Alvard, M.S., 1986, "Polygyny as a Human Female Reproductive Strategy". *Contribution to Anthropology,* 5: pp. 42-56.

Ansari, S.A., 1991, *Manipur: Tribal Demography and Socio-economic Development.* Diya Publishing House, Delhi.

Beals, R. L.; H. Hoijer; and A. R. Beals., 1977, *An Introduction to Anthropology* (5th edition) Macmillan Publishing Co. New York.

Blumberg, R.L. and R.F. Winch., 1972, "Societal Complexity and Familial Complexity: Evidence for the Curvilinear Hypothesis". *American Journal of Sociology.* 77: pp. 898-920.

Boserup, E., 1970, *Woman's Role in Economic Development.* George Allen and Unwin. New York.

Burton, M.L. and K.P. Reitz., 1984, "The Plow, Female Contribution to Agricultural Subsistence and Polygyny". *Behaviour Science Research.* 16 : pp. 275-305.

Carey, B.S. and H.N. Tuck., 1976, *The Chin Hills*. Volume I (First Published: 1896), Gian Publishing House, New Delhi.

Chaki-Sirkar, M., 1984, *Feminism in a Traditional Society - Woman of the Manipur Valley*. Shakti Books, New Delhi.

Das, R.K., 1988., *Tribal Social Structure: A Study of Maring Society of Manipur*. Inter India Publications, New Delhi.

Das. T.C., 1945, *The Purums : An Old Kuki Tribe of Manipur*. University of Calcutta, Calcutta.

Dorjahn, V.R., 1959, "The Factor of Polygyny in African Demography". In W.R. Bascom, and M.J. Herskovits (Eds.): *Continuity and Change in African Cultures*. pp. 87-142. University of Chicago Press, Chicago.

Dow, J., 1983., "Woman Capture as Motivation for Warfare". In R. Dyson-Hudson and M.A. Little (Eds): *Rethinking Human Adaptation: Biological and Cultural Models*. West View. Boulder. pp. 97-115.

Ember, C.R. and M. Ember., 1994, *Anthropology* (7th edition). Prentice-Hall of India, New Delhi.

Ember, M., 1974, "Warfare, Sex Ratio, and Polygyny". *Ethnology*. 13:197-206.

Ember, M., 1984-85, "Alternative Predictors of Polygyny". *Behaviour Science Research*. 19: pp. 1-23.

Engle, R., 1985, *The Origin of the Family, Private Property and the State*. First Published, 1884. Progress Publishers. Moscow.

Epstein, A. L., 1979. "The Case Method in the Field of Law". In A. L. Epstein (Ed): *The Craft of Social Anthropology*, pp. 205-230. Hindustan Publishing Corporation, Delhi.

Goode, W.J., 1975, *The Family* (2nd Indian reprint). Prentice-Hall of India. New Delhi..

Goody, J., 1973, "Polygyny, Economy and the Role of Women". In J. Goody (Ed). *The Character of Kinship*. Cambridge University Press. Cambridge, London. pp.175-190.

Goody, J., 1976, *Production and Reproduction*. London.

Goody, J. and S.J. Tambiah, 1973, *Bride Wealth and Dowry*. Cambridge University Press, Cambridge, London.

Goswami, M.C. and H. Kamkhenthang, 1975, "Clan among the Paite". *Bulletin of the Department of Anthropology, Gauhati University*. 4: pp. 19-64.

Gougin, T., 1986, *History of Zomi* (2nd edition). Zomi Press, Churachandpur, Manipur.

Grossband, A.S. 1976. "An Economic Analysis of Polygyny: The Case of Maidugiri". *Current Anthropology*. 17 : pp. 701-707.

Grossband, A.S., 1980, "The Economics of Polygamy". In J. L. Simon and J. DaVanzo (Eds.): *Research in Population Economics.* JAI Press, Greenwich. C. T. Volume 2. pp. 321-350.

Hartung, J., 1982, "Polygyny and the Inheritance of Wealth". *Current Anthropology*. 23: pp. 1-12

Heath, D.B., 1958, "Sexual Division of Labour and Cross-cultural Research". *Social Forces*. 37 : pp. 77 - 79.

Hodson, T.C., 1908, *The Meitheis*. David Nutt, London.

Hodson, T.C., 1984, *The Naga Tribes in Manipur* (First published, 1911) Neeraj Publishing House. Delhi.

Karong, T., 1976, "The Koms". In K.B.Singh (Ed.): *An Introduction to Tribal Language and Culture of Manipur*, Manipur State Kala Akademi, Imphal. pp. 62-78.

Khothang, T.J. and H. K. Khenthang., 1976, "A Brief Introduction to the Language and Culture of the Paites (Teddim Chins)". In K.B. Singh. (Ed.): *An Introduction to Tribal Language and Culture of Manipur,* Manipur State Kala Akademi, Imphal. pp. 108-136.

Kottak, C.P., 1978, *Anthropology: The Exploration of Human Diversity*. Second Edition. Random House. New York.

Lee, G.R., 1979, "Marital Structure and Economic Systems". *Journal of Marriage and Family*. 41: pp. 701-713.

Linton, R., 1936, *The Study of Man*. Appleton-Century-Crofts, New York.

Lowie, R.H., 1920, *Primitive Society*. Boni and Liversight, New York.

Mair, L., 1975, *An Introduction to Social Anthropology* (Second reprint) Clarendon Press. Oxford.

Majumdar, D.N. and T.N. Madan., 1977, *An Introduction to Social Anthropology*, Asia Publishing House, New Delhi.

ManiBabu, M. 1991a. "Meetei Family and Status of Women: An Anthropological Preliminary Account". *Manipur Today*, 11, 1: 47-52.

ManiBabu, M. 1991b. "Education and Social Change among the Tribals of Manipur". *Manipur Today*, 11, 3. pp. 37-39.

Martin, M.K. and B. Voorhees. 1975. *Female of the Species*, Cambridge University Press, New York.

Mead, M., 1950, *Sex and Temperament in Three Primitive Societies* (First published, 1953), New American Library, New York.

Murdock, G.P., 1949, *Social Structure*, Macmillan, New York.

Osmond, M. W., 1965, "Toward Monogamy: A Cross-cultural Study of Correlates of Type of Marriage". *Social Forces*, 44: pp. 6-16

Redfield, R., 1972, "How Human Society Operates". In H. L. Shapiro. (Ed.): *Man, Culture and Society* (reprint) pp. 345-368, Oxford University Press, New York.

Sachchidananda., 1979, *Changing Munda*, Concept Publishing Co, New Delhi.

Shakespear, J., 1975, *The Lushei Kuki Clans* (reprint). Tribal Research Institute. Aizawl.

Shimray, R.R., 1985, *Origin and Culture of Nagas*, Brahma Printing Press, New Delhi.

Shimray, Y.K., 1976, "Tangkhul Language and Culture". In K.B. Singh (Ed.): *An Introduction to Tribal Language and Culture of Manipur* pp. 1-30. Manipur State Kala Akademi, Imphal.

Singh, K.M., 1991, *History of Christian Missions in Manipur and Other Neighbouring States*, Mittal Publications, New Delhi.

Srinivas, M.N., 1966, *Social Change in Modern India*. Allied Publishers, Bombay.

Verdon, M., 1983, "Polygyny, Descent, and Local Fission: A Comparative Hypothesis". *Journal of Comparative Family Studies*, 14: pp. 1-22.

White, D.R. and M. L. Burton., 1988, "Causes of Polygyny: Ecology, Economy, Kinship, and Warfare". *American Anthropologist*, 90: pp. 871-887

White, M.K., 1978, *The Status of Women in Pre Industrial Societies.* Princeton University Press, Princeton, NJ.

Whiting, J.W.M., 1964, "Effects of Climate on Certain Cultural Practices". In W. H. Goodenough (Ed.): *Explorations in Culture Anthropology.* pp. 511-544. McGraw – Hill, New York.

5

Demographic Statistics of Mate Tribe of Manipur

— S. Jibon Kumar Singh

The population of India, in spite of all its efforts to stabilise, is increasing fast with the consequence that, it is the second largest in the world just next to Republic of China. It is neither surprising nor exaggerating that only the absolute increase of its population (180 millions approx.) during the period 1991 to 2001 is much larger than the total population of Brazil (170 millions approx.) which ranked fifth in the world population ranking. Though India has experienced a considerable decrease in the fertility level of its population during the last three-four decades, yet it is growing fast because of its already too large base population. This fast growing India's population simply means fast growing population of its constituent States and Union Territories, even though there may be variability within and among them. Demographic variability is a phenomenon observed everywhere. No population so far is reported to be stationary, obviously because of variability in the population variables - more particularly fertility and mortality patterns. This ever on-going process of variation in fertility and mortality pattern has drawn the attention of many scholars. As a result, a number of earlier studies on various populations of different places of India have well documented the causative factors of population dynamics. However, such data are particularly lacking for Manipur – a tiny State in the north eastern corner of Indian sub-continent. Such a paucity of data, therefore, ultimately demands for envisaging into the matrix of population dynamics of different ethnic groups, having different genetic, socio-cultural, socio-economic and geo-ecological variations. Keeping this in view, an earnest attempt is being made in this Chapter to envisage the population dynamics of Mate tribe of Manipur.

Mates – a socio-culturally distinct and very much discrete in physical appearance, but not one among the recognised Scheduled Tribes of Manipur, are a little known tribal community seeking official and administrative recognition from the Union Govt. of India. They are found settling mainly in 35 villages of three hill districts of Manipur *viz,* Chandel, Churachandpur and Senapati, and also sporadic distribution of a few households in Imphal - the capital of Manipur.

Excepting a very brief ethnographic profile (Singh *et al.*, 2000) and a few stray references (Das, 1990; Singh, 1990; Mate, 1997), this tribe which is generally backward and the poorest of the poor, remained almost untouched from academic point of view. The phenomenon of tribal scenario and social reality observed among the minor and numerically insignificant tribe is the problem of decline in its population size heading towards numerical extinction. This is because of a number of exogenous factors—more particularly socio-cultural exploitation and absorption by some major tribes who are socio-culturally dominant, technologically more advanced and numerically superior. With not an exception, Mates who are demographically virgin may also face similar situation and, if proper attention is not paid, then their demographic virginity may end in tears. Therefore, it is on this context that the Mate tribe of Manipur has been selected for the study.

Material and Methods

The present chapter is based on the demographic data collected from the entire population of Mate tribe settled in 35 villages of three hill districts in Manipur during the month of September, 2003. Altogether, 1054 households were surveyed for census enumeration using structured schedule.

The data include information like name, age, sex, clan, marital status, educational attainment, occupational status, income, age at marriage, house type, livestock count, electronic gadgets used in the houses, means of transport, health condition, number and cause of death during the last one year etc.

For a detailed fertility survey a random sample of 200 married women were interviewed using structured interview schedule. This sample constitutes 12.00% of the women belonging to reproductive period of life span. The data of fertility study include age at menarche, age at marriage, age at the first child birth, age at menopause, reproductive performance (serial outcome of each pregnancy), use of contraceptive devices etc.

Appropriate statistical and mathematical treatment was given to the data for calculating relevant statistical constants and various rates and ratios.

Results and Discussion

Table 5.1 displays the demographic profile of the Mate tribe of Manipur settled in 35 villages distributed in 3 hill districts of Manipur. The total population of the tribe as per the census enumeration of a total of 1054 households is 6682. This figure constitutes 1.60% of total Scheduled Tribe population and 0.29% of the total population of Manipur. Out of the total population, 3254 (48.69%) are males and 3428 (51.30%) females, thus giving a sex ratio of 1053. High sex ratio observed in this population may be attributed to differential mortality pattern caused particularly by higher incidence of death of males consequent upon the demolition of their villages in the ethnic classes which took place during 1997 to 1999. This population can be considered as a young population on the basis of high young dependency ratio (65.72) and comparatively high crude birth rate (29.03). The natural growth rate is 18.67 which is much higher than that of Manipur total (13.10) and 17.40 for India (Bose, 2001).

Table 5.1: Demographic Profile of Mate Tribe: Age and Sex Composition

Age Group in years	*Male*	%	*Female*	%	*Total*	%
0-14 years (Children)	1240	38.11	1312	38.27	2552	38.19
15-64 years (Active person)	1891	58.11	1992	58.11	3883	58.11
65+(Aged)	123	3.78	124	3.62	247	3.70
	3254	48.69	3428	51.30	6682	

Sex Ratio – 1053 (females per 1000 male)
Total number of household – 1054.
Average number of members per house – 6.34.
Young Dependency Ratio – 65.72.
Old Dependency Ratio –6.34.
Total Dependency Ratio -72.08.
Crude Birth Rate – 29.03.
Crude Death Rate – 10.36.
Natural Growth Rate – 18.67.

Menarcheal age which marks the beginning of reproductive span is one of the important biological factors determining fertility of a population. It is at the same time influenced by environmental factors as well (Johnston, 1974; Barry, 1988; Tanner *et al.*, 1967). Variation in age at menarche of 24 different countries ranges between 10 to 18 years (Shah, 1958, cited in Bhasin *et al.*, 1993). At the same time secular trend in age at menarche is also demonstrated (Hoshi *et al.*, 1981; Tanner *et al.*, 1967; Barry, 1988). As for the present study is concerned, age at menarche of Mate tribe range from 12 to 17 years, with the highest frequency (38.00%) at the age of 14 years and mean age being 14.48 ± 0.08 years (Table 5.2). On the other hand, age at menopause which marks the termination of reproductive life span is not as sharply defined as that of menarche. Among the Mates it ranges from 39 years to 56 years. The average age at menopause of the population is 45.50 ± 0.47 years (Table 5.3) and does not show much

Table 5.2: Distribution of Women According to Age at Menarche

Age in Years	*Married Women*	
	No	%
12	4	2.00
13	30	15.00
14	76	38.00
15	54	27.00
16	31	15.50
17	5	2.50
Total	200	100.00

X = 14.48±0.08 years

SD = 1.08±0.05 years

deviation from the norm of 46 years (Pearl, 1939). The time interval between age at menarche and menopause therefore, clearly indicates the reproductive span to be 31.02 years.

Table 5.3: Distribution of Women According to Age at Menopause

Age in Years	*Women*	
	No	%
39-40	2	3.57
41-42	10	17.86
43-44	12	21.43
45-46	14	25.00
47-48	10	17.86
49-50	4	7.14
51-52	-	-
53-54	2	3.57
55-56	2	3.57
Total	56	100.00

X = 45.50 ± 0 .47 years

SD = 3.53 ± 0.33 years

Age at marriage is one such factor which plays a significant role in determining the fertility status of a population. It has been demonstrated by many of the earlier studies (NSS, 1961-1962; Agarwala, 1970; Mutharayappa, 1988; Sharma *et al.*, 1990) that women getting married at an earlier age experience longer period of reproductive span and usually have more number of children as compared to those getting married at a later age. On the other hand, a magnitude of variables such as age at menarche, educational qualification, socio-economic status, cultural beliefs and practices, urbanisation and employment status etc. have been reported to have influenced in bringing variation of age at marriage in different populations (Caldwell *et al.*, 1983; Choudhury et *al.*, 1997; Maheo, 2004).

Age at marriage (Table 5.4) among the Mate women ranges between 14 years (1.00%) to 26 years (1.50%). The

Table 5. 4: Distribution of Women According to Age at Marriage

Age in Years	*Married Women*	
	No	*%*
14	2	1.00
15	22	11.00
16	33	16.50
17	28	14.00
18	42	21.00
19	13	6.50
20	22	11.00
21	13	6.50
22	11	5.50
23	4	2.00
24	5	2.50
25	2	1.00
26	3	1.50
Total	200	100.00

X = 18.36±0.19 years

SD = 2.64±0.13 years

highest number of women (21.00%) gets married at the age of 18 years. Their mean age at marriage (18.36 ± 0.19 years) is almost equal to that of Indian women (18.32 years) as reported by Bhasin, *et al.*, 1993.

The outcome of pregnancies according to the age of mothers is shown in Table 5.5. Number of live births per women increases with the increase in chronological age of the mothers. Women of age group 15 - 19 years give only 1.25 live births per woman while those belonging to age group 45 and above give birth to as many as 6.61 live births during the whole course of their reproductive period. Obviously, it is because of exposure to married life for a longer period.

Incidence of pregnancy wastage also nevertheless, shows a similar trend of increase with the increasing age of mothers as observed in case of live births (Table 5.5). This in fact may be because of the fact that with the increase in chronological age more particularly, after 35 years and after having 3 or more children, decline in the efficiency of reproductive system takes place thereby increasing the risk of pregnancy wastages. It is also evident from the table that when the average number of live birth per woman is 4.83, pregnancy wastage accounts for 0.67 (0.28 still births and 0.39 abortions) per woman. This indicates that approximately for every 8 pregnancies 7 turned out to be live birth and 1 pregnancy wastage. The other ways round the ratio of number of pregnancy to abortion and number of pregnancy to still birth are 14:1 and 20:1 respectively. If we combine the percentage frequency of still births (5.10%) with abortion (7.10%), the total pregnancy wastage comes to 12.20% of the total number of pregnancies. This comparatively higher incidence of prenatal death is also evident from comparative statement with other populations may be attributed to lethal effects of homozygosis of gene loci consequent upon consanguineous marriage (cross cousin marriage as reported by Singh *et al.*, 2000), a preferential form of marriage prevalent among them. Similar findings are also reported for other populations as well (Basu, 1975; Ansari *et al.*, 1978; Pandey *et al.*, 2000). Moreover, some of the Mate villages located in the interior part of Manipur lack modern health care facilities. Therefore, poor health care measures accompanied by under nutrition of expectant mothers during gestation period and child birth might be another cause of higher pregnancy wastage among them.

Table 5.5 : Age Group-wise Distribution of Pregnancy Outcome.

Age group in years	No. of Women	No. of Pregnancy	Live Birth No.	Live Birth Per Woman	Still Birth No.	Still Birth Per Woman	Abortion No.	Abortion Per Woman
15-19	4	5	5	1.25	-	-	-	-
20-24	26	50	39	1.50	2	0.08	9	0.35
25-29	26	86	82	3.15	4	0.15	-	-
30-34	28	132	119	4.25	6	0.22	7	0.25
35-39	37	226	200	5.41	12	0.32	14	0.37
40-44	20	155	130	6.50	5	0.25	20	1.00
45+	59	445	390	6.61	27	0.45	28	0.48
Total	200	1099	965 (87.81%)	4.83	56 (5.10%)	0.28	78 (7.10%)	0.39

Pregnancy per woman = 1099 ÷ 200 = 5.5.

As regards the birth order (Table 5.6), higher number of women of both the categories (all the women and who completed reproductive period) have birth order 4 and above. Sixth birth order shows the highest frequency (14.50%) when all the women are considered together, while for the women of completed fertility, highest frequency (21.43%) of them has a birth order of 8 live births. But on the whole, the average number of live births per woman account for 4.83 and 6.60 for the first and second categories of women respectively.

On comparison of these values with the available data of other population of Manipur (Singh, 2004), the present findings show a higher number of live births (Table 5.7) per woman. This certainly is because of their early marriage and their main economic activities (agriculture) which demands for more working hands.

Table 5.6 : Percentage Distribution of Women by Birth Order

Order of birth	*Women*			
	All the age group		*Completed fertility*	
	No	*%*	*No*	*%*
0	5	2.50	4	7.14
1	17	8.50	2	3.57
2	23	11.50	-	-
3	21	10.50	2	3.57
4	26	13.00	4	7.14
5	27	13.50	5	8.93
6	29	14.50	7	12.50
7	21	10.50	6	10.71
8	17	8.50	12	21.43
9	5	2.50	5	8.93
10	6	3.00	6	10.71
11	2	1.00	2	3.57
12	-	-	-	-
13	-	-	-	-
14	1	0.50	1	1.79
Total	200	100.00	56	100.00

Average number of live birth per woman (all the age group)-4.83.

Average number of live birth per woman who completed fertility-6.60.

Table 5.7: Fertility Pattern among the Mate and Other Population Groups of Manipur

Population	*Live birth per woman*	*Completed fertility per woman*	*Still birth per woman*	*Abortion per woman*
Mate (present study)	4.83	6.60	0.28	0.35
Meitei (Singh, 2004)	4.01	6.19	0.04	0.30
Pangal (Singh, 2004)	4.35	6.39	0.13	0.21
Nepali (Singh, 2004)	4.15	6.35	0.19	0.07
Kabui (Singh, 2004)	4.12	6.29	0.12	0.22

Mortality measures on the basis of total enumeration, presented in Table 5.8 reveals that during the period of September 2002 to September 2003, a total of 22 infants (12 neonates and 10 post neonates) and 58 adult (of all ages) deaths took place, while the total number of live births being 194. Accordingly, the corresponding IMR, NMR, PNMR and CDR are 113.40, 61.86, 51.55 and 8.68 respectively. These rates are higher than the corresponding figures of Manipur State in particular and India in general.

Table 5.8: Mortality Measures among the Mate Tribe

I.				
No. of death	***Infant***	***Neonates***	***Post Neonates***	***Total (all ages)***
	22	***12***	***10***	***58***
II.				
Death Rates	IMR	NMR	PNMR	CDR
	113.40	61.86	51.55	8.68

(Calculated on the basis of 194 total live births and 6682 total population.)

High Infant Mortality Rate observed among these people may be consequent of a number of factors. Higher rate of Neonatal Mortality Rate may be mainly due to endogenous factors apart from chronic malnutrition of the fetus during gestation period. Most of the Mate villages, being located in the interior areas of Manipur, lack maternal child welfare facilities. People are less aware of the immunisation of the children. Because of lack of crèches and child welfare centers as well as by the nature of their economy, children are carried on their mother's back to the work-site where they are exposed to various health-hazard environments resulting to higher infant mortality rates.

However, in spite of high mortality rates, fertility rate is high, first because of the fact that high infant mortality is a very great indirect inducer of higher fertility. The death of a child is often compensated with another conception. Secondly, to compete in the struggle of identity crisis among the tribal groups whereby numerically superior and politically dominant recognised tribes exploit and suppress the lesser ones, they have an inclination towards increasing the population size. Then only they feel they can get recognition and constitutional benefits.

REFERENCES

Agarwala, S.N., 1970, *A Demographic Study of Six Urbanized Village.* Asia Publishing House. Bombay.

Ansari, N.A and S.P. Sinha. 1978. "Survey on the Effect of Inbreeding in Two Populations of Bihar". *Indian Medical Research Journal.* 68: pp. 295-299

Barry, B. 1988. *Patterns of Human Growth.* Cambridge University Press, New York.

Basu, S.K. 1975. "Effects of Consanguinity among North-Indian Muslims". *Journal of Population Research.* 2: pp. 57-68.

Bhasin,V. and M.K. Bhasin., 1993, "Ecology, Population Dynamics among Transhumant of Himalayas: A Case Study of Gaddis of Himachal Pradesh". *Journal of Human Ecology,* 3: pp. 171-219.

Bose, A., 2001., *Population on India: Census Results and Methodology.* B.R. Publishing Co., Delhi.

Caldwell, J.C.; P.H. Reddy and P .Caldwell., 1983, "The Causes of Marriage Change in South India". *Population Studies,* 37 : 343.

Choudhuri, B.: and M. Devi., 1997, "Fertility Differentials in Manipur: A Study of the Meiteis and the Muslims". *Journal of Human Ecology,* 8, 1: pp. 51-59.

Das, R.K., 1990, *"Tribal Identity in Manipur".* In B. Pakem (Ed): *Nationality, Ethnicity and Cultural Identity in North-East India.* Omson Publication, New Delhi.

Hoshi, H. and M. Kouchi., 1981, "Secular Trend of the Age at Menarche of Japanese Girls with Special Regard to the Secular Acceleration of the Age at Peak Height Velocity". *Human Biology,* 53: pp. 593-98.

Johnston, F.E., 1974, "Control of Age at Menarche". *Human Biology.* 46: pp. 159-71.

Maheo, L.M., 2004, *The Mao Naga Tribe of Manipur.* Mittal Publications, New Delhi.

Mate, L. D.,1997, *The Mate Tribe.* Mate Anthropological Society, Manipur.

Mutharayappa, R., 1998, "Fertility and Family Planning Among Jenu Kuruba and Kadu Kuruba Tribes of Karnataka". *Man in India.* 78, pp. 1-2: 119-126.

National Sample Survey, 1993, *Tables with Notes on Couple Fertility*. 17th Round, September 1961 to July 1962, No. 175. Indian Statistical Institute, Calcutta.

Pandey, B.N., S.K. Mishra, S. Yadav and P.D. Sharma., 2000, "Foetal Wastage and Infant Mortality in Four Endogamous Population of Purnia District (Bihar)". *Journal of Human Ecology*, 11, 6: pp. 477-81.

Pearl, R., 1939, *The Natural History of Population*. Oxford University Press, New York.

Sharma, K. N. N. and S. K. Abdul., 1990, "Fertility and Mortality Trends of Khairwar Tribal Women of Madhya Pradesh". *Man in India*. 70, 4: pp. 446-53.

Singh, J., 2004, "Differential Fertility among Four Population Groups of Manipur". Paper presented in the National Seminar on Population and Development in North- East India, February 2004. pp. 25-27.

Singh, R.K. R., 1990, "Emergent Ethnic Processes in Manipur: A Re-appraisal", In B. Pakem (Ed): *Nationality, Ethnicity and Cultural Identity in North-East India*. Omson Publication, New Delhi.

Singh, W. N. and L. Doukhosei., 2000, *The Mates of Manipur: Their Ethnographic Profile*. Government of Manipur, Imphal.

Tanner, J.M. and O.B. Keeffe., 1967, "Age at Menarche in Nigerian School Girls with a note on their Height and Weight from Age 12-19 years". *Human Biology*, 39: pp. 187-96.

6

Nutritional Status of the Children of Tarao Tribe of Manipur

— *Ksh. Vedmani Devi* and *K. Saratchandra Singh*

A few anthropometric measurements are often used as a tool for assessment of nutritional status especially among the growing children (Jelliffe, 1966; Johnston, 1981; Helene *et al.*, 1988; Gorstein, 1989; etc.). Such anthropometric parameters have been commonly called as nutritional anthropometry. Often growth and nutritional status of the children are done with the use of height or weight for age, and with the simple index of height and weight, i.e., Body Mass Index (BMI). Normally, height indicates the rate of temporal growth, while weight indicates the sum total of the growth of an individual. Body weight in particular has long been used as an index of Protein Energy Malnutrition (PEM). But BMI is an indicator of obesity (Weisell, 2002) and reduced BMI is known as indicator for Chronic Energy Deficiency (CED).

Health and nutrition are one of the priority areas of the public health organisation in the world today. To map out the magnitude and geographical distribution of malnutrition to discover and analyse the ecological factors that are directly responsible, has been emphasised by the World Health Organisation (WHO). Optimal nutrition is necessary for optimal health (WHO, 1983). Sharma (1991-92) says health is a composite and cumulative effect of a host of factors including the availability of food and food habits, safe drinking water, hygienic living conditions, improved purchasing capacity and, above all, education and not just immunity against communicable diseases. Rao (1996) reported that nutritional status of the tribes seems to be influenced by their habitat and socio-economic status. According to the National Nutrition Monitoring Bureau in India, the prevalence of malnutrition between the period of 1969 and 1975 was as high as 18 to 20 percent (Gopalan, 1988).

Data on the nutritional status of the tribes of India are scanty. The National Institute of Nutrition (1971) and the Planning Commission of India (1980) reported high protein calorie malnutrition along the rice eating belt. Among the tribes of Assam, high incidence of goiter, angular stomatitis and Vitamin A deficiency have been reported (Gopalan, 1971). Studies, on the food habit and the nutritional status of the people of Manipur including that of the tribal populations, are either scanty or has not been taken up systematically.

In the present study, an attempt has been made to assess the nutritional status of the children of Tarao Tribe of Manipur by using height for age, weight for age and body mass index (BMI).

The Tarao tribe is one of the scheduled tribes of Manipur. Their distributions are confined in four villages in the hill district of Chandel and one in Ukhrul district. As per household census conducted during 2003, for the present study, the total population of the Tarao is 689 only. In language and custom, they are, closely akin to the Kuki-Chin groups and referred to be an old Kuki tribe of Manipur (Shakespear, 1912; Bose, 1934; Levi-Strauss, 1969; etc.). At present, they identify by themselves as a Naga-ethnic community. They observe clan exogamy and they follow patrilineal descent. Of late, they have adopted Christianity.

Rice is the staple food for the Taraos. Cultivation of rice and other vegetables are done on the *Jhum* fields. Scarcity of rice is the normal order amongst them and during such time, their requirements are often supplemented by roots and tubers, maize and pumpkin, etc. Varieties of wild vegetations are identified for consumption. They are non-vegetarians and meats of various animals are relished by them. Simple boiling is the chief medium of cooking for various forms of vegetarian and non-vegetarian cuisines with a pinch of salt. They take two major meals—once in the early morning and another in the evening.

Material and Methods

With an aim to study the gastronomy, the nutritional ecology and the demographic profile of the Tarao tribe, a large component of data including a few anthropometric measurements, haemoglobin level and clinical observations have been collected during a span of one complete year in 2003.

For the present study, only height and weight measurements have been considered for the purpose of assessing nutritional status of the Tarao children belonging to 1-19 years of age group. The measurements were taken following the standard techniques given by Weiner and Lourie (1969) by using anthropometric rod and weighing machine. Height for age as recommended by WHO (1976) and weight for age which was originally proposed by Gomez *et al.* (1956) and modified later on by Jelliffe (1966) were scored. BMI which expresses the ratio of weight to height square has also been calculated.

A total sample of 141 children of both sexes (male = 71, female = 70) have been collected at random following cross sectional survey.

Analyses and Results

Results from the findings of the estimation of the nutritional status of the Tarao children out of the three measures are given as below.

Nutritional grades in terms of Height for Age percentage reference among the Tarao children have shown that out of the 71 male children (Table 6.1), 22.54% were found to belong to normal group, while the rest were found to be suffering from Grade I (32.39%), Grade II (29.58%), Grade III (7.04%) and Grade IV (8.05%) malnutrition levels. Among the female children, only 17.14% were normal, which is much lesser than that of the males. The remaining of them was found to be suffering from different malnutrition Grades of I (31.43%), II (38.57%), III (7.14%) and IV (5.71%).

Table 6.1: Nutritional Grades among the Tarao Children in Respect of Height for Age

Grades	*Percentage of reference*	*Male*		*Female*		*Total*	
		f	*%*	*f*	*%*	*f*	*%*
Normal	95	16	22.54	12	17.14	28	19.86
Malnutrition							
Grade I	90-95	23	32.39	22	31.43	45	31.91
Grade II	85-90	21	29.58	27	38.57	48	34.04
Grade III	80-85	5	7.04	5	7.14	10	7.09
Grade IV	> 80	6	8.45	4	5.71	10	7.09
	Total	71	100.00	70	100.00	141	100.00

The estimation of Weight for Age percentage reference (Table 6.2) has indicated that the number of normal group of children were rather high (55.32%) in this population being

Table 6.2: Nutritional Grades among the Tarao children in respect of Weight for Age

Grades	*Percentage of reference*	*Male*		*Female*		*Total*	
		f	*%*	*f*	*%*	*f*	*%*
Normal	80	42	59.15	36	51.43	78	55.32
Malnutrition							
Grade I	70-80	17	23.94	14	20.00	31	21.99
Grade II	60-70	5	7.04	12	17.14	17	12.06
Grade III	50-60	4	5.63	4	5.71	8	5.67
Grade IV	> 50	3	4.23	4	5.71	7	4.96
	Total	71	100.00	70	100.00	141	100.00

59.15% for the males and 51.43% for the females. The rest (male children) who suffered from malnutrition, are 23.94% in Grade I, 7.04% in Grade II, 5.63% in Grade III and 4.23% in Grade IV levels. The female children, who suffered from different malnutrition grades are 20.00% in Grade I, 17.14% in Grade II, 5.71% in Grade III and 5.71% in Grade IV malnutrition. In this estimation of weight for age percentage too, the female children appears to suffer more, due to malnutrition, than their male counterparts.

Classification of BMI has shown (Table 6.3) that the normal children are again found to be quite few among their population being 23.94% among the males and 17.14% among the females, in a trend more or less similar to those percentage references of height for age. The numbers of underweight children are very high with 42.55% of which 39.44% are the males and 45.71% are the females. A total of 7.09% children are at the risk of obesity in this group, whereas male children (9.86%) outnumbered the female children (4.29%). A good number of children are also suffering from Obese Grade I (17.02%) and Obese Grade II (12.77%) levels and it has been evident that the female children are more than that of the male children in both the categories.

Table 6.3: Body Mass Index among the Tarao children

Body Mass Index	*Classification (IOTF)*	*Male*		*Female*		*Total*	
		f	%	*f*	%	*f*	%
< 18.5	Under weight	28	39.44	32	45.71	60	42.55
18.5 - 22.9	Normal	17	23.94	12	17.14	29	20.57
23.0 - 24.9	At risk of obesity	7	9.86	3	4.29	10	7.09
25.0 - 29.9	Obese - I	10	14.08	14	20.00	24	17.02
> 30.0	Obese - II	9	12.68	9	12.86	18	12.77
	Total	71	100.00	70	100.00	141	100.00

Statistical comparisons have, however, shown (Table 6.4) that no significant bisexual variations have been found in the manifestations of the normal and other forms of malnutrition in all the above three measures, i.e. height for age ($\chi^2 = 0.64$, d.f = 1), weight for age ($\chi^2 = 0.85$, d.f = 1), and BMI ($\chi^2 = 1.0$, d.f = 1) at 5 percent probability level.

Table 6.4: Test of Significance: Bisexual comparisons in the distribution of Normal and Malnutrition Tarao children

Measures	*X^2 values*	*Probability level*	
Height for Age	0.64	P>0.05, df=1	Not significant
Weight for Age	0.85	P>0.05, df=1	Not significant
Body Mass Index	1.00	P>0.05, df=1	Not significant

N.B. All the frequencies of malnutrition grades or classifications have been grouped together in all the measures for the purpose of χ^2 test.

Summary and Conclusion

The three measures, for the nutritional status, as discussed above, have revealed that the numbers of normal Tarao children are only 20.00% according to the height for age (19.86%) and BMI (20.57%) except in weight for age in which the normal group of children are appreciably high with 55.32%. In the former two measures, height as a factor is common for the estimation of nutritional index of the population and it may be pointed out that height has a rigid plasticity. Lesser number of normal children, perhaps, also indicates poorer growth rate among these children. Weight, on the other hand, is more sensitive and fluctuates on little stress. It, therefore, appears that height as a parameter reveals more appropriate pictures of the nutritional level compared to body weight, in a broader perspective. Although weight for age has shown comparatively higher number of normal children, still the numbers of children who show mild to severe form of malnutrition are proportionately high suggesting the Tarao children being suffered more from protein energy malnutrition (PEM). At the same time, reduced BMI has indicated the chronic energy deficiency (CED) amongst them. The presence of significant number of obesity possibly among the higher age group children may be indicative of morbidity and mortality (Weisell, 2002; Saroja, 2003). High incidence of malnutrition cases among the population has also been pointed out by Vedmani (2006) from the assessment of haemoglobin level and certain clinical observations. There is a clear indication of inadequate intake of protein source food despite of the Taraos having non-vegetarian food habit. A serious review of the food quantity and quality consumed by the Taraos is the need of the hour if their health is to be improved.

REFERENCES

Bose, J.K., 1934, "Dual Organisation in Assam", *Journal of the Department of Letters*. Calcutta University. 25. 1: pp. 1-29.

Gomez, F., R.R.Gatvan; S.Frank; J. Cravioto; R.Chavez; and J. Vosquiz., 1956, "Mortality in Second and Third Degree Malnutrition", *Journal of Tropical Paediatrics*, 2: pp. 77-83.

Gopalan, C.1988., "*Combating Malnutrition - Practical Leads from Scientific Research in India*", C.V.Raman Memorial Lecture. 5th Oct. 1988, Indian National Science Academy. Delhi.

Gorstein, J.,1989, "Assessment of Nutritional Status: Effect of Different Methods to Determine Age on the Classification of Under Nutrition". *Bulletin of World Health Organization*, 67, 2: pp. 143-50.

Helene, D; N. Gayle; J.Binkin; W. Norman; F. Stachlingand; and L. Trowbridge., 1988, "Arm Circumference Vs Weight for Height in Nutritional Assessment. Are the Findings Comparable?" *Journal of Tropical Paediatrics* 34 : pp. 213-17.

Jelliffe, D.B.,1966, *The Assessment of the Nutritional Status of the Community*. World Health Organisation Monograph, 53:69 World Health Organisation, Geneva.

Johnston, F.E.,1981, "Anthropometry and Nutritional Status". pp 252 – 264. In *Assessing Changing Food Consumption Patterns*, National Press Academy, Washington.

Levi-Strauss. C.1969, *The Elementary Structure of Kinship*, Oxford University Press. Oxford.

Planning Commission of India. 1980. *Report of the Sixth Five Year Plan*, Government of India, New Delhi.

Rao, D.H., 1996, "Nutritional Profile of Indian Tribes". *Nutrition News*, 17:2: pp. 1-4.

Saroja, P. 2003, "Nutritional Status of Adolescent Girls Residing in a University Hostel", *Indian Journal of Nutrition and Dietics,* 40, pp. 274-279.

Shakespear, J.,1912, *The Lushei Kuki Clans,* Macmillan and Co., Ltd., London.

Sharma, J.C., 1991-92, "Nutritional Factor in Health, Physical Growth and Development and Politics", *Proceedings of 79th Session of Indian Science Congress Association,* Part II, Presidential Address.

Vedmani Devi, Ksh., 2006, Gastronomy and Nutritional Status of TaraoTribe of Manipur, Unpublished Ph.D. Thesis, Manipur University.

Weiner, J.S. and J.A.Lourie., 1969, *Human Biology: A Guide to Field Methods.* International Biological Programme, Handbook No.9, Blackwell Scientific Publications. Oxford and Edinburg.

Weisell, C.R., 2002, "Body Mass Index as an Indicator of Obesity". *Asia Pacific Journal of Clinical Nutrition.* 11: pp. 681- 83.

World Health Organization., 1976, *Methodology of Nutritional Surveillance.* Technical Report Series No. 593

World Health Organisation., 1986, "Use and Interpretation of Anthropometry Indicators of Nutritional Status". *Bulletin of World Health Organization,* 64, 6: pp. 929-41.

7

Elements of Disintegration in Khasi Matrilineal System

—M. Sasi Kumar

Matrilineal systems in its traditional form are hard to find to exist anywhere in the world. Matrilineal descent groups gradually disintegrate under economic changes brought about by contact with western industrial nations (Schneider and Gough, 1961). Fortes (1949) sees that unstable social system produced by occupational differentiation, stratification by income, education and rank, geographical and social mobility, as well as disparate values in religious beliefs are root causes for disintegration of matrilineal systems. Economic changes brought by changes in production relations as a result of culture contacts tempt communities like Rabhas to choose the path of change (Raha, 1989). Introduction of cash crop farming and subsequent economic changes have brought radical kinship changes among many matrilineal communities like, Tonga, Ndembu, Yao, Ashanthi and Nayar (Colson, 1961; Turner, 1957; Mitchell, 1956; Fortes, 1949; Schneider and Gough, 1961).

Though matrilineal system was much more widely distributed in India, the matrilineal communities and the communities bearing matrilineal elements are chiefly found in the northeast and southwest parts of India (Raha, 1989). In south India most communities like Nayars, Kurichians, Thiyyar and Mappila (Kerala) have given up many of the elements of matrilineal system and adopted the elementary family mode. The Arumbukuttom Vellalas of Tamil Nadu numbering a few thousands of people still follows the matrilineal systems of descent and inheritance (Sasikumar, 1999). Rabhas, a tribal community of West Bengal and Assam, which traditionally followed matrilineal system, is in a transitional stage from matriliny to patriliny.

The Khasi and Garo of Meghalaya are the important tribal groups, who follow the matrilineal system in the northeast part of India. Though neighbours, geographically, the two communities are distinct with reference to the structure and composition of the descent groups and with relation to inheritance and residential patterns. Other communities, who show matrilineal features in the eastern and north eastern parts of the country, are the Pani-Koch and Lalung (Raha, 1989).

The People

The Khasi is a Scheduled Tribal community found mainly in the East and West Khasi Hills District of Meghalaya. The main feature of Khasi society is its matrilineal social structure. The Khasi speaks a dialect that belongs to Mon-Khmer branch of the Austric family.

Four subdivisions of Khasis are generally identified. They are the Jaintias, the War Khasis, the Lyngam Khasis and the Khasi proper or the mainland Khasis or the Khynriam Khasis. These sub-divisions of Khasis are not strictly endogamous groups. But they are not exogamous as well. Marriages between them though uncommon are not prohibited. The Lyngams are said to be half Khasi and half Garo (Gurdon, 1907). Some of the authors like Gurdon (1907) and Chowdhury (1996) considered the Bhois also as a sub-group of Khasi, though there is certain admixture of Mikir elements in them. The Bhois themselves claim that they are Khasi and many Khasi customs and social traits are reported to be present side by side with Mikir influences in their culture. Though all the sub-groups of Khasi share many things in common, differences are observed as far as many of their cultural elements such as economy, dialects, customs and rituals etc. are concerned. All these sub-groups follow matrilineal system of descent and kinship though there are differences in minutiae. Each of these sub-divisions again is sub-divided into a number of clans, lineages and families. The main feature of Khasi society around which the whole fabric of Khasi social organisation is woven around is clan exogamy. The present study confines itself to the Khynriam Khasi inhabiting the Shillong plateau.

Elements of Disintegration

The Khasi society is not immune to the types of changes that are taking place among the matrilineal societies, the world over. But the process and direction of changes are different. An alternative value system is gradually emerging giving tremendous pressure to the matrilineal systems in that society and this shift is not due to a 'single factor' but it is a cumulative outcome of wide variety of factors evident in that society today. Though the impingement has been considerable in some respects, in many other respects their traditional more have continued unaffected.

One of the integrating principles of the Khasi society is its value system based on its religious beliefs and practices. The matrilineal system also exists surrounding this value system rooted in religion. As far as the Khasis are concerned, religion and worship were matrilineal family affairs performed by the matrilineal male usually the *kni* (the eldest of the maternal uncles) at the *khadduh's* residence. Presently Christianity offers an alternative organised belief system that has a patrilineal bias and it conflicts and even contradicts matrilineal beliefs. It is a known fact that in the Christian preaching, the father, not the maternal uncle, figures prominently. Among the Christians though the presence of maternal uncles and maternal males bring honour to the occasion, yet it is the father who is preferred. During marriages it is the father who gives the bride away publicly. The maternal uncle does it only in his absence.

The spread of education among the Khasis during the last few decades, has brought some structural changes. Many of them, after getting education, could enter the Government Service, which brought occupational and spatial mobility among them. Most of them who could get into Government Service, settled in and around the Shillong town. They could also engage in different businesses and non-traditional and non-agricultural jobs and thus becoming part and parcel of the urban affluence. This has also helped in inculcating in them certain western values that is not in conformity with their traditional norms and value systems. In the little stratified Khasi society, a middle class is gradually emerging, based on the urban centered affluence, education and wealth. The urban centered self-sustainability and spatial mobility results in the decreasing influence of the matrilineal groups on its members.

The role and control of maternal uncles on their sisters and their children is also becoming thin and slacken for the lack of proximity and presence due to spatial mobility. He has to give prominence to his own career, entertainment, and his own children with whom they have more emotional attachment. They use their earnings primarily for their elementary families and neglect their traditional obligations to matrilineal kin. As the maternal authority relinquishes, the paternal responsibilities and authorities are on the increase. The tendency among the youth, especially among those settled in the cities and among the educated, is to socially identify with their father and not with their maternal uncles.

Earlier spatially close frequency of social contacts was regular. Change of residence from rural to urban settings and change of occupational pattern caused for the changes in interactional pattern as well. Social interaction is evidenced in the major areas of deaths, engagements, marriages and births. Among the Christian Khasis as the traditional rites are not practised as vigorously as earlier interaction is also cut down in this area as well.

In the present day Khasi society, the male members are physically unavailable to his matrilineal descent group, due to the matrilocal pattern of residence. Traditionally, this problem was solved by the custom of village endogamous marriages so that his accessibility to his own descent group is not a problem. Now-a-day due to spatial mobility of a Khasi due to education, occupation etc., this proximity was cut down to a considerable extent. A man is thus gradually alienating from his own descent group. Due to his emotional attachments to his children and wife and also due to the pattern of matrilocal residence, he weans away from his own group and assimilates himself with his wife's descent group. The degree of alienation, from his own group and assimilation with his wife's descent group, has great repercussions, as it will obstruct the continuity of the matrilineal descent group.

Though it was not uncommon among the educated Khasis, especially among the Christian Khasis, to adopt the father's title, it has made a reversal in recent years under the pretext that it may hamper the very sanctity of clan exogamy on which the structural existence of the community was rooted. The Khasis fear that adoption of fathers' titles may lead to marriages between blood relatives on the mothers' side, which they considered to be a taboo and the greatest sin a Khasi can ever commit. Still the practice of adopting father's title was a style, at least among some, who live outside the Khasi domain; but whenever they come back to the Khasi fold, they revert to mothers' titles.

But the urge to identify themselves with the father, among the Khasi living in urban areas, is found irreversible though they are fond to use different methods. One recent trend is to use the titles of both the parents; the father's title being prefixed to that of mother's. Yet another method is to suffix father's personal name to one's personal name followed by mother's title.

Specific areas of role performances and decision-making of maternal uncles and fathers were not clearly defined in the traditional social and familial set-up of the Khasis. As the avenues widens, the father is to expand his sphere of family responsibilities as well. The maternal uncles have their added responsibility in his own household as the father of his kids. These dual roles, as father of his kids and maternal uncle of his nephews and nieces, make him incapable to perform his traditional role as maternal uncle as satisfactorily as the custom demands. Other factors, influencing the role performances are level of education, economic stability, physical proximity, personal interest and involvement. Modern values conflict with the traditional norms. It is the corporate responsibility, however, of all the maternal male members of the *Iing* (matri lineage) to be involved of the main issues that concerns their *Iing* members.

The father in the modern context find himself confronted with new roles and duties, to perform with a greater responsibility to shoulder, than in the past. In the past the role of the father was limited to that of the breadwinner. He took care of the small domestic problems that may arise. He even assisted his wife in the management of her ancestral property. Now as the sphere of day-to-day life widens, the involvement of father in the activities of the family, especially, those pertaining to the children, also widens. As the spheres of duties to be performed were limited in the traditional way of life, the duties and responsibilities of the father and the maternal uncles were not precisely defined. The father had only a limited role to perform in a family. The elder males' responsibilities were more of religious and of social nature and the maternal uncle usually met it. Today what is expected to be delivered to the youngsters are more than the religious and social needs, but they have to take care of their education, socialisation, careers, food and clothing and a lot others the modern world demands. The father now acts also as the legal guardians of their children and not the maternal uncles. In all these spheres of life, the maternal and paternal responsibilities are not so defined and the fathers' involvement is more visible. Thus when the responsibility of a Khasi man as a maternal uncle dwindles, the responsibility as a father is on the increase. Nevertheless in decisions regarding the sale of ancestral property and in disputes among siblings, the maternal uncle has not lost his influence.

The modern transport and communication facilities have helped them to shift from traditional subsistence-based agricultural productions to cash crops. This shift in their production pattern introduced them to a commercial economy, bringing tremendous changes in their life style. As a result, the little stratified Khasi society emerges as a stratified society based on property and income. A middle class based on economic prosperity is gradually emerging among them. In such a society, negative sanctions, by the community against the deviants, seldom work and ultimately affect the continuity of the matrilineal group.

Land was largely controlled by matrilineal descent groups and was never alienated or transacted without the consent of the *kur durbars*. This property would have been looking after by the *kur* or clan and may be distributed among its needy members for cultivation and erecting houses. The traditional laws forbidding the sale of matrilinealy owned lands ceased to be observed in practice and such sales are now in practice. Now the sale of ancestral lineage-owned property has become common and private owned property (*ri-kynti*) has correspondingly increased. Traditionally, the land among the Khasis was owned by the family and was managed by the maternal uncle of the youngest daughter who latter inherits the property. But now-a-days, some differences are observed to this pattern and in many cases the *ka khadduh* (youngest daughter) seeks co-operation and participation of their husbands in the management of properties under her custody. In the case of *ri kynti*, the family concerned has all the freedom to use the land as per their wishes. As a result many mothers are now-a-days setting apart a portion of land for their destitute sons as well.

The underlying principle of ultimogeniture rule of inheritance negates the rights of daughters, other than the youngest, over the property of their parents. This is one of the areas of stress and strain felt even by the female members of the community. Even though the youngest daughter was only the custodian of the ancestral property in the past, the situation has changed a lot and now she is more or less considered as the legal heiress. As the community has advanced from subsistence-based society to stratified society, this system of inheritance matters a lot. It creates imbalances as far as the economy of the members of the family is concerned. It is observed that while the youngest sister living in posh houses, enjoying a lot of economic liberties, her own siblings have to try hard to make a living.

In the towns, especially among the working husbands, it is found that the husbands instead of settling in the wife's family or locality is either leaving his wife behind temporarily with her parents or else take her to live in his locality. Some are found living with the husband's mother itself if he is the only child of his mother or living in a separate house built by the husband's mother for his son in her land. This pattern is generally found among those living in urban settings.

The matrilineal system among the Khasis is not continuing unchallenged. There is a section among them who are not satisfied with the sort of affair happening with in the system. Though isolated, the attempts to change the system are more than five decades old. An organisation called *Ka Seng Iktiar Longbriew Manbriew*, was formed in 1961 to spearhead a movement for change in the matrilineal system in favour of patriliny, especially in the matters of descent, inheritance and succession. The organisation with this objective continued their activities but could not make much headway. The State Government in 1980's requested its Law Commission to draft a Bill enabling the parents to bequeath their self-acquired property to distribute among their children as per their wish. The Law Commission prepared a Bill accordingly and the Bill was duly passed by the Meghalaya Legislative Assembly as the Meghalaya Succession to Self-Acquired property (Khasi and Jaintia Special Provision) Act 1984 which received the assent of the President of India in 1986. The above Act does not apply to the ancestral properties. But the Act of 1986 still lies in the 'cold storage' as the Government failed to formally notify it to give effects to its application. In the year 1990, a new organisation named *Syngkhong Rympei Thymmai* was formed with more or less the same objective of the earlier organisation and replaced the other one.

Conclusion

The Khasis still follow the matrilineal system of descent and inheritance pattern. But elements of changes are visible in several aspects of their culture which survive around the matrilineal system. The close link of matrilineal system, with their traditional religion, helped them to restrain change elements to a great extent. The Khasi is a tradition-bound society. It often persuades its members to cling to their old age customs and traditions by enforcing various kinds of sanctions on deviants. In a close-knit society, no one can live as a social isolate and hence they observe the traditional norms and values as strictly as possible.

Several extraneous elements are gradually penetrating into the social self of the community. Some elements like Christianity, with a strong patrilineal bias, have already made deep inroads into their socio-religious life. Those, who embraced Christianity, began to neglect many of their customs and practices and rites and rituals without observing them as strictly as earlier. Christianity often prefers the paternal to maternal involvements in their socio-religious observances.

Adoption of Christian faith, spread of education, introduction to commercial economy, enrolment in Government Services and the consequent occupational and spatial mobility, have brought them in contact with other cultures. Among the youth there is a growing tendency to imbibe more and more elements from other cultures and to neglect their own. Today the whole fabric of matrilineal system of Khasi is facing the threats of changes from various quarters and as a result it evolves certain social mechanisms that will help to maintain, adopt, adjust and that will ensure the survival and continuity of the society. There may not be any sudden change as far as the descent and kinship pattern are concerned, but changes could be observed as far as inheritance, succession, authority patterns, decision making etc. are concerned.

REFERENCES

Chowdhury, J.N., 1996, *The Khasi People*. Shillong.

Colson, E., 1961, "Plateau Tonga", in D.M. Schneider and K. Gough (Eds): *Matrilineal Kinship*. University of California Press. Barkley.

Fortes, M., 1949, "Time and Social Structure: An Ashanti Case Study". In F. Eggan and M. Fortes (Eds): *Social Structure*. Oxford University Press, London.

Gurdon, P.R.T., 1907, *The Khasis*. Cosmo Publications, Delhi (Reprint, 1975).

Mathur, P.R.G., 1979, *The Khasi of Meghalaya*. Cosmo Publications, New Delhi.

Mitchell, W. E., 1956, *The Yao Village*. Manchester University Press, Manchester.

Nakane, C., 1961, *Garo and Khasi: A Comparative Study in Matrilineal System*. Mounton and Co. Hague.

Raha, M.K., 1989, *Matriliny to Patriliny: A Study of the Rabha Society*. Gyan Publishing House, New Delhi.

Sasi Kumar, M., 1996, "Kurichia", In T. M. Menon and M. Sasikumar. (Eds): *The Encyclopaedia of Dravidian Tribes*. Vol. II. International School of Dravidian Linguistics, Thiruvananthapuram.

Schneider, D.M. and K. Gough., 1961, *Matrilineal Kinship*. University of California Press, Barkley.

Turner, V., 1956., *Schism and Continuity in an African Society*. Manchester University Press, Machester.

8

Spatial and Temporal Dimensions of Matriliny Among the Garo of Meghalaya

—Sankar Kumar Roy

Under same ecological and technological system, two cultures stand distinct. It happens so ,when the two are close to each other. Why it happens so, is a matter of debate. This we may say that each ethnic group has cultural language peculiar to its own. Each is a repertoire of experience which it acquires through its journey over time and space and that an ethnic group hardly parts with. For this, we see the patriliny and matriliny exist under the same ecological and same technological systems.

This reality becomes obvious when we examine the cultures and ecology of North East India. There are a number of remote corners in North East India, which encapsulate even today the pre-literate populations with such a level of technology that has not undergone any major change. This state is comparable to either the food gathering or the early level of food producing economy that made its beginning during prehistoric past (Roy, 1981, 1994; Ashraf, 2004). However, such a state exists on the contemporary time plane, where the chronologically modern cultures stay with economically prehistoric ones. When the juxtapositions of the two are considered, time tends to lose its horizon, the past breaks its barrier and merges with the present.

The present era in which we line is overwhelmed by market economy where the ethno-cultural groups are mostly patrilineal. But among them, the three matrilineal cultural groups, the Garo, the Khasi, the Pnar thrive on their distinct socio-cultural identity in their traditional abodes of Meghalaya and beyond that as well. The three matrilineal cultural groups stand as islands, widely encircled by the patrilineal cultural groups of differential economic contours (Hutton, 1921, 1932; Shakespeare, 1921; Mills, 1922, 1937; Roy, 1992, 1994; Goswami, 1994).

The historicity of mother based society antedates the father based one (Childe, 1952: 28). Schematic arguments were put forward as to the replacement of matrilineal system by the patrlineal one. Such arguments are based mostly on economic grounds. The emergence of plough is assumed to be a cause of the reduction of the women role in the sphere of production and that led to the decline of this system and consequently her power; but here economic environment in family does not recede. But the question is. Why among the shifting cultivators in North East India the matriliny exists? Not only that among some plough using ethnic groups of the plains adjoining the habitation of the Garo, patriliny and matriliny exists for tracing the lineages—for the son through the father's and for the daughter through the mother's clans, respectively (Roy, 1999). Therefore, the male's instrumental role in the food production economy cannot be taken as a sole cause of decline in matrilineal system.

Ember (1983 : 285 – 286) commented that the relative decline in women's economic contribution to agriculture started with its intensification, this was fostered by the introduction of plough and that ultimately pulled the women out of the main productive system. She was more burdened with the domestic works and with increased rate of fertility.

Crown and Fish while building current model of Hohokam prehistory, commented that the main cause in the decline of women's status was increased occurrence of warfare during the classical period (1996: 804). The ethnographic accounts from the shifting cultivators of North East India record the inter-tribal and inter-clan feuds during the early part of twentieth century (Hutton, 1921, 1932; Shakespeare, 1921; Mills, 1922; Dutta, 1978). In such feuds, the women need protection from the males; last, the opponents should carry her off as war booty. The males protect her as she has a major economic contribution. She gets protection from the males; and that also by sacrificing her status. She has to accept the domination of the males. The main idea behind juxtaposing the examples from North East India aims to have an understanding that in addition to economic factor, others are there that work behind determining the status of women.

It is a fact that with the invention of improved food producing technology, the economic power shifted to the hand of the males from the females. The ethno cultural socio-economic and socio-cultural scenario of North East India, as a whole, is dominantly patrilineal and that of the Garo, the Pnar and the Khasi – the matrilineal ethnic groups of Meghalaya, almost insularly in their extreme, offer us an interesting area for study. If this system is viewed against the perspective of economy and time, it is a phenomenon of the past resounds in the present. The three groups with their so-called 'primordial' system thrive.

The Garos are not the only matrilineal groups in Meghalaya, there are other two – the Khasis and the Pnar. The inner content of the two vary in their inner texture as well. Of the three matrilineal groups, the Garo are brought under examination for two reasons. Firstly, this cultural group remains encapsulated cohesively within their given geo-cultural territory. Although migration has taken place, they remains confined to their territory, mostly with their traditional cultural elements.

Secondly, the traditional habitat of the ethno-cultural group under study is a rich archaeological material. Of that, the typological analogy between the lithic hoe blades of Neolithic culture and the present-day used metallic ones, and their location in some *jhum* field, carries the positive clue to their functional continuity. This is being supported by the same edge-wearing pattern. Hence, the economy of the Neolithic past and the ethnographic present of this area do not present a dichotomy; it is continuity rather (Roy, 1981). The economic base underpins the socio-economic structure and the kinship network gets oriented accordingly to ensure the economic existence. This is seen among the culture that remains at a low level of technology. The Garo with their subsistence economy offer a Stone Age economic pattern on the contemporary time plane. Against this background, let us examine the prevailing socio-economic system of the ethnic group under study.

Geographic and Ethno-cultural Situation

The populations we are concerned with are distributed with the greatest density of concentration over the highland of the Garo hills district of Meghalaya. This highland zone is situated in between 25.9" and 26.0" N latitude and 80.47" and 91.2" E longitude. It is enclaved on its east by Bangladesh and on the west by Goalpara district of Assam. The major part of this district is covered by three major hill-ranges – the Tura, Rongru and Arbella; their altitude varying from 1500 to 4600 ft. (Sharma, 1972: 24 – 30). This area comes under sub-tropical zone where the heat and cold are equally contrast and torturous. The density of annual rainfall recorded varies. It starts in between February and March and continues up to July; after that the rainfall and temperature recedes and the moisture content becomes low and it is followed by cold.

There are altogether five rivers, of these there is only one river, named Simsang in Garo hills which is more or less navigable towards its down streams; it becomes fully navigable and creating a wide flood plain when it enters into Bangladesh. Others cruise through the rocky gorges of Garo Hills. They are fed by innumerable inlets from the different areas of hills and hillocks. In fact, none of the rivers creates any barrier to human movement.

The people, inhabiting adjacent to the river Simsang, use dugout canoe (Roy, 1980) as a transport between their horticultural field and the village. In the western part, owing to the absence of navigable river, human energy is solely utilised. However, the traditional socio-cultural or socio-economic pattern of the two (i.e. western and eastern part of this district) remains unchanged. The difference, seen here in the technology of horticulture of this area as a whole, limits too little only. The construction of the canoes necessitates the collective effort and the use of a set of carpentry tools known as *Rua* (cutting tools including axes are known as *rua*) in Garo dialect (in eastern part). The collective involvement in making the canoe is followed by collective usufruct right over the same (Roy, 1980). While moving towards the western hilly part, the use of *Rua* gets ineffective as the canoe cannot be used here. *Ate mongreng* or *ate* – the chopper for felling trees and for serving other purpose emerges as a main tool, subservient to the horticultural technology.

The dialect, they speak in, is included in Bodo group that comes under the Tibeto-Burman linguistic family (Grierson, 1903). Barring some minor variations, the Garo (the Achik) maintain homogeneity in dialect (Roy, 1996).

As regards their origin and migration, there remain conflicting opinions. Playfair (1909: 7 – 14) while recording the legends of their migration, stated that the Garo who now-a-days call themselves Achik (Hillman) traced their original place of habitation AS Tibet. Their present day distributional pattern shows that they are mostly distributed over the southern valley of the mighty river Brahmaputra. The physical feature of this population as described by Playfair (1909: 2 – 4) appears to be somewhat at variance with the population inhabiting Tibet now. Not only this, but the present days subsistence technological pattern of this population is very close to that of the technology adopted to the tropical highland ecology of the South East Asia (Roy, 1977). The stone tools collected from the Neolithic horizon of this area bear a distinct ethnicity with tools collected from its neighbouring South East Asian cultural zone. The economic pattern this area presents even today bears a close similarity with that of its South East Asian counterpart.

May it be that this ethnic group have migrated to this area during the Neolithic period, from the neighbouring South East Asia and have not get submerged under the successive waves of the Mongoloid or the Indo-European speaking population settling on the flood plains of North East India. This process as it appears is stalled here owing to its geographical location.

Issues as to the cultural or ethnic homogeneity or isolation are very often considered to be of geographical origin. However, sometimes, contrast linguistic difference between the two populations may be a cause of isolation; the same phenomenon distanced the Mayans of America from the neighbouring counterparts (Coe, 1975: 36-41). Similarly, the Garo living in dense forest-covered area maintained cultural isolation from its neighbouring (plains) cultural groups, viz., the Bengalee as late as the end of nineteenth century A.D., the barter operated between the two hostile and linguistically alien populations at some truce spots of the *hatta* (weekly market) in the form of 'dumb show' (Das, 1982). Very often, the linguistics difference coupled with cultural contrast forms a barrier insurmountable. That had, what exactly, been here until the recent past as well.

Ethno-archaeology and Ethno-history

As said earlier, the Neolithic culture artifacts became archaeologically defunct, but its function exists in the typologically similar iron hoe blades. The Neolithic population of this area entered in the historic period when they accepted the iron version of Neolithic Celts from their neighbouring populations who knew the technology of iron smelting. There are two such populations adjacent to Garo Hills; one in the flood plains Assam and another Khasi Hills. The latter one has been inheriting the indigenous method of iron smelting from an unknown past (Gurdon, 1975). Nevertheless, they traded or exchanged their iron sword *(Melan)* with the Garo from an unrecorded past. Hence, a uniform period of acceptance of iron tools (not technology) cannot be ascribed to all over the area; rather it depended on their relative proximity to the iron using cultures. However, there is a logical reason to believe that the Garo, living nearer to the population of the Plains, procured the iron blades or chopper as early as the middle or late part of historic era. The acceptance of metal marks the beginning of metal using era in this area.

Now the question remains whether this quantitative change in horticultural tools really brings about any qualitative difference in the economic sphere or productive pattern. The study conducted in this area gives a negative picture (Roy, 1981).

The cultural pattern or the economy is nothing but a resultant of how the technology negotiates with the given ecology. In fact, the cultural pattern or the socio-economic condition of this people hinges on a delicate relation between the ecology and technology. Majority of the people remain encapsulated even today in the forest cover and their culture is in a state of maintaining courtship with ecology, and the mode of exploiting nature remains more or less same as it was during the Neolithic past (Roy, 1981).

They live in a close co-operation with the nature by evolving an eco-friendly farming or horticultural technology. Their socio-economic system is as such where the sex-wise division of labour is coupled with balanced sharing of authority and wealth. Each family is economically self-contained; although the technological level is not sufficient to take a family beyond the subsistence level. When such economic pattern is viewed against the evolved agricultural economy of the Plains, the technology in operation at this area (i.e. Garo Hills) is nothing but a 'continuation of Stone age Economy' of the past exists chronologically in the present.

Again, it becomes pertinent to shed some light on the ethno-historic or the ethnic affiliation of the population thriving on in their present habitat. Already said that the present day economic pattern of this ethnic group is an extension of Neolithic economy; but this doubt lurks whether the present people are the same ones who abandoned their stone hoe blades in favour of the iron hoe blades, which are typologically considered replica of the stone ones. The Neolithic Cultures developed at Bankao, Thailand (Soresen, 1967: 110) entered into iron using culture retaining the previous pottery types more or less unaltered. Similar situation exists in this area as well. What more is that the hoe blades – the lithic and iron carry almost the same feature in respect of their size, shape and edge wearing patterns. All these speak of the fact that both the lithic and iron hoe blades were used in horticulture in a same manner (Roy, 1981). The baton of culture was relayed from the past to the present. Time passed on but economy remaining the same.

The horticultural economy practised here is not sufficient. One has to depend on the naturally available material like the culturally nonderilict types of root and tuber to compensate the deficit of horticultural or shifting agricultural products. For the collection of such product, tools for grabbing are required. For such purpose i.e., for digging out roots and tuber that form a vital part of diet during the prehistoric past. Sumatraliths (Sharma and Roy, 1978) which is described as 'handadze' suited for digging out the roots, and tubers was used during Hoabinhian Culture (Solheim II, 1967), might have been used here as well. The second one, he inferred, the wide utility of the wooden artifacts during Old Stone Age in South East Asia. He described it as one of the major substitutes, for the stone tools discharged similar function of digging. This, he dabbed as 'lignin culture '(Solheim II, 1969). Issac comments that digging stick was very much an integral part of food gathering economy, it entered into the Neolithic economy in an unaltered form (1970 : 43 – 44). Its transcendence, in the present days shifting cultivation system, speaks of the inheritance of food gathering elements by this ethnic group. Further, the presence of concave scrapers in the Stone Age collection speaks of its utility in dressing the digging stick. Similar inference is made on the scraper from the Stone Age site distributed in the sub-tropical areas of India (Allchin, 1983: 50).

The use of metal except for the hoe blade and chopper is found to be restricted to a major extent even today. This is evident from the extensive use of bamboo, wood, fodder as raw materials for house construction. The extensive use of bamboo slip for house construction was preferred to other e.g., iron wire or riveting, materials even today. Here is a constant attempt to meet the needs from within the given available resources; the natural or artificial. People enjoy material plenty by reducing their needs. It has become an economy of concrete and finite object (Shalins, 1972: 27). Since all here derives resource from the same ecology in a uniform way and scale, there is no rich, nor is there poor also.

'Time' in the cultural sense is a concept that is reckoned with the level of technological formation and that level is made to relate with some geological formation, or else with some historical events. The very item 'time' is of little use to the people whom we are concerned with. They come into being in the same area / territory; use same iron hoe as their father did, that in turn is handed over to the next. Same tradition rolls on. Past and present becomes an indivisible entity; the people simply stand in between with their culture.

Material culture

The material cultural content of the people consists of limited items only and almost all are functionally integrated with the needs. The term material culture has its wider connotation. But for the present purpose, a certain items forming indiscrete part with the economic pursuit and socio-cultural life have been referred to (Table 8.1).

In fact, under this technological pattern, the involvement of each tool is systematically conditioned. For example, the hoe blade, its total span of involvement is 1010 hours (approx)

Table 8.1: Material Cultural Items of the Garo

Items	*Name English*	*Loca name*	*Raw material*	*Availability*	*Function*	*Ceremonial*	*Sex who uses it*	*Remarks*
Costume/ Textiles	Turban	*Fagri*	Cotton	Obtained from the Bengali trader	Decorative	N.F.	Male	Used by Nokma
	Lower garment	*Ganao*	Cotton	-do-	Ulitarian		Male	
	-do-	*Rikhing*	Cotton	-do-	Ulitarian	N.F.	Female	
	Shawl	N.K.	Cotton	-do-	Utilitarian	N.F.	Female	
	Shawl	*Marang -jaksa*	Silk	Obtained from Assamese people	Ulitarian	N.F.	Female	
	Head dress	*Orua*	Cotton	N.K.	Utilitarian		Female	
	Bark blanket	*Salachala*	Bark	Locally available	Utilitarian tree		Male & Female	
	Dancing costume	*Pandera*	Cotton	N.K.	Decorative	N.F.	Female	
	Waist band	*Senki*	Cotton and bead	N.K.	Decorative	N.F.	Female	
Ornament	Ear ornament	*Penta*	Ivory	N.K.	Decorative	Obsequres	Female	
	-do-	*Penta*	Silver	Assam		Functional	Female	
	Conch shell bead	*Necklace*	Conch shell	N.K.	Decorative		Male	Chiabak Garo
	Heavy ring	*Jaksa*	Silver/Brass			Functional	Male	Used during hunting
	Circlet covered with cloth	*Kancisil*	Brass					
	Comb	*Filna*	Bamboo		Decorative	N.F.	Female	

Items	Name English	Local name	Raw material	Availability	Function	Ceremonial	Sex who uses it	Remarks
War and chase	Shield	*Sepi*	Wood	Locally available	Decorative		Male	
	Shield	*Danil*	Animal hide		Utilitarian	Functional	Male	
	Sword	*Melan*	Iron	Obtained from the Khasi	Utilitarian		Male	
	Bow and Arrow		Bamboo/Iron				Male	
Agriculture	Axe	*Rua*	Bamboo/Iron	Obtained blade from Bengali trader	Decorative	N.F.	Male	
	Heavy chopper cum axe	*Ate Mongren*	Bamboo/Iron	-do-	Utilitarian		Male	
	-do-	*Ate*	Bamboo/Iron	-do-	Utilitarian		Male	
Utensil	Cooking Pot	*Medak*	Clay	Indigeneously made	Utilitarian		Female	
	Basket strainer	*Ganchi*	Bamboo	-do-	Utilitarian		Female	
Musical Instrument	Drum	*Knam*	Wood and animal hide	Indigeneously made		Functional	Male	Sometime used entertainment
	Drum	*Nadik*				Functional	Male	-do-
	Flute	*Adil*	Bamboo	-do-		Functional	Male	-do-
		Singa	Cattle horn	-do-		N.F.	N.K.	
		Otekara		-do-				
Fishing trap	Fishing gear/trap	*Nagil*	Bamboo	Indigeneously made		N.F.	N.K.	
		Chekka	Bamboo	-do-	Decorative		N.K.	

Abbreviation: N.K. for not known
N.F. for non-functional

throughout its working span (Roy, 1981: 201). The women are the traditional manipulator of the hoe in horticultural operation while the male's traditional involvement is hardly above 90 hours throughout the season. A woman has to work from dibbling to harvesting; in terms of hours, it is the maximum. A male dispenses his traditional involvement in horticultural operation with clearing the jungles and setting fire to that when it gets dry (Table 8.2).

If we see the role of each sex involved in the production of artifact, a certain observations can be made. The female is manipulator of the hoe but she is not its maker; it is male who makes it; so is the case for basket for containing and carrying product from field. In final analysis it becomes clear, that a balanced equation in techno-economic level is maintained. The technology that underpins the relation between the male and female has its direct impact on their kinship pattern. The low level of technology of material culture here at this area has two dimensions; it makes the economy go never above subsistence level; secondly this has made the relation between man and land close and thereby generating a strong force of cohesion among the clan members; that ultimately culminates in forecasting a wider sense of cohesion among all clans and makes this group exist with a distinctive identity. This develops owing to the fact that there exists a true form of democracy in material culture. To understand the socio-economic aspect of this matrilineal ethnic group, quantitative and qualitative evaluation of material culture becomes essential.

Seen that the traditional relation between artifact and gender is fixed almost and that debars the female from making basket, so is the relation between the hoe, the digging stick and the male. This works in silent or in subconscious level. In between the artifact and the gender, there exists an unseen phenomenon, this is a culturally patterned involvement of a given gender towards a given type of artifacts. This in the words of Dobres and Hoffman (1994) ".......technology thus serves as an arena in which different kinds of interests can be

Table 8.2: Time Schedule for Weeding and Harvesting Crops from Shifting Cultivation

Crops	*Months of sowing*	*Months of harvesting*	*Weeding period and approximate hours*	*Remarks*
1	*2*	*3*	*4*	*5*
Millet (E) Millet(L) Paddy (L)	March	August	March 707 hours	Taking 9 hours per day, less 2 hours (approx.) leisure period a day. The initial 3 months experience heavy rainfall and weeds grow rapidly, hence the involvement of tools becomes greater [b]
Melon/gourd/ other vegetables		September		
Brinjal / Chili		October	August 160 hours	Taking 8-7 hours a day, leisure period as above
Paddy Manioc/ yams Deccan hemp/ginger/ arum		November	September 120 hours	Working hours decline steadily through October-November
Beans sesame and similar seeds		October 10C hours		

1	2	3	4	5
Cotton		December	November (exact hours not known)	
Lai		January		
Paddy(L) changing				

Source: Roy, 1981: 201

Notes: (a) Weeding starts 20-25 days after sowing

(b) The main tool used is the hoe. The *dao* is not uncommon, but its use is extremely limited. The area covered by each person is approximately 0.55 acre per day, but cannot be ascertained exactly, since one individual will use his own hoe to help another during the peak period. The period and location of the hoe blade's use are, therefore, not restricted to one individual's area.

E = early; L = late variety

defined, expressed and negotiated" (cited from Dobres, 1995: 27).

Field prepared by the male for *jhum* cultivation, while the female broadcast seed over that. The male built the house, the female own it with the offspring of her lineage. Almost, everything of the house – movable or immovable is traditionally owned by the females. When a man and a woman is examined against the previously mentioned material items, it becomes apparent neither male nor a female is in a position to maintain an insularly existence in economic sphere; rather one feeds back another. Here the qualitative, not the quantitative involvement of the male or the female is important, what is important that how this system works now with its strong socio-economic viability. Under this system, the co-ordination between quantitative and qualitative aspects of the material culture is very tacitly made. The male act as a starter; the women keep the system on.

Resource Management

The density of population away from the urban and peri-urban areas ranges from 5 to 6 persons per square kilometer. The low carrying capacity is not due to the insufficiency of land, it is rather a reverse. For the development of such phenomenon, the traditional technology under the given ecological condition plays an important role (Roy, 1981). Under such horticultural technology, the major part of the land appears to remain underexploited, but the field situation reveals this is something a requirement of this system itself. At material, cultural or economic level, one unit is opposite to another, this completes the functional cycle.

A given plot of land once brought under cultivation is left fallow for a period of 5 to 20 years, with a view that the lost of vegetation results from burning returns to its original state so that it gets ready for coming agricultural operation. This appears now, that this is the best means to maintain an economic balance whereto technology (hoe and chopper) contributes its vital share. The traditional pattern of land tenure that helps in the continuation of this system needs to be understood against its proper perspective. Here the technology and the mode of distribution of land work in close harmony and they underpin the traditional economy of this population. The technology and the ecology are not the last words. It is equally important to examine the social relation that determines the production system of this population since ancient past.

Land Tenure System

Shifting cultivations practised in this part of Meghalaya, is not a unique phenomenon ; rather it is a commonly adopted means to raising agricultural crops from the highland areas of Nagaland (erstwhile Naga Hills) by the ethnic groups viz., Lotha Nagas (Mills, 1922 : 97 – 98), Sema Nagas (Hutton, 1921 : 44 – 51), Ao Nagas (Smith, 1925 : 127-28), Lakhers (Hutton, 1932 : 75 – 82), the Lushai Kuki clans (Shakespeare, 1921) etc. In Arunachal Pradesh similar practices are still in currence among the Nocte (Dutta, 1978), the Boris (Kumar, 1979), the Nishis (Shukla, 1959), the Tagins etc. This type of agricultural pattern is reported as well from the highlanders of South East Asia. The main features that differentiates the system of this ethnic group from that of others not by virtue of its mode of technological operation but by the distinctive way the system works. In fact, the given land brought under cultivation is not individually owned; a clan possesses it. The clans are matrilineal where the females traditionally inherit the property. Hence, the women have authority over the agricultural land and its product in an explicit manner. However, the power of demarcation of land remains at the hand of the males; with this power, he is entitled to take the decision over the demarcation of plot of land allotted to this family. Covertly, he acts as attaché to his wife.

Each village has traditionally demarcated area of its own, termed as *a'dok* (a land for cultivation). An *a'dok* may be a part of *a'king* (a village exclusively of homogeneous or same clan member). In course of time, some new *a'king* may grow out of an *a'king* village. For such newly grown *a'king*, a particular area is allotted. When demarcated, it is *a'dok* having a series of area which is taken up for cultivation in a cyclic order. The *Nokma* (a village headman) does this allotment.

Now the question that comes to one's mind whether this type of land tenure system, method applied to *Jhum* cultivation technology and social organisation work in an integrated manner. The whole system hinges on their balanced relation. Authority and power distribution system are not independent entities; these are interlocked, each has to work as within the wider system. All works in a structured manner within the mother based kin system. It is vertically shared between the two sexes – the female exclusively shares the economic power and authority over the household matter, but the decision-making or political power rest in the hand of the males. The female keep it on and conserve it; for its disposal or distribution, may be in part, male's approval is required. One opposes another; through opposition, the system exists.

Nature offers resources; from that, technology generates energy. This energy is economy, it is the blood for culture, while the kinship system is artery and arteriole, through which it is transmitted to the different limbs or institutions. At a first glance, it appears here that the technology holds the rein of the system. Males and females are nothing but the components working under the dictation of this system. A little introspection leaves an impression that the existing form of the Garo culture is nothing but a symphony of different variables; geography cradles it and time tunes it when demanded.

Settlement Pattern

The settlement pattern of this ethnic group deserves special attention for a number of reasons. Of that, for the present purpose of study, its symbolic aspect is very much important. Each village stands for a particular clan. The clan in its form and content do not vary from one another; so does their house pattern. A village means a clan village wherein a member of another clan cannot stay with his separate identity permanently. Expansion in the number of houses in village means the increase in the members of the same matrilineal clan.

The process starts with the migration of the male after his marriage to his wife's house permanently but not all daughters can stay in their mother's house permanently. The tradition or custom reserves the right of the youngest daughter to be the heir of her parent's residence and property. So, a male after his marriage to a youngest daughter needs to stay in his in-law's residence, wherein he has to past his whole life.

The other daughters after their marriage have to release their usufruct right over the residence of their parent by constructing houses somewhere within the same village boundary to start life anew. If the given space of a hillock proves insufficient for further enlargement, one has to construct one's house on a nearby hillock; that is within one's own clan territorial limit.

Such a construction of new settlements acts as bud of the natal village. However, in due course, with the establishment of new families, its size grows; and finally the cluster of residences with homogeneous clan population emerges as an independent village with a social structure like that of its natal one.

As said earlier that a male adds a new lease of life to the preexisting system. He cannot bring any change in the vernacular architecture; because here he simply participates in a preexisting system. He merely acts, not directs, he protects; but cannot create anything new.

At an interval of certain years, the male members of the clan renovate a house together in a day. The women's participation remains confined to the preparation of meal for the participating members only. The males make the preexisting tradition, as it appears, perpetuate. This may be owing to the fact that the cultural equilibrium has not been disturbed since its beginning by the external agencies like inter-ethnic conflicts or warfare like other patrilinial shifting cultivators of North East Indian highlanders as earlier mentioned. Nor did the settlers of the plain culturally or economically come in confrontation with this group of people until 18th century (Das, 1983: 115 – 116). The time rolls on, but the kinship system, which remains as a strong core around which everything; non-material or material or economic system revolves; this withstands the onslaught of time. Settlement pattern as it exists in traditional milieu responds in a same way as the other non-material aspects do.

The geographical, linguistic barriers and the ethnic situations around this cultural group are very much conducive to the preservation of traditional system until a few decades back. It maintained an insular existence until the historic period; their contact with other neighbouring people was maintained for economic reason; but that was in the form of 'silent or mute trade' (Roy, 1992: 83; Das, 1983: 15 – 16).

However, its impact was less on this culture living in a non-mechanic stage; here the crisis or needs are met with from within its given resources available locally. People here, barter their deficit and seasonal surplus, almost equally among themselves. This is a culturally accepted reality to them; all are psychologically oriented towards facing the uncertainty. The cultural system is balanced here as such that it absorbs uncertainties, deficit and seasonal excess, if there be any, in it.

Economy

The geomorphic condition has not undergone any major variation; nor does the technology suited to this geographical condition from the Neolithic to the recent past show any shift. The quantum of production, from the traditional technology and Neolithic one, does not show any major variation (Roy, 1981). A family under this type of subsistence economy is a producer and a consumer at the same time and the similar feature is found among the other shifting cultivators of North

East India (Roy, 1994). As already mentioned that under such system, patrilineal societies in respect of status and role, the male predominate over the female. This remains not only confined to between the two sexes; the same tendency leads one member to the road of giving leadership to his clan that culminates in the creation of chieftainship while assuming the authority over a clan with all its clan members. This leads to the centralisation of power in the hands of a chieftain. Once such power is acquired, there is a tendency to retain it and it devolves upon the successors of his lineage. It becomes a system. This system retains the seed of centralisation in it. Economy here has not reached beyond the subsistence level; as under exploitation of natural resources with low level, technology in an unfavourable ecological condition, acts a negative pull. This negates the very process of State formation.

The economic centralisation means slicing away other's economic resource or power in favour of the chieftain. The subsistence economy of the shifting cultivator comes under strain. This generates the very force of the fission within a homogeneous clan. In order to get rid of such strain, some members, of a clan in part, splinter out of its nodal clan and emerge out as a new one with the same force of centralisation that is in operation in the nodal clan. In fact the force of fission, which results from the challenge to the authority and power of the chieftain, is very much a manifestation of internal dynamics in the patrilineal based subsistence economy.

The Garo culture is opposed to the above; the females are the sole inheritress of the residence and other heir looms. It is inherited through female line. Females retain it and their husband protect the same. The women reserve their exclusive authority over the conservation of property but she cannot dispose it of her own; the managerial authority rest with her husband or in his absence, the elders of her *machong* or *chara* act as substitute (Majumdar, 1980: 21).

This is how the economic power among this matrilineal society is balanced at a family level. But when the management of the village organisation is taken into account, the role of the female has little weightage. The husband and the male members of her *machong* or *chara* play the decisive role. Here again the role of *Nokma* becomes decisive and his decision becomes mandatory almost.

In Khasi hills the *Syiemship* in its form and content goes to represent a crude level of State formation under the matrilineal system. According to Mathur (1975: 68) several *raids* or communes join to form the State or *Syiemship* with an elected chief, the *Syiem*. Gurdon observed that in some parts of this hill, as many as eight clans took part in electing a *Syiem*. Through this process, a *Syiem* centralized the political power over the State under his jurisdiction. Such a centralisation of power in the hand of a male does not lead to an aberration in the traditional pattern of heirship; the heirship to *Syiem* is always through female line (Gurdon, 1975: 68 – 74).

Under such a system, a *Syiem* is vested with the political power no doubt; but here he acts as an attaché of the matrilineal clans. He is a spectrum whereon the female power and authority reflects in a tacit manner. In fact, despite the structural difference between the Garo *Nokma* and the *Syiem*, uniformity becomes obvious that their matrilineal system through its balanced distribution of wealth and power delimits the mobility of the males; it cannot go beyond a given level.

In fact, the political position of a *Nokma* is bound up with the traditional authority of his wife. The youngest daughter, by virtue of traditional custom of inheritance, becomes the sole heiress of the residence (*Nok*) and other property of her mother, the rest while married daughters start a new life in a residence, built within the same *a'king* village; in case of lack of residential area within the same *a'king*, they built new residence outside the present village, which should be within the demarcated area of her clan. The youngest daughter does not change her residence. The *Nokma* adds a new lease of life to the preexisting residences of his wife in particular and *a'king* as a whole. He simply infuses himself to the already existing system. The process of fusion instead of fission comes to pass through the centripetal nature of matrilineal system. The very force of fusion is inherent in Garo polity. Such force originates from the family level and extends wide over to encompass *Mahari / Machong* and *Catchi* level.

The economic structure of the traditional population is conditioned by the finite factors or conditions like the partial utilisation of land with a low level of technology and definite time limit set by erratic monsoons and the nature of inclination of slope (Roy, 1981: 205). It makes the relation between man, nature and society or culture very intimate or direct. Reciprocity and co-operation in the sphere of economy spills over to each and every aspect of economic spheres. The reflection of the same is seen in kinship formation and pattern. Under this system everybody is served, an invalid or an orphan, a widow or an old; *Mahari* of one is one's last resort.

Kinship, Marriage and Family

Already said that the Garo reckon their lineage through the mother. For men, children of their sister or sister's daughters are very important. For women, children of their sister's are equivalent to those of their own daughters. The mother's brother's daughter type of cross cousin marriage is mostly preferred among the people. A man must marry a woman from an opposite *catchi*. The relation between the *machong* of two opposite *catchi* once established, perpetuate from one generation to another. Utmost endeavour is made to maintain the same through MBD type of marriage; the least it breaks. The reason behind is that property should not go to the hand of *machong* or *mahari* other than the preexisting ones. Even after the death or divorce of a spouse, the *a'king* relation continues. It is the responsibility of the deceased's *machong* to provide a replacement spouse of the surviving partner. It is thought proper for the *mahari* of a widow to provide a virgin girl as a co-wife (*Jikgite*) to the second husband (if the second husband is a bachelor). It is a custom that after the death of the father-in-law, his widow (i.e. mother-in-law) is theoretically considered as his wife. Not only that there was evidence from Matchakholgiri, a young man married to a daughter of a widow who had her mother in the same residence, and thus theoretically he became the husband of all the three women (Majumdar, 1980: 81).

Goswami (1994: 187-94) dabbed *mahari* as a pivot of social system; around this, all economic and social activities nucleate. It is a solid plank that underpins the Garo social structure wherein the *a'kings* or *a'khem* acts as another plank that cements the relation between two *mahari*. These two are very much important to understand the Garo polity as well. Introduction of Christianity and modern education have not been yet able to induce a difference in the traditional structure. *Mahari* in true sense is a unit that shares joint responsibility, when somebody has to pay compensation, the *mahari* jointly has to subscribe to that; and it is equally divided among the household of the *mahari* (Majumdar, 1980: 92). It reserves right as well to interfere with the activities of the members of its households.

In fact, the system of matriliny is so much penetrating that it influences the personality formation of both the sexes from their initial stage. A boy psychologically gets himself prepared that his residence is somewhere else than his existing one. This is expressed in their mode of choosing playmates and rearing up process. Goswami (1994: 192) records the statement of a Garo boy. This is as such; the girl say, "Come and join us in our play". Come the retort - "No, we shall not join you. You are girl. You are destined to stay here throughout your life; we are destined to go away from you. What is the benefit to play with you"? What more is that a man says "my mother and sister are my sheet-anchor like the bamboo stump – whereas my wife and children are like hornets (which stung)" (Goswami, 1994: 189). Here it is seen that 'push and pull', the two forces are in operation in the socio-economic sphere of this society. This constitutes the essence of the Garo social organisation.

A man goes to his wife *mahari* after his marriage, but his relation with his mother's *mahari* continues through the *a'king* bond as earlier stated. Here his authoritative role does not die out as long as he survives. The effective role of *mahari* transcends the boundary of one's village and sometimes far beyond that. A Garo couple may remain outside of their traditional territorial limits but the very force of *mahari* does not loose its strength. Under new situation, he is no more than a stranger; he cannot exert his identity in isolation, psychologically his *mahari* / *machong* bond remains equally active when he moves away from his own village. It continues to give him kinship coverage from distance as well. The moment he comes back to his village, his village (mother) returns him the authority. Here time and space difference does not matter at all, what is important that he is an indivisible part of a system.

A Garo, outside his traditional abode, continues to be a Garo, as long as he keeps the attachment alive at his mental level. System or structure exists and works at mental level consciously even if a Garo stays in an alien culture. As already said that the Garo are not the only matrilineal society or culture in North East India, there are other two—the Khasis and the Pnars of Meghalaya.

When the matrilineal system of the Garos is compared with the matrilineal system of the Khasis (Gurdon, 1975) and the Pnar of the Khasi and Jaintiya hills respectively, the contrast between the Garo and the Khasis is not so much obvious as it is between the Garo and the Pnar. The relation of mother's siblings and father among the Pnars when considered, it gives an example of extreme case of matriliny. In case of the Khasis and the Garo, the husband add a new lease of life to the preexisting family and discharge specific roles—economic and social till they survive. Among the Pnars the husband's role limits to be instrumental to procreation only. To a wife, the husband comes at night and leaves at dawn (as a visiting mate) to his mother's or sister's home. He has neither socio-economic obligation to his wife or to progeny after their birth.

A boy grows and is reared up in his mother's family. As a result, psychologically and economically a male becomes dependant upon and an inexorable part of his mother's or sister's family, which provides him socio-economic security throughout his life. In fact, a husband here is a stranger, having no obligation to his progeny. The identity of the progeny and his status nucleates round the mother (Mannoorumpily, 1982: 53 – 64).

Conclusion

Through this study an attempt has been made to infer that matriliny, the so-called primordial or archaic system existing in Garo Hills on contemporary time plane was cradled in the 'stone age economy' of the Neolithic past. Here the Neolithic phase archaeologically broke off when the people inhabiting this area accepted metal and entered into metal using phase; but the 'stone age economy' of the Neolithic past with its structure and content has been continuing uninterruptedly as a stable and viable system withstanding the onslaught of time.

The matriliny exists for certain reasons. The economic level under *jhum* cultivation hardly allows the traditional economy to go beyond the subsistence level; thus arresting the tendency of generating surplus. Deficit both in resource management and in human labour exists. This makes the economy to develop the principle of economic 'cut off' on the one hand and on the other to generate the very obligatory force of 'reciprocity and co-operation' in the economic sphere among the respective clan members. The deficit perpetuates in traditional economy. As a result, the chances of centralisation of political power in the hands of the individuals, gets nipped in the bud. The possibility gets reduced further; since the females act as Central or Pivotal point of kinship system and of the traditional heiress of the property. This skirts the authoritative role of the males and his mobility to a major extent.

Nevertheless, in any social or economic crisis one's *mahari* acts as a last resort for and gives coverage to either the males or the females equally. The relation between the two clans, once got cemented through marriage, is traditionally perpetuated through MBD type of marriage. This is a means to recycle the resources between the two such clans to arrest the further division of the meager resource the clans possess.

True that the matrilineal group, we are concerned with has its inner stress and strain, but that does not lead to the emergence of a new system or make them deviate identifiably from the preceding ones. Any problems generated within it are internalised within the ambit of given system. This is a unique feature that characterises this cultural groups charged with centripetal force.

One may move out beyond one's traditional territorial limit. With that one's kinship bond does not die out. The moment one returns to one's own clan, one gets back one's previous rights. The interesting and significant reality is here, the male's masculine superiority is tacitly counter balanced with the female's traditional right of the inheritance of wealth and the kinship system centering round the mother. This has hedged the tendency of centralisation of power at the hands of the males.

This system seems to be simple but in practice, it proves more effective by working in a dynamic, peculiar to its own. By that it distances itself from the patriarchal groups around its. The ethos stands on mother based kinship or socio-economic system is so strong among this group that the Christianity, (a historical representative of patriarchy) which has already made an inroad among this group, never challenges this traditional system. The bell of change rings, but this traditional system cradled by the Stone Age economy rhythms of its own independent of time and socio economic changes are already set in.

REFERENCES

Allchin, F.R., 1983, *Rise of Civilization in India and Pakistan.* Select Book Service Syndicate, Delhi.

Childe, V.G., 1952, *Social Evolution*. Watts and Co, London.

Coe, V., 1980, *The Maya*. Pelican Publication, Delhi.

Crown, P and S.K.Fish., 1996, "Gender and Status in Hohokam Pre-class to Pre-classic Transition". *American Anthropologist*, 94, 4: pp. 803 – 17.

Das, K.N., 1983, Social Dimension of Garo Language. Unpublished Ph.D Thesis, Gauhati University, Assam.

Dobres, M.A., 1995, "Gender and Prehistoric Technology: On Social Agency of Technological Strategies". *World Archaeology*, 27, 1: pp. 25 – 49

Dutta, P.C., 1978, *The Noctes*. Directorate of Research, Government of Arunachal Pradesh. Shillong.

Ember, C.R., 1983, "Relative Decline in Women's Contribution to Agriculture Intensification". *American Anthropologist*, 85, 2: pp. 285 – 304.

Goswami, M.C., 1994, "Garo Matrilineal Matrix". *Journal of the Indian Anthropological Society*. 1 – 2: pp. 187 – 94.

Gurdon, P. R.T., 1975, *The Khasis*. Cosmo Publications, Delhi.

Hutton, J.H., 1921, *The Angami Nagas*. Macmillan and Co. Ltd., London.

Hutton, J.H., 1932, *The Lakhers*. Macmillan and Co. Ltd., London.

Issac, E., 1970, *Geography of Domestication*. Prentice Hall, New York.

Kumar, K., 1979, *The Boris*. Directorate of Research, Government of Arunachal Pradesh, Shillong.

Majumdar, D.N., 1980, *A Study of Cultural Change in Two Garo Villages of Meghalaya*. Gauhati University Press, Guwahati.

Mannoorapil, T., 1982, The Sociology of the Pnars of Meghalaya. "Unpublished Ph.D Thesis", Gauhati University.

Mathur, P.R.G., 1979, *The Khasis of Meghalaya: A Study in Tribalism and Religion*. Cosmo Publication, Delhi.

Mills, J. P., 1922, *The Lotha Nagas*. Macmillan and Co. Ltd., London.

Mills, J.P., 1937, *The Rengma Nagas*. Macmillan and Co. Ltd., London.

Playfair, A., 1909, *The Garos*. David Nutt and Co., London.

Roy, S.K., 1977, A Study of Ceramics from Neolithic to Mediaeval Period of Assam: An Ethno Archaeological Approach. Unpublished Ph.D Thesis, Gauhati University. Assam.

Roy, S.K., 1980, "A Note on Carpentry Tools (Rua) in Eastern Garo Hills". *Bulletin of the Department of Anthropology, Dibrugarh University*, pp. 9: 202 – 05.

Roy, S.K., 1981, "Aspects of Neolithic Agriculture and Shifting Cultivation, Garo Hills, Meghalaya". *Asian Perspectives,* 24: pp. 193 – 221.

Roy, S.K., 1992, "Garo". In P. Hokings (Ed): *Encyclopedia of World Cultures.* pp 81- 84, Volume III, G. K. Halls and Co, Boston.

Roy, S.K., 1994, "Dimensions of Barter and Exchange in North East India". *Journal of the Indian Anthropological Society,* 29, 3: 227 238.

Roy, S. K., 1996, *Museum News Letter,* Department of Anthropology, Gauhati University. 1,1 : pp. 1– 8.

Sahlins, M., 1972, *Stone Age Economics.* Tavistock Publications, London.

Sangma, M., 1971, "Garo Law of Inheritance". *Pines,* 1, 1: pp. 14 – 16.

Shakespear, I., 1921, *The Lushai Kuki Clans.* Macmillan and Co. Ltd. London.

Sharma, H.C., 1972, Stone Age Cultures of Garo Hills. Unpublished Ph.D Thesis, Gauhati University, Assam.

Sharma, H.C. and S. K. Roy, 1978, "On Discovery of a Pebble Tool Industry in the Garo Hills, Meghalaya" In P. Bellwood and V. N. Mishra (Eds): *Advances in Indo Pacific Prehistory.* IBH and Oxford Publication, Delhi.

Shukla, B.K., 1959, *The Dafla.* Directorate of Research, Government of Arunachal Pradesh. Shillong.

Smith, W.C., 1925, *The Ao Naga Tribes of Assam.* Macmillan and Co Ltd., London.

Solheim – II, W. G., 1967, "South East Asia and the West". *Science,* 157 (3791): pp. 896 – 902.

Solheim – II, W.G., 1969, "Reworking in South East Asian Prehistory". *Paideuma,* 15: pp. 125 – 139.

Sorensen, P., 1967, *Ban-Kao: Archaeological Excavation in Thailand.* Volume II, Munksgaard, Copenhagen.

9

Is Dorbar Shnong Still A Traditional Institution?

—*A.K. Nongkynrih*

In the last five years, we have been engaged in community development extension programme covering the Khasi-Jaintia hills District of Meghalaya. Under this programme, we visit and interact with people, local organisations, and elders of the village. During formal and informal interactions, varied issues are discussed but one issue that keeps cropping up is the village council. It is an important institution in the villages, because it is the keeper of social order and also a body, through which government schemes are implemented. Besides these, there are many aspects related with village councils. On the basis of the information, we have gathered from the field this Chapter has been written The present study tries to examine this particular social institution, from the perspective of change and the impacts. It is not an exhaustive study, but it only examines some key issues, and much more intensive work is required for a comprehensive understanding.

It is important for the general reader to know that the village council we are discussing is not only a socially recognised institution. According to the Sixth Schedule of the Constitution of India, clearly stated in its provisions as to the management of the tribal areas in the State of Assam, Meghalaya, Tripura and Mizoram. The basic objective is to protect the tribal societies. To protect the tribal societies, the Constitution of India created the Autonomous District Councils (ADCs). The role of the ADCs is to manage, preserve the customary beliefs and practices of the tribes, including the traditional institutions. Further, the powers of the Sixth Schedule is that it specify categorically that the President of India, may, with respect to any Act of Parliament, order that it will not be applicable to the Autonomous District or Region of the concerned State. The Constitution of India legitimises the existence and practice of tribal institutions and their customary beliefs and practices. In the State of Meghalaya there are three tiers of administration: The Legislative Assembly, the Autonomous District Councils and the traditional institutions (Gassah, 1998). In Khasi-Jaintia hills, the traditional institutions is organised into a three-tier system or two-tier system, depending on the clustering of villages and the type of political formation. The structural arrangements have evolved over generations. The first process is the formation of villages. In each settlement, the domestic groups belonging to more than one clan, collectively organise themselves to form a *Shnong*, i.e., village. Over generations, these villages together formed a cluster and also maintaining their own individual village autonomous entity. This process, of clustering of villages, created a second tier known as *Raid*. Over generations, different *Raids* formed levels maintaining their *Raid* entities. The addition of various *Raids* into different bodies are known in different names—*Hima, Doloiship, Lyngdohship, Wahadadarship*, and *Sordarship*. Each has a representative head, known as- *Syiem, Doloi, Lyngdoh, Wahadadar* and *Sordar* (Dorbar Hima Mylliem, 2001).

The case, we are referring in this chapter, is the village council of the State of Meghalaya and in particular, the Khasi-Jaintia hills district. Meghalaya is one of the States of the North Eastern Region of India. A population of 17, 74778 persons (1991 census) inhabit its total area of 22,429 sq. km. Within the State of Meghalaya, there are many ethnic groups. One, of the large ethnic groups, is known as "*Hynniewtrep*", which occupies 4 districts out of a total of 7. These districts are East Khasi Hills, West Khasi Hills, Jaintia Hills and Ri Bhoi. The erstwhile British government coined the word 'Khasi-Jaintia' after the invasion and annexation of the area. Since then, the terms, Khasi and Jaintia are being used in administrative and intellectual vocabulary. But the society perceives itself, as *'Ki khun Ki Ksiew U Hynniewtrep Hynniewskum'* (The offspring of *Hynniewtrep*).

'*Hynniewtrep*' is a legend of the genesis of the group. The oral tradition, coming down through generations, narrates that: God, the maker of heaven and earth, human beings and flora and fauna, created land with water for the human beings to live on it. At this point of time there were 16 human families living in *'Haneng'* (God's abode). They were given the freedom to move between *'Haneng'* and *'Hatbian'* (earth). They shuttled up and down freely. From amongst the 16 families, 7 families expressed their desire to live on *'Hatbian'*. God granted their wish and placed them on *'Lumsohpetbneng'* (Mount Navel of Heaven located in Ri Bhoi area). From this mount the 7 families migrated to different parts (north, east, west and south). These 7 families belonged to 7 clans. The Khasi-Jaintia of today is their descendants. The numerical numbers 16 and 7 mentioned are not to be understood as the absolute numbers, 16 or 7 can mean any number.

These 7 families of 7 clans migrated and settled in different parts as small communities, known as *"Shnong"* (village). The *'shnongs'* and the people residing on the upland plateau are referred to as 'Khynriam' running east to west. The eastern part of the 'Khynriam' plateau is referred to as 'Pnar' or 'Synteng'. Those residing in the southern slopes adjoining Bangladesh are referred to as 'War' and the 'Bhoi' who settled in the northern slopes bordering the plains of the present State of Assam (Nongkynrih, 2001).

Khasi - Jaintia society is a clan-based society. Every member of the society traces the line of descent through the mother and, besides one's own name, one has to add the mother's clan name. This is the identity card that one belongs to the Khasi-Jaintia society. Besides being a member of the clan, one is also a member of a *Shnong* i.e., village. In a *'Shnong'*, a member is identified as belonging to it, when such a member is born in an *'Ïing'* (domestic group). *'Iing'* can be viewed commonly, as a domestic group of three or four generations, consisting of male and female consanguine, and may or may not have any husband in any generation residing with their wives and children, and may also include married brothers living with their sisters but without their wives and children. Every *'Ïing'* belongs to a *'Kur'* i.e., clan. *'Kur'* identifies every member of an *'Ïing'*, at the larger level of collectivity of social relationships. There are more than 3500 *'Kur'* spreading over 2848 villages, meaning that there are 2848 village councils, approximately in Khasi-Jaintia Hills. Every village has a *Dorbar Shnong* i.e., village council and every male adults from each *Iing* are members of the village council (ibid, 2001). One can safely say, that village council is the council of male adults, representing the constituent domestic groups and takes decision on their behalf. One male assumes and occupy the position of *Rangbah Shnong* i.e., Headman. The position of Headmanship is either hereditary or consensus selection, and with some peculiar criteria being followed. This aspect we will explain shortly. The Headman is the representative head of the village, and acts according to the advice of the village council.

It is true that every village has a village council, but there are some peculiarities, we observed amongst them. These peculiarities are important to understand, because they do have a bearing on the structure, function, and role of the village council. The causal factor for such peculiarities is because of the process of formation of the village. We categorize these peculiarities as follows:

1. In a village with multi-clans, the traditional authority of Headmanship is hereditary. Only the males a particular clan can occupy this office.
2. In a village with multi-clans, the traditional authority of Headmanship is vested with few founding clans of the village, and they share on rotation basis.

3. In a village with multi-clans, the traditional authority of Headmanship is usually meant for the males of those domestic groups belonging to the category of the first settlers and founders of the village.
4. In the villages the position of Headman is both political and religious. He performs annual rites and rituals, invoking the God for good health and prosperity of the village.
5. There are villages with only 10 domestic groups, between 30 to 50 domestic groups, between 50 to 150 domestic groups, and some are very large with more than 300 domestic groups.

From the above description, we can say that the general features found common across villages are, that members of the village councils are adult males only, permanent resident of the village and are identified on the basis of their mother's house or, for some males through their wives' house. The types of variation found can be said to be at the level of number of domestic groups constituting the village, and the exclusive right of some clans or domestic group in occupying the traditional authority of *Rangbah Shnong* or *Waheh Chnong* (Headman). It should be noted, that non-Khasi-Jaintia domestic groups are debarred from village councils, even though they may be permanent residents of the village.

II

With the brief background cited above, the chapter will further elaborate on the meaning, structure and function, and the guiding value of the village councils. According to the customary beliefs and practices of the society, Village Council (*Dorbar Shnong*) was created and formed as one of the institutions of the society. It is a body comprising of permanent resident adult male members. From among them, they select a person of integrity, as the leader and he occupies the office of Headmanship. He is the legitimate authority of the village and functions on the advice of the village council. The term of office vary from village to village but generally it is one year and depending on the village council he may be requested to continue. In some cases, there are headmen, who by dint of their quality leadership continue to occupy the position for many years, and some after one year the council replaces them by selecting another. Decision-makings are taken on the basis of consensus and are enforced by the headman. Collectively, the members of the council are responsible for any decisions and actions taken.

The village council is created and formed with a definite purpose, role and responsibility. As one of the social institutions, it has to perform different and specific tasks in the society. These are as follows:

- Keeper and protector of peace and social tranquility
- Keeper of customary beliefs and practices
- Resolves any misunderstanding amongst the members of the village
- Disciplines any wrong doer and punishes the culprit
- Formulates rules and regulations
- Controles and manages its population, territory, common property resources, and other matters
- Care and security of the children, women and especially the poorest and the marginalised
- Works for the benefit of the people and assist them in crisis
- Educates, cares and controls the youth

The function of the village council is embedded into a guiding and binding values and referred to as "*Ka Hok*" (means the righteous ways of living or the prescribed modes of behaviour). The principle role and responsibility of the village council is following and practising of *Ka Hok*. In its deliberation, decision, control and management, and actions, it has to bear in mind that it speaks, acts, and teaches the righteous ways or the prescribed mode of behaviours. This is because the society believes that *Ka Dorbar Shnong dei ka Dorbar*

Blei, meaning that the village council is not only the council of male adults but also a council consecrated with sacredness. Therefore, *Ka Hok* is the guiding principle and values of controlling and managing the population, its resources and any other affairs concerning the village. The people also believed that if the village council deviates from the guiding principle and values of *Ka Hok,* then such a village invites itself all sorts of troubles, confusion, hardships, and conflicts (Rymbai, 1990 ; Sullai, 1990 ; Sngi, 1990).

Is it the same situation today? Or has it changed? What has changed? And what are the impacts on the institution and society? It is difficult to answer all these questions, but on the basis of our interactions we have with more than 300 villages, we can provide a preliminary understanding on the subject. We will do this by describing part by part so that one can understand the type of change and at what level. We have selected few aspects that we consider crucial for this particular institution of the society and these are as given below.

The village council is an autonomous political unit and it is one of the constituents of the traditional state mentioned earlier. Before 1950, its legitimacy and recognition is derived from the traditional state of which it is a part. After 1950, according to the Constitution of India under the Sixth Scheduled, the traditional institutions are under the control of the Autonomous District Councils.

The entry of modern organisations and modern institutions in the hills, from 1829 onwards, and through the process of cultural contact and diffusion of ideas did affect the structure and function of the village councils. We observed that every village council, besides the position of headmanship, has also adopted, created, formed and integrated within the traditional structure, a body known as Executive Committee, and has also created additional positions like those of the Secretary, Treasurer and few members of the Executive Committee. The occupants of different positions cited above are selected from the adult male members of the village council, and they assist the headman in day-to-day functioning of the village council.

After 1950, the Government of India has formulated various types of induced development schemes for reducing poverty, especially for the rural areas of the country. In the State of Meghalaya, the process of selection of beneficiaries and implementing of village level activities is carried out through the village councils, since it is considered as people's institution.

The legal status of the village council demands that any applicant for any job or any scheme from government departments or financial institutions or applying for the Scheduled Tribe Certificate or identifying real beneficiaries for government schemes or certifying the residential status and issuing of character certificate to any person or permitting the "Non-tribals" to reside or to carry out business and trade, has to be certified or issuing of No Objection Certificate by the village council.

The institutionalisation of party based parliamentary system in the country has also led to the interaction and interface between representatives of political parties and representatives of the village councils in particular and the village population in general. Over the span of fifty years, more various political parties have managed to create their own supporters and setting-up of party-based unit in the villages. We also observed that during the process of election campaign's the headman has to act as a Chairman of every meeting organised by different political parties. This is done with the intention of controlling political behaviours and at the same time maintaining political neutrality of the village.

The coming of different Christian denominations into the villages has also brought other types of interaction and interface between the village councils and the denominations. Mostly, such interaction relates matters of setting-up of educational institutions and places of worship, organising religious programmes. The entry of religious organisations has also led to change of belief because we found that many domestics groups are today followers of different denominations or one particular denomination (Syiemlieh, 1989).

The influence and impacts of moderniszation, on the society in general and the village councils in particular, can be observed at various levels. We will try to describe the impact of the change by broadly categorising them into two parts, that is, merits and demerits.

Merits

The adoption and integration of new functionaries into the traditional structure of village councils like, the positions of Secretary, Treasurer, and the Executive Committee have provided additional assistance and support for the headman in controlling and managing the affairs of the village, and leadership.

The recognition of village councils as a people's institution by the State government has widen its active role in executing and implementing schemes or projects of the Community and Rural Development Blocks Office, and other government departments. Its role has widened and its status has grown in the society, because its authority of certification is mandatory.

The process of democratic election, of local representatives for the States' Assembly, has led to participation of the people and increased the bargaining power of the village councils for development or change of policies affecting the people.

Demerits

Under the Sixth Schedule of the Constitution of India, the Autonomous District Council (ADCs) has the power to introduced a law that headman needs the final approval of the ADCs after being selected by the village council. In many cases, the headman does not seek the approval of the ADCs, but only the approval from the *Hima* or *Wahadadar* or *Lyngdoh* or *Doloi* or Chief of the *Elaka*. There are many instances where villages have two headmen, one approved by the traditional chief and another by the Autonomous District Councils. This has created confusion, tension, and strain of social relationships among the members of the village

The integration of new positions, like the Executive Committee in the structure and management of the village councils, has also led to change in its practices. According to the spirit and values of the society, traditional institutions have to place every issue or subject before the village council, for open and free discussions so that every member is kept informed and can participate in the deliberations. It seems many issues or subjects are first discussed in the Executive Committee and then placed before the village council. Majority of the villagers, we discussed, think that this method of few people meeting is not according to traditions. This has created some kind of mistrust, because it is not transparent. Some elders argued that whether village councils today are traditional in the real sense. Or it seems that it is becoming a body representing an image of tradition, but in actual reality, their role and function are gradually being replaced.

There are few important areas where people have complained that the headman and the Executive Committee do not provide proper information on various schemes received from the government departments. Questions are raised on the lack of transparency and accountability. The identification and selection of "beneficiaries" has been another issue of debate, because the people say that the right ones are left out and the wrong ones are selected. Another area, which has been a source of strain for the village councils, is the lack of accountability of funds received from various sources or money collected as local tax from transactions of land or from issuing of No Objection Certificates, and the amount spent for various community services is not recorded properly and the people do not know the details of expenditure.

The party-based politics and election of public representatives has influenced individuals to the extent that within the village councils, members are divided along party lines and has created conflict in the village and village council. There are instances where village councils are not able to function and carry out its responsibilities because of political factionalism.

The changes of beliefs and practices from traditional religion have brought radical changes in the fragmentation of villages on religious lines. This can be understood on the basis of the fact that we have single-religion-based villages, and it is more common in Jaintia hills district and few regions of other districts of Khasi-Jaintia hills. For example, in Jaintia hills Christian dominated villages are known as *Skur* and indigenous religion dominated villages are referred to as *Chnong*.

The merits and demerits discussed above can be further elaborated by citing the example of two villages. There is a village 120 kms from the city of Shillong. Its name is Mookaiaw and twenty-five years back this village is economically backward with low literacy rate. The then headman and secretary of the village initiated various community programmes, like cleaning drive, health camps, and promoting education as a very important part of change. Besides these activities, it formed a transport cooperative society, and various other committees are formed with specific role and responsibilities in bringing about changes for the village. Within a span of twenty years, the village council transformed the village into one of the most developed villages and is considered as a model village of development for the State of Meghalaya.

Another village by the name of Umbir, not far off from the city of Shillong, say approximately 15 Kms, is an opposite example of the above. People of the village and especially the village youth organisation have been complaining that the Headman and the Executive Committee are running and managing the village without holding the annual village council for the past ten years. The community lands of the village is being sold to private parties without the sanction of the village council and the money transacted out of sale of such lands is not known. The youth leader of the village said that the sale of land has brought two major problems, decrease of community lands and the poor people of the village are not able to find plot of land for agricultural cultivation to sustain their livelihoods.

III

From the beginning of our discussion, we have highlighted various aspects concerning the village councils. On the basis of the description in the preceding pages, we are in a position to comment and remark on the village council. These comments and remarks are:

The term *Dorbar Shnong* or *Dorbar Chnong* (village council) has not changed but continues.

It is still a male dominated institution because only adult male members are active participants of it.

There are variations from one village council to another at the level of occupying the position of headman and other positions. Different practices are found and not every male has an equal right to occupy position of authority. The rules of protective discrimination seems to apply here too.

There is a modification in its structure and function with the integration of new positions.

Its role is beyond the maintenance of social order, because it has also been used by the government for implementing government schemes or programmes.

Its legitimacy is derived from (if I am permitted to use the Weberian notion of authority) the traditional authority.

It continues to function according to the traditions and customs, even when it has integrated some modern structural elements in the traditional structure.

Individuals occupying the position of authority are defining its role and function.

The members of traditional institutions seems to be facing problems in tackling, handling and separating between their party-based-allegiance versus their role and responsibilities as adult male members of the village council. Due to this factor, some villages have succumbed to political factionalism leading to political fragmentation and conflict. But some other villages have been able to overcome this factor and use the political parties for the development of the village.

On closer examination we find that there are two factors causing the change. One, the exogenous factor like the Autonomous District Councils and its power over the village council, and the modern bureaucratic organisations like religious organisations and the government, and the parliamentary politics, secondly, the village council itself integrates new forms in its structure is an example of an endogenous process. We can tentatively conclude by arguing that the village council has not undergone any structural change as such. But there are some aspects of change as we have observed above. At this juncture one finds difficult to articulate as to whether this particular institution is in real sense traditional. The reason for arguing so is because over generations with the process of modernisation of the society, it too has adopted and adapted, and integrated new elements from the modern bureaucratic organizations into its structure. The partial structural modification has led to the process of change at the level of decision-making. The traditional collective authority of male adults and the spirit of consensus seem to be replaced by Executive Committee. This is a shift from its traditional values and norms. Another important feature of the village council is, its power and authority has expanded because of its legal status. Take for example its authority and certification in the selection of beneficiaries for government schemes, implementing community schemes and various other transactions. This is not its traditional role and responsibility. This new role and responsibility has also contributed to the rise of conflict within the village council and among members, and also given rise to the exploitation of power and authority by the few, at the cost of the village population. Besides the above points, there are two exogenous factors that have pervaded across the society and are very influential elements. These are parliamentary politics and religion. Village councils are unable to handle or deal with the party-based politics in a rational way. There is a problem of separation as a member of the village council devoid of any party-based politics and as an active member or supporter of political parties. The increase politicisation of village councils is a major threat on the resiliency of this traditional institution. The formation of villages has never been based on religion, but after 1929 onwards there are many villages which have been formed on the basis of religion. The same ethnic group but villages are segregated and separated from each other on the ground of religion.

We have been discussing on various aspects of change and its impact on the village council as one of the institution of the society. It is also important to highlight on those structural aspects where exogenous factors have not been able to influence any change and endogenously too the society is not initiating any change, and these are:

Customs and traditions govern the rules of participation in village councils. Women are yet to be accepted as equal partners in decision-making. The traditional political domain is still male dominated.

Even amongst male members, the rules of participation differentiate between permanent residents and non-permanent residents. Only permanent residents are allowed to participate. Among permanent residents there is further distinction on the basis of earlier settlers versus later settlers in some villages, and founding clans versus clans who came and settled later. Males belonging, to the category of founding clans or earlier settlers, have more privileges because only they can occupy positions of authority in the village council.

Compounding all the issues and points we have been discussing so far, we may be in a position to argue that, village council is still an institution defined by customs and traditions. But its structure has been modified and the way it functions, can be said to be restrictive consensus decision-making. Women do not enjoy equal rights, and among men the rights of equal opportunity of occupying positions of authority is being determined by traditional rules and regulations of protective discrimination. Therefore, the rules of inclusion or exclusion apply according to one's residential status in the village. Lastly, it seems that it is resilient even when different exogenous and endogenous forces are penetrating it.

REFERENCES

Gassah, L.S., 1988. *Traditional Institutions of Meghalaya*. Regency Publications, New Delhi.

Gassah, L.S., 1990, "Ka District Council Bad Ki Tymmen Shnong". Paper Presented in a Seminar on Ka Bynta U Tymmen / Rangbah Shnong Ha Ka Imlang-sahlang Bad Ha Ka Sain Hima-sima, Hynniewtrep Endeavour Society, Shillong.

Lyngdoh, S., 1990, "U Rangbah Shnong Bad Ka Dorbar Shnong: Ka Thymmei Ka Synshar Ka Khadar U Hynniewtrep". Paper Presented in a Seminar on Ka Bynta U Tymmen / Rangbah Shnong Ha Ka Imlang-sahlang Bad Ha Ka Sain Hima-sima, Hynniewtrep Endeavour Society, Shillong

Nongkynrih, A.K., 2001, "Ka Shnong: The Microcosm of Hynniewtrep Society". In *Indian Horizons*, Indian Council for Cultural Relations, New Delhi.

Office of the Dorbar of Hima Mylliem, *Memorandum*, Hima Mylliem, Shillong.

Rymbai, R.T., 1990, "Ki Rangbah Shnong". Paper Presented in a Seminar on Ka Bynta U Tymmen / Rangbah Shnong Ha Ka Imlang-sahlang Bad Ha Ka Sain Hima-sima, Hynniewtrep Endeavour Society, Shillong.

Shullai, L.G., 1990, "Ki Dorbar Shnong Bad Ki Tymmen Shnong". Paper Presented in a Seminar on Ka Bynta U Tymmen / Rangbah Shnong Ha Ka Imlang-sahlang Bad Ha Ka Sain Hima-sima. Hynniewtrep Endeavour Society, Shillong.

Syiemlieh, D.R., 1989, *British Administration in Meghalaya*. Heritage Publishers. New Delhi.

10

The Marngars of Meghalaya— A Bio-anthropological Perspective

—*R. Khongsdier*

One of the fascinating facts regarding modern human species, or Homo sapiens, is its variability characterised by innumerable characteristics, which can be looked from different angles, depending upon the interest of the researchers or observers. Physical anthropologists and other human biologists may be interested in those genetic or biological characteristics of the human species. On the other hand, social anthropologists and other social scientists may be interested in behavioural, psychological, economic, political, social and other cultural aspects. Thus the beauty of the human species consists in its variation. Such a variation is useful in some cases, harmful in others and neutral in some others. From the evolutionary point of view, human variation is the result of evolution, although we have learned little about just how it has happened.

Human variation, in phenotypic (morphological) and genetic traits at the population level, has been a major focus of attention in physical (or biological) anthropology. In the last 50 years, an attempt has also been made, not only to disseminate the nature and types of human biological variation, but also to understand the causes of such variations between and within populations all over the world. As for Indian populations, thousands of publications relating to human variation, have also been made by physical anthropologists, although many of them are purely descriptive of population variation with respect to phenotypic and genetic traits. Many more works are yet to be carried out in order to understand the causes of micro-differentiation in different populations all over the country. This chapter is concerned with admixture as an important evolutionary force to bring about genetic variation and similarity between human populations, with special reference to the Marngars of Meghalaya and other neighbouring populations.

The Marngars

The people living in Marngar village are also known as Marngars. They speak a language, which is a mixture of Assamese and Boro languages and those, who do not embrace Christianity, follow the Khasi religion. At present, they are regarded as one of the members of the Bhois—one of the Khasi sub-groups. Therefore, they enjoy the same Scheduled Tribe status with the other Khasi sub-groups, namely, Khynriams, Pnars, Bhois, and Wars. According to a tradition, the Marngars were not the offshoots of the Khasi population. It is told that few members of the Lalungs (or Tiwas) migrated to Ri Bhoi district of Meghalaya from Kamrup district of Assam. When they reached at Marngar, they found that it was good for paddy cultivation and decided to settle at the present village Marngar. Another story says that the first inhabitants of Marngar were the Rabhas who migrated from Assam. Thus the ethnic affinity of the present Marngars is not clear. However, it is likely that the first inhabitants of Marngars were neither the Mikirs (Karbis) nor the Bhois. It is believed there is intermixture between the Marngars and other communities such as the Bhois, Mikirs, Garos, etc. They are taller and bigger than the Bhois and other Khasi groups. In other words, the Marngars are of medium to tall stature, have brown skin colour, straight and black hair, medium nose and face with epicanthic fold.

At present, the Marngar society is divided into 14 clans, namely, Syiem, Lyngdoh, Shilliang, Damlong, Sohkhwai, Majhong, Pombeh, Baro, Giri, Marwet, Makdoh, Binong,

Pombah and Pator. It is said that these clans came from different areas, perhaps through marital alliances or otherwise. For example, Syiem clan was originally a Kopha clan, which came from Nowgong to settle the land dispute between the Binong and Damlong clans, who were believed to be the first lineage groups to settle at Marngar. Lyngdoh clan came from Nongshlur village of Ri Bhoi district. Sohkhwai clan was originally a Lalung clan, and Baro is originally a Boro Kachari clan, while Marwet came from Byrni area of Ri Bhoi district. Of these clans, 9 clans—Syiem, Lyngdoh, Shilliang, Damlong, Sohkhwai, Majhong, Pombeh, Baro and Giri – should always be involved in running the political and religious organisation of the village, under the leadership of the *Syiem* (Village Chief) of the Syiem clan.

At present, about half of the total households follow the matrilineal pattern of the society, while the rest follow the patrilineal pattern of society. It is told that they followed the matrilineal system of society as in the case of other Khasi sub-groups, but during the last 30 years or so, there has been a strong tendency among them to follow the patrilineal system of society. There are many reasons, why the Marngars have started following the patrilineal pattern of society. Firstly, it was believed that the first inhabitants of the Marngar village were, in fact, the followers of the patrilineal system of society. But due to political compulsion and admixture with the Bhois and other Khasi groups, they adopted the matrilineal system of society. In olden days, it was possible that the Chief of Mylliem State might have compelled them to follow the matrilineal system of society, since Marngar has been under the political jurisdiction of Mylliem State till the present day. Secondly, a high intermixture with other patrilineal communities like Boro Kachari, Lalungs, etc., has often given rise to a problem of descent, especially when the female is from patrilineal society. This is also a common problem in the Khasi society which is largely responsible for the formation of many clans (Khongsdier, 1996). In such type of marriage, where male and female are from matrilineal and patrilineal systems of society respectively, the common solution is to form another clan in the Khasi society, because clan members of the male do not generally allow him to take his children to his own clan. But in the Marngar society, the clan members of a male allow him to take his children to his clan, thereby resulting in adoption of patrilineal system of descent. This is also likely to prompt the other Marngar men, who married other females belonging to other Khasi sub-groups, to take their children to their own clan.

Monogamy is the general practice of the people here in this village. In the case of matrilineal system, the bridegroom goes to stay at the bride's residence after marriage. In the case of patrilineal system, the bride goes to stay at the bridegroom's residence after marriage. Like in other societies, clans are strictly exogamous. No one is allowed to marry within one's clan.

The main occupation of the people in this village is agriculture. The major agricultural products include paddy, pineapple, ginger, banana, vegetables, tea and broomstick. Some people are also engaged in business and services. Some other has trade and commerce relation with other populations at the centers like Umden, Nongpoh and Shillong.

Gene Flow into Marngar Population

The admixture between two or more populations of separate gene pools, through marriage, is important in bringing about genetic differences and similarities. It takes place generally through migration. Thus the terms "migration" and "gene flow" are synonymously used in population genetics, although genes may flow into a population from outside without migration cf individuals (especially males). However, such a casual gene flow is considered to be less important in changing the genetic composition of populations (Spuhler, 1973). The importance of gene flow can be observed, when there are frequent intermarriages between members of a given population and those from neighbouring populations. Secondly, if genetic data are available, one can estimate the rate of gene flow into the study population from the neighbouring populations. In this connection, it may be appropriate to take the Marngar population into consideration. Recently, the Department of Anthropology, North-Eastern Hill University, conducted a genetic study of the Marngars with respect to the ABO blood groups and PTC taste sensibility (Chumikam, 2002; Kiran Devi, 2002). Table 10.1 shows that the present Marngars were, by and large, similar to the Bhois, Mikirs and Lalungs, although they differ significantly from the Mikirs with respect to PTC taste sensibility. One of the possible explanations for such genetic similarities of the Marngar population with these populations, may be due to the different recombination of genotypes as a result of admixture. With this end in view, we take into consideration the genetic contribution of the Bhois, Lalungs and Mikirs to the gene pool of the contemporary Marngar population with respect to the ABO and PTC alleles. On the basis of Bernstein model (Workman, 1973) of gene flow from two parental populations, the following equation was used to compute the genetic contribution of the three parental populations to the gene pool of the contemporary Marngar population:

$$M = [\{G / (D_1 + D_2 + D_3)\} / (N - 1)]$$

Where

M = estimated gene flow in the hybrid population from one of the two parental populations

H = observed allele frequency in the hybrid population

P_1 = observed allele frequency in parental population one

P_2 = observed allele frequency in parental population two

P_3 = observed allele frequency in parental population three

D_1 = $(H - P_1)$, or $(P_1 - H)$, depending upon whether P_1 or H is greater in frequency of a given allele

D_2 = $(H - P_2)$, or $(P_2 - H)$, depending upon whether P_2 or H is greater in frequency of a given allele

D_3 = (H – P_3), or (P_3 - H), depending upon whether P_3 or H is greater in frequency of a given allele

G = (D_2 + D_3), if we wish to estimate gene flow from parental population P_1

Or

G = (D_1 + D_3), if we wish to estimate gene flow from parental population P_2

Or

G = (D_1 + D_2), if we wish to estimate gene flow from parental population P_3

N = Total number of parental populations

For example, the frequencies of allele p of the ABO blood groups in Marngars (H), Lalungs (P_1), Bhois (P_2) and Mikirs (P_3) are 0.2856, 0.1944, 0.2184, and 0.2467, respectively (Table 10.2). The differences between Marngars and the three populations in this allele are as follows:

Marngars and Lalungs = (D_1 = H – P_1 = 0.2856 – 0.1944 = 0.0912)

Marngars and Bhois = (D_2 = H – P_2 = 0.2856 – 0.2184 = 0.0672)

Marngars and Mikrs = (D_3 = H – P_3 = 0.2856 – 0.2467 = 0.0389)

The sum of the three differences (D_1 + D_2+ D_3 = 0.0912 + 0.0672 + 0.0389) = 0.1973.

Therefore, the genetic contribution of the Lalungs to the Marngars with respect to allele p = (D_2 + D_3) / (D_1 + D_2+ D_3) /[{N – 1}] = [{0.1061 / 0.1973}/ 2] = 0.2689].

The genetic contribution of the Bhois to the Marngars in respect of the same allele = (D_1 + D_3) / (D_1 + D_2+ D_3) / [{N – 1}] = [{0.1301 / 0.1973} / 2] = 0.3297].

And the genetic contribution of the Mikirs = (D_1 + D_2) / (D_1 + D_2+ D_3) / [{N – 1}] = [{0.1584 / 0.1973} / 2] = 0.4014].

The M value in the above equation describes the proportion of the total gene pool of Marngar population, which is derived from the parental populations, irrespective of the number of generations. The equation makes no assumption whether the hybridisation is due to a single instance of intermarriages, or due to the consequence of gene flow in different proportions from the parental populations. In the present analysis, it is simply a description of the sum total of gene flow from the three parental populations (Lalungs, Bhois and Mikirs).

Table 10.1: Differences Between the Marngars and Other Neighbouring Populations with Respect to ABO Blood Groups and PTC Taste Sensibility

Genetic markers	*Marngars (N = 160)*	*Bhois (N = 192)*	*Mikirs (N = 245)*	*Lalungs (N = 114)*
ABO blood groups (%)				
O	29.38	37.70	30.20	33.33
A	36.25	30.40	33.06	26.32
B	21.25	23.00	26.53	31.58
AB	13.13	7.80	10.21	8.77
X^2 with the Marngars		5.45, $P > 0.05$	2.14, $P > 0.05$	6.28, $P > 0.05$
PTC taste sensibility				
(%)	70.63	78.10	83.67	71.05
Tasters	29.37	21.90	16.33	28.95
Non-tasters				
X^2 with the Marngars		2.69, $P > 0.05$	9.77, $P < 0.01$	0.01, $P > 0.05$

Sources: Das (1978); Das *et al.* (1980); Chumikam (2002)

Applying the above equation, the genetic contribution of the Lalungs, Bhois and Mikirs to the gene pool of the Marngar population is given in Table 10.2. It is found that, on the basis of the ABO blood groups and PTC taste ability, the average genetic contribution of the Mikir population to the Marngar population is about 0.3508 or 35.08%. In other words, the contemporary Marngars derived approximately 35.08% of their genes from the Mikirs, about 33.43% from the Lalungs

Table 10. 2 : Estimate of Gene Flow into the Gene Pool of Contemporary Marngars

Allele	*Marngars*	*Lalungs*	*Bhois*	*Mikirs*	*Gene flow from Lalungs*	*Gene flow from Bhois*	*Gene flow from Mikirs*
p (ABO)	0.2856	0.1944	0.2184	0.2467	0.2689	0.3297	0.4014
q (ABO)	0.1880	0.2278	0.1694	0.2045	0.2343	0.3758	0.3899
r (ABO)	0.5264	0.5778	0.6161	0.5487	0.3427	0.2255	0.4318
t (PTC)	0.54198	0.5381	0.4680	0.4041	0.4912	0.3285	0.1803
Average genetic contribution per allele					0.3343	0.3149	0.3508

and about 31.49% from the Bhois, thereby indicating a higher degree of the Mikir ancestry as compared with the Bhois and Lalungs. Thus the contemporary Marngars may be considered to have a higher degree of Mikir ancestry, compared with the Bhois and Lalungs with respect to the ABO blood group and PTC taste ability. This is contrary to the general belief that the Marngars are an offshoot of the Lalungs who migrated to the Ri Bhoi district of Meghalaya. In addition, although the Marngars are treated as members of the Bhois (one of the Khasi sub-groups), the genetic contribution of the Bhois is the lowest as compared with the Mikirs and Lalungs.

Limitations of the Present Study

Although it appears that the contemporary Marngars derived most of their genes from the Mikirs and Lalungs, one should be cautious of interpreting such a trend. In this estimate, we have assumed that the contemporary Marngar population is a tri-hybrid group due to admixture among the Bhois (Khasis), Lalungs and Mikirs, i.e., without taking into consideration the intermarriages between the Marngars and other communities like the Garos and so on. If intermarriage with other communities also takes place frequently, our interpretation of the genetic contribution of the Lalungs, Mikirs and. Bhois to the Marngar population would be different, or even more complicated. Secondly, our assumption that the Marngars are the product of the Khasis, Mikirs and

Lalungs would be totally wrong, if the Marngars belong to a different ethnic group like the Rabhas. Thirdly, the present analysis does not take into account the problem of sampling errors in explaining the genetic relationship of the study populations. Moreover, genetic markers such as the ABO blood groups and PTC taste ability are now-a-days considered to be weak genetic markers in establishing the population relationship. The problem is more complicated when a hybrid population derives its genes from the populations living in different environmental conditions, because the selective pressure acting on genes tends to vary between populations of different environments (Workman, 1973). In addition, the present analysis has taken two loci, namely, ABO blood groups and PTC taste sensibility, which may be different in the parental populations. For example, Table 10.2 shows that the contemporary Marngars had a higher Lalung ancestry with respect to PTC taste sensibility (about 49.12%). In other words, the genetic contribution of the Lalungs is the highest (49.12%) followed by the Bhois (32.85%) with respect to PTC taste sensibility. Thus the present analysis does not take into consideration the number of loci; rather it takes into account only the number of alleles while estimating the gene flow from the parental populations.

The classification of Marngar population, as a tri-hybrid group in this presentation, should also be treated as a classificatory device in order to understand the gene flow from one population to another. It has little to do with those issues relating to linguistic and socio-cultural identities of the Marngar population as one of the sub-groups of the Khasis. Many of the earlier scholars were of the opinion that the Khasis might be one of the earliest inhabitants of this part of the country (Das, 1978). It is believed that the founding ancestors of the Khasis were the Proto-Australoids of Austric speakers (Mon-Khmer), who changed their genetic make-up and physical features due to the admixture with the Mongoloid populations. Therefore, from this point of view, the present-day Khasis are also the result of the admixture and other evolutionary forces, and some of their sub-groups are hybrids of hybrids. In this connection, if one looks at the evolutionary history of the other Khasi sub-groups, such as, the Bhois, War Jaintias and War Shellas, etc., one should acknowledge the fact that intermixture plays a very important role in patterning their genetic composition and physical characteristics. Of course, earlier studies have revealed that the Khasi population, as a whole, is highly heterogeneous in genetic make-up (Das, 1978; Khongsdier and Ghosh, 1994, 1996), which may be regarded as a result of evolutionary mechanisms that may be essential for its long-term survival in relation to the changing environment. Understanding of such genetic variation within the Khasi population is very important for understanding of a variety of ways that are beneficial to the society. For example, understanding of health and diseases in a population always needs our knowledge of the genetic variation within such population.

Biological Consequences of Admixture

It has long been established that admixture or intermixture could produce a hybrid population. The hybrid population may be different or similar to its parental populations. For example, the present findings are different from those reported for another hybrid group in Meghalaya known as "Lyngngam" population, which is different from both the parental populations, namely, the Khasis and Garos (Ahmed *et al.*, 1997; Khongsdier, 2004). The Marngar population does not appear to emerge as a separate genetic entity as did the Lyngngam population by deviating itself from the parental populations with respect to the ABO blood groups and PTC taste sensibility. Perhaps, the Marngar population is not as old as the Lyngngam population or it is simply because of frequent intermarriages especially with the Bhois. Nevertheless, it is obvious from the present analysis, that admixture also brings about genetic similarities between hybrid and parental populations. Admixture does not by itself produce new genes in the population, as did mutation, but it brings about different combinations of genes from two or more populations. Many other populations in the world have also followed such a trend (Workman, 1973).

Along with other evolutionary forces, such as, mutation, natural selection and genetic drift admixture is a very important evolutionary mechanism that brings about genetic and phenotypic diversity and similarity. By increasing genetic diversity, admixture enhances the long-term survival of the population in coping with the changing environment, i.e., environmental change is an on-going process. On the other hand, if environmental quality remains constant, admixture may be disadvantageous for the population which is optimally adapted to such a constant environment. For example, the high frequencies of sickling gene in areas of West Africa is due to the selective advantage of sickling-gene carriers in those areas, where malaria is endemic (Allison, 1964). Admixture with non-sickling peoples would result in a decreased average fitness of the hybrids in those areas, where malaria is constantly endemic. However, if malaria is controlled or eradicated, the situation will be different in which the hybrids with lower incidence of sickling gene are likely to show their increased fitness as compared to the native population.

From the genetic and medical points of view, hybrid population is expected to show a higher prevalence of Mendelian genetic disorders/diseases, if the parental populations happen to be the carriers (heterozygote) for such diseases. On the other hand, the most frequent diseases, due to recessive alleles of a highly endogamous population, are likely to reduce when admixture with other populations takes place. To the best of our knowledge, there are no such reports for both the Lyngngam and Marngar populations. Physical anthropologists should also deal with such problems, rather than simply documenting the genetic differences and similarities, due to admixture or other evolutionary forces. From the biomedical point of view, it may be imperative to find out the correlation between the proportion of admixture and susceptibility to certain diseases that are more prevalent in one or more parental populations. For example, it is suggested that the prevalence of Type 2 diabetes in different Native American populations is positively correlated with the proportion of Native American genes (Chakraborty, 1986). It is also reported that the non-diabetic Pima Indians have about twice the European gene ancestry compared with the diabetic members of the same population (Williams *et al.*, 2000).

Human populations also harbour different populations of pathogens to which they have previously developed an immune resistance. The flow of these pathogens into a native population with less immune resistance could result in an increased prevalence of infectious diseases. For example, it is well-known that Europeans have a better resistance to tuberculosis due to the selective process brought about by repeated outbreaks of tuberculosis during the 18th century. Immigrants from Europe brought this disease to the United States of America in the early part of the 19th century, resulting in a large number of deaths especially in cities with large immigrants, such as New York, Philadelphia and Boston (Volpe, 1990). Indeed, such type of intermixture may be largely social in nature, i.e., social and economic intermixture rather than genetic or marriage intermixture. But the implication is for certain recessive genes relative to immune systems and other phenotypic characteristics, that may be spread in the native population through admixture. It is often cited in literature that American immigrants introduced Rh-negative gene into Chinese populations; whereas Chinese immigrants introduced more Rh-positive genes into American populations. The intermarriage between Chinese men with Rh-positive genes (RR) and American women with Rh-negative genes (rr) would increase an incidence of hemolytic disease or Rh-diseased infants. Among the Marngars, the frequency of Rh-negative gene is about 2.50%, which is still low like in the Khasi groups and other populations in North East India.

Our recent study of the growth and nutritional status of Muslim Khasi children, whose one of the parents were the migrant Muslim males, seems to support the contention that admixture could produce certain phenotypic (physical) variation in the hybrid population. It was found that the growth and nutritional status of Muslim Khasi children (i.e., who were the offspring of the Muslim males and Khasi females) was much better than that of the Khasi children whose both the parents were Khasis (Khongsdier and Mukherjee, 2002a, 2002b). On the other hand, Muslim Khasi children were less disadvantageous, compared with Khasi children. Thus future studies on the Marngars are expected to throw much more light on the role of admixture in bringing about a decreased or increased fitness of the population in terms of the genetic component of phenotypic variation, such as diseases and anthropometric traits. As for growth and nutritional status, it is likely that the Marngar children would be superior in fitness to the Khasi groups (Bem Bem, 2002).

Anthropological Implications of the Present Study for Population Classification

The present study has many anthropological implications and questions. The immediate implication should be related to the main focus of attention in physical anthropology, i.e., to understand the processes of human biological evolution and variation. The present study is also an attempt to understand the gene flow or genetic relationship, between the Marngars and other neighbouring populations. We have considered the Marngar population as a tri-hybrid population, on the basis of historical background and geographical location with other neighbouring populations, namely, Bhois, Mikirs and Lalungs. The admixture between these population groups is assumed to have produced the gene pool of the contemporary Marngar population. However, we are not sure about the original inhabitants of the Marngar village – whether they were the Lalungs or Mikirs. As mentioned in the limitations earlier, our classification of Marngar population as a tri-hybrid group should be treated as a classificatory device, to estimate the gene flow from one population to another.

We have observed that the Marngars are similar in blood groups to the Bhois, Mikirs and Lalungs. But they are significantly different from the Mikirs with respect to PTC taste sensibility, despite evidence of greater average gene flow from the Mikirs. This appears as if the Marngar population had got no coherent biological entity as claimed by some anthropologists and serologists while denying the biological concept of race. In other words, the Marngars are similar in blood groups to the Mikirs, but they deviate significantly from the Mikirs with respect to PTC taste sensibility, indicating the absence of correlation between the two genetic traits. This is the crux of the problem in defining a biological population or race. Our present study does not also guarantee, that the greater genetic contribution of the Mikirs to the Marngars is valid or real, especially if future studies will be conducted and tested statistically with more genetic and phenotypic traits. Thus our definition of the Marngar population as a biological entity is arbitrary, which is also one of the major limitations of many other reports on bio-anthropology of human populations. As a matter of fact, this is one of the causes leading to the denial of the biological concept of race, which also calls for the denial of the biological concept of a given population like the Marngar population.

In addition, the misuse of population classification by linking social behaviour or functional capabilities, with certain races or population groups, is the greatest obstacle to the study of human biological diversity. The Hitlerian postulation of the race concept, or racism (a doctrine that one race is superior or inferior to another), is one good example of the misuse of population classification. Anthropologists have been exhorted not even to use the term "race" after what the Nazis did to the Jews. Meanwhile, they use or cannot deny the biological concept of race and/or sub-races, although they substitute it with terms, denoting different hierarchies of

Mendelian populations, such as meta-populations, populations, sub-populations and demes—the smallest breeding units after family. Some have suggested the use of the term "clines" instead of "races." A cline is a gradient of change in the distribution of a phenotypic or genetic trait, through space from one breeding population to another. For example, human skin colour is distributed in a clinal pattern from north to south of the globe. This gradient of change in skin colour suggests adaptation to climatic variation, as we move from north to south. Similarly, the high frequency of B-blood group in Eastern China diminishes as we move westwards. All these suggest the importance of gene flow and adaptive value of phenotypic or genetic trait.

But it is debatable to suggest that "there are no races, there are only clines" (Brace, 2000), if we also mean clines as sub-species variations of Homo sapiens. On the other hand, if we accept there are no sub-species of Homo sapiens, we should also question about the scientific utility of studying human biological variation or phylogenetic relationship between human populations. As noted above, the denial of the biological concept of races or sub-species also calls for the rejection of the biological concept of any Mendelian population. In addition, how should anthropologists and human biologists combat racism, if they deny the biological concept of race? Earlier anthropologists believed that the best way to combat racism, was to openly discuss the subject of race, and to teach courses on human races and racism. Despite a long-standing controversy within biomedicine, anthropology and other disciplines about the biological meaning of race, its use seems to be inevitable especially for developing a comprehensive design of a given study. This can be observed in modern medical literature. On the one hand, the biomedical community claims the biological unreality of race, but it utilises racial and ethnic categories for biomedical study design. If race is a concept without scientific utility, the question arises: why do we use it in the scientific literature?

Nevertheless, many physical anthropologists have still supported the biological concept of race if "it is considered merely as an arbitrary grouping of populations identified for the purpose of a particular study" (Molnar, 1992). They tend to see nothing wrong in defining and naming the different populations of Homo sapiens into hierarchical order ranging from races to demes – the smallest breeding unit. For the study of biological variation, there is nothing wrong to classify the entire Homo sapiens according to skin colour. But it is wrong to treat the individuals belonging to any particular skin colour as superior or inferior in function and capabilities, because such capabilities are products of the interaction between genotypes and the environment. The interaction between genotypes and environment depends, in turn, on the norm of reaction, which is highly unpredictable (Khongsdier, 2005). Similarly, the distribution of ABO blood groups may be classified according to clines or different population groups or races, depending upon the purposes of a given study. According to Gill (2000), the biological reality of race depends on the definition of reality than on the definition of race. The point to be made here is that any group of Homo sapiens such as the Marngars, Bhois, Khasis, etc. possesses its biology and culture relative to the environment where it lives. There is nothing wrong to study the biology or culture, or both culture and biology, of any group of humankind.

Physical anthropologists and biologists must, however, admit, that they have failed to provide accurate criteria for defining a biological or Mendelian population, ranging from demes to races. It is a fact that many phenotypic and genetic traits follow a clinal pattern of distribution. According to Gill (2000), "serologists who work largely with blood factors will tend to see human variation as clinal and races as not a valid construct, while skeletal biologists, particularly forensic anthropologists, will see races as biologically real. The common person on the street who sees only a person's skin colour, hair form, and face shape will also tend to see races as biologically real. They are not incorrect. Their perspective is just different from that of the serologist." In the present analysis, we have observed that the Marngars are similar to the Mikirs with respect to the ABO blood groups, but they are significantly different from the Mikirs with respect to PTC taste ability. While Europeans and Chinese are closer to each other in skin colour than either one of them is to Africans, the distribution of the ABO blood groups indicates that Europeans and Africans are closer to each other than either one of them is to Chinese. Similarly, sickle-cell anemia is so often regarded as an African disease, although its origin might be from the Middle East (Brace, 2000). In fact, it represents a kind of adaptation that aids survival in populations where malaria is endemic. These may be regarded as facts of human variation ranging from the individual to the population level. Any two individuals of a given population may be similar in skin colour, but different in blood groups, because humans are highly polymorphic, i.e., composed of individuals with different genotypes. Thus there is also a possibility that two individuals resemble each other in skin colour and blood groups, but different with respect to height and other genetic markers. The same is true with race or population variation because Homo sapiens are also polytypic species, i.e., composed of different populations or races with different gene pools (Dobzhansky, 1962). The point is that what is real in one individual may be real or unreal in another, and what is real in one population may be real or unreal in another.

The classification or categorisation, of human populations on biological basis, is inevitable to understand human evolution and variation. In order words, the basic idea for the biological classification of the species Homo sapiens is to understand the processes of human evolution and the phylogenetic relationship between human populations. Although there is controversy over the concept of race, physical anthropologists agree that there is intra-variation within the human species, or Homo sapiens. Such intra-variation may be in the form of clines or traditional-racial criteria. Human origins and evolution or variation remain the main focus of attention in biological and anthropological studies.

Race or population differences within the human species are facts of nature, and to say that there are no biological differences between races, is just like we are denying the genetic and phenotypic differences between populations, which have been reported by anthropologists and biologists for the last two centuries. Of course, genetic variation between races is smaller (about 6.3 percent) than that between populations within races (about 8.3 per cent), and the genetic differences between individuals within populations of races account the highest proportion (about 85.0 per cent) of the total diversity of the human species (Lewontin, 1972; Jorde *et al.*, 2000; Rosenberg *et al.*, 2002). Such pattern of genetic differences between and within races should be questioned and verified in order to enhance our knowledge of genetic variation, that patterns the life and well-being of the human species. For example, it is not clear what does it mean by 6.0% to 8.0% of genetic differences between populations or races? It simply suggests greater genetic variation within races than between races or populations of Homo sapiens. If genetic variation between races is more than 50.0%, for example, what would be the consequences to the Homo sapiens? Is there a possibility for the formation a separate species? The point is that the processes and mechanisms of human evolution and variation are not yet fully understood; it is highly complex depending upon genetic and environmental factors. "After all, it is possible that some traits are adaptively neutral and others are governed by heterotic, diversifying, or sexual selection. It would certainly be interesting to discover which differences – individual; inter population within a race, and inter racial - belong to these classes. The data gathered by anthropologists studying racial variation in mankind should not be underrated" (Dobzhansky *et al.*, 1977).

Thus the sub-division of human species ranging from races to demes is ubiquitous and there should be no surprise with regard to the classification of Marngar population as a tri-hybrid group. However, such classification is less meaningful if anthropologists just simply account for the similarities and differences without any reference to the well-being and benefit of the society. What is the health condition of the Marngar population? Are there any advantages or disadvantages for the Marngars in relation to the Khasis and other populations, especially with respect to health and diseases? What is the progress of sustainable development and welfare among the Marngars? How to improve the well-being of the Marngars? Besides academic interests, these are few questions that anthropologists and other scientists of today are expected to deal with, in the interest, the human society including the Marngar society.

Concluding Remarks

Human variation as the product of human evolution has been the major focus of attention in anthropological study of modern human species, or Homo sapiens. Despite a long-standing research in this area, the nature of human variation is not yet fully understood, especially with respect to defining the biological boundaries of variation within the human species. Some traits of variation are highly plastic, such as height, weight and other phenotypic traits, and others are more rigid such as blood groups and other genetic traits. However, facts remain facts that all phenotypic and genetic traits have their own limits, thereby defining the characteristics of human species. In short, human biological variations between individuals, populations or races are within the limits of being Homo sapiens. In other words, human variation beyond the limits of being Homo sapiens is bound to produce a separate species. The present chapter has got nothing to do with such human variation beyond the limits of being Homo sapiens, because there is no such evidence as yet. Thus human biological variation refers to any trait or evidence of human evolution, within the limits of being a dynamic Homo sapiens, as a result of the changes in hereditary endowment, or genotype, due to gene recombination or mutation, and to the modification during growth and development, due to interplay between genetic and environmental factors.

In order to understand human biological variation, classification of human species on the basis of certain criteria into different sub-species or population groups is inevitable. However, such classification is sometimes misused, despite its practical value relating to the biological facts of human species. Racism is one good example of the misuse of population classification. It is true that the long-term residents in various parts of the world have patterns of features that we can easily identify as characteristics of the geographical areas from which they come. This is exactly the stem of controversy, whether these long-term residents of the different parts of the world should be called "races"?

Genetic anthropologists and serologists tend to see human variation as clines and races as not a valid construct, while forensic anthropologists consider races as biologically real. The common persons on the street who see only observable variations such as skin colour, hair form, and face shape, also tend to see races as biologically real. These observations are not incorrect but different in perspectives. The above question on the concept of race is also similar to the question whether we should consider the Marngar as an evolutionary unit or population group within the Khasi population? From the social and political point of view, the Marngars are treated as one of the Khasi sub-groups. In the present study, we consider the Marngar as a tri-hybrid group with higher Mikir ancestry. These classifications are not incorrect but different in perspectives. On the other hand, the difference in perspectives or approaches enhances our knowledge of human variation. Thus the division or classification of human species into different sub-species, ranging from races to demes, should be regarded as a classificatory device to understand human variation and evolution. However, such classification is less meaningful if anthropologists just simply account for the similarities and differences without any reference to the well-being and benefit of the society as well. In addition, biological differences between human populations reflect both hereditary and environmental factors. In most cases, the differences are due to the interaction of both, and the degree, to which environment or heredity affects any particular trait, varies greatly (American Association of Physical Anthropologist, 1996).

Population geneticists and anthropologists are concerned with such sub-divisions of the human species that are based on certain concentration of genetic traits, and now-a-days with special emphasis on neutral molecular traits, with a view to understand the evolutionary relationship between human populations. At the same time, they must also acknowledge human capacity for developing and learning culture, as a universal phenomenon, that has a considerable bearing on human evolution or genetic variation. Human capacity for culture is the function of the brain, that is genetically determined, but it is wrong to say that culture is genetically determined. For example, humans learn language from their parents and other human beings, or resources, because they have that capacity to speak a language or languages. This capacity to learn language or other behaviour is genetically determined, but heredity or genetic factors have nothing to do with what type of language or behaviour that a person should learn. The type of language, learned by a person, depends to a great extent on the type of communication, followed or shared by other members of the society, where he or she lives. Similarly, the human desire for food is triggered by physiological characteristics, which are determined by heredity, but heredity does not determine which type of food to be taken by an individual. The type of food and drink wanted and taken by an individual, depends largely on the food habits of the society in which he or she lives. On the other hand, the food habits or type of language, in this instance, are parts of the shared tradition and custom of a given society, or group of individuals. The same is true with the Marngar population. The influence of the Bhoi society (Khasi society), on the cultural aspects of the Marngar society, cannot be disputed. For example, the adoption of the matrilineal system of Khasi society by the Marngars is a good example of the impact of the Khasi society. The point is that, although the Marngars may be genetically or physically different from the Bhois and other Khasi groups, they have the same capacity for developing and learning culture. And the culture or behaviour, developed and learned by them, depends largely on the society and the environment in which they live. Thus different questions may arise regarding their habitat or environment. How are the Marngars coping with the variation or change in their environment? How has their culture a bearing on their biology and vice versa? Anthropologists and other scientists need to explore more on this area, with regard to the Marngar population. From the modern anthropological point of view, a study of genetic variation between and within populations would not become so meaningful, if the variation in environmental conditions (including socio-cultural conditions) is not taken into consideration. Population sub-divisions may be considered the product of the interplay between genetic and environmental factors, and culture should be considered the principal means of human adaptation to environment, thereby influencing human biological evolution. In fact, an attempt, to understand the human biological evolution, would not become so meaningful without taking into consideration the nature of cultural evolution.

REFERENCES

Ahmed, T. J., S. Sengupta and A K. Ghosh. 1997, "Genetic Study on the Lyngngams of Meghalaya". *Journal of Human Ecology*. 8: 473-475.

Allison, A. C. 1964. "Polymorphisms and Natural Selection in Human Populations". *Cold Spr. Harb. Symp. Quart. Biol.* 29. pp. 137-49.

American Association of Physical Anthropologists, 1996. "American Association of Physical Anthropologist Statement on Biological Aspects of Race". *American Journal of Physical Anthropology*. 101. pp. 569-70.

Bem Bem. 2002, "A Study of Growth and Nutritional Status of the Marngars of Ri Bhoi District, Meghalaya". Unpublished M.Sc. Dissertation. Department of Anthropology. North Eastern Hill University. Shillong.

Brace,C.L.,2000, Anantagonist'sperspective.http://www.pbs.org/wgbh/nova/first/gill.html, http://www.pbs.org/wgbh/nova/first/gill.html;

Chakraborty, R., 1986, "Gene Admixture in Human Populations: Models and Predictions". *Yearbook of Physical Anthropology.*, 29, pp. 1–43.

Chumikam, T., 2002, *"A Genetic Study of the Marngar Population of Ri Bhoi District, Meghalaya"*.Unpublished M.Sc. Dissertation. Department of Anthropology, North Eastern Hill University. Shillong.

Das, B. M., 1978, *Variation in Physical Characteristics in the Khasi Population of North East India*. Dutta Barua and Co., Guwahati.

Dobzhansky, T., 1962, *Mankind Evolving*. Yale University Press, New Haven and London.

Dobzhansky, T.; F. G., Ayala; C. L. Stebbins; and J. W. Valentine., 1977, *Evolution*. W. H. Freeman and Co., San Francisco.

Gill,G.W.,2000,.*AProponent'sPerspective*http://www.pbs.org/wgbh/nova/first/gill.html;http://www.pbs.org/wgbh/nova/first/gill.htm.

Jorde, L.B.; W.S. Watkins ; M.J. Bamshad ; M.E., Dixon ; C.E Ricker ; M.T. Seielstad ; and M.A. Batzer., 2000, "The Distribution of Human Genetic Diversity: A Comparison of Mitochondrial, Autosomal and Y-chromosome Data". *American Journal of Human Genetics*. 66: pp. 979–88.

Khongsdier, R., 1996, "A Note on Micro-social Variation in the War Khasi with Special Reference to Inheritance of Property". *Journal of North-East India Council for Social Science Research*. 20. pp. 46-50.

Khongsdier, R., 2004, "The Lyngngams as a Hybrid and Evolving Population". *The North Eastern Hill University Journal*, 2. pp. 1-14.

Khongsdier, R., 2005, "Malnutrition, Social Inequality and Natural Selection in Human Populations". *Journal of Human Ecology*. 14.

Khongsdier, R. and A. K.Ghosh., 1994, "Bio-demographic Study among the War Khasi of Meghalaya". *Journal of the Indian Anthropological Society*. 29. pp. 195-202.

Khongsdier, R. and A. K. Ghosh., 1996, "Relevance of Population Study in Physical Anthropology", in F. A. Das and I. Barua (Eds): *Communities of North-East India*, pp.64-74, Mittal Publications. New Delhi.

Khongsdier, R. and N. Mukherjee., 2003a, "Growth and Nutritional Status of the Khasi Boys in North East India Relating to Exogamous Marriages and Socio-economic Classes". *American Journal of Physical Anthropology*. 122: pp. 162-70.

Khongsdier, R. and N. Mukherjee., 2003b, "Effects of Heterosis on Growth in Height and its Segments: A Cross-sectional Study of the Khasi Girls in Northeast India". *Annals of Human Biology*. 30. pp. 605-21.

Kiran Devi, B., 2002, "Genetic Demography of the Marngars of Ri Bhoi District, Meghalaya". Unpublished M.Sc. Dissertation. Department of Anthropology, North Eastern Hill University, Shillong

Lewontin, R.C., 1972, "The Apportionment of Human Diversity". In T. Dobzhansky, M. K. Hecht and W.C. Steere (Eds): *Evolutionary Biology*. pp. 381-98. Appleton-Century-Crofts. New York.

Rosenberg, N. A.; J. K., Pritchard ; J. L.Weber ; H. M., Cann ; K. K., Kidd ; L. A. Zhivotovsky; and M. W Feldman. 2002. "Genetic Structure of Human Populations". *Science*, 298: pp. 2381-2385.

Spuhler, J. N., 1973, "Anthropological Genetics: An Overview", In M.H. Crawford and P.L. Workman (Eds): *Methods and Theories of Anthropological Genetics*, pp. 423-451. University of New Mexico Press. Albuquerque.

Volpe, E. P., 1990, *Understanding Evolution*, 5th edition. Universal Book Stall. New Delhi.

Williams, R.C.; J.C. Long; R.L Hanson; M.L. Sievers; and W.C. Knowler., 2000, "Individual Estimates of European Genetic Admixture Associated with Lower Body Mass Index, Plasma Glucose, and Prevalence of Type 2 Diabetes in Pima Indians". *American Journal of Human Genetics*. 66: pp. 527–38.

Workman, P. L., 1973, "Genetic Analyses of Hybrid Populations", in M.H. Crawford and P.L. Workman (Eds): *Methods and Theories of Anthropological Genetics*, pp. 117-50, University of New Mexico Press. Albuquerque.

11

Socio-economic Profile of the Scheduled Tribes Inhabiting the Hill Areas of Assam—An Empirical Study

— Girindra Nath Das

The State of Assam, administratively divided into 23 districts, occupies a geographical area of 78,438 sq.km. and a total population of 2.24 crore as per 1991 Census. Physiographically, the State may be divided into three units, viz., the plains of the Brahmaputra Valley comprising 18 districts in the north, the plains of the Barak Valley with three districts in the south and the Karbi plateau and North Cachar hilly region with two districts in the middle. The last unit consisting of the Karbi Anglong and the North Cachar Hills autonomous districts is commonly known as the Hill Areas of Assam. The Karbi Anglong district has a surface area of 10,434 sq.km. and a total population of 6.62 lakh, while the North Cachar Hills district has an area of 4,888 sq.km., and a population of 1.50 lakh as per 1991 Census. In other words, the Hill Areas of Assam, with an area of 15, 322 sq.km. and a population of 8.12 lakh, constitute 19.50% and 3.60% of the geographical area and total population of the State respectively.

According to the Scheduled Castes and Scheduled Tribes Amendment Act 1976, the following 14 tribes have been specified in the two autonomous hill districts of Assam: (1) Chakma (2) Dimasa Kachari (3) Garo (4) Hajong (5) Hmar (6) Khasi, Jayantia, Synteng, Pnar, War, Bhoi, Lyngngam

(7) any Kuki tribe (37 groups) (8) Lakher (9) Man (Tai speaking) (10) any Mizo (Lushai) tribe (11) Mikir (Karbi) (12) any Naga tribe (13) Pawi and (14) Synteng. Besides, settlements of some Scheduled Tribes (Plains) such as the Boros and the Tiwas, etc., are also observed. However, the Karbi Anglong district is predominantly inhabited by the Karbis. On the other hand, the major tribe in the North Cachar Hills district is the Dimasa Kacharis.

The rate of literacy excluding 0 - 6 years age group, as per 1991 Census, is 45.57% (Male 55.55%, Female 34.35%) in Karbi Anglong district and 57.76% (Male 66.39%, Female 47.34%) in North Cachar Hills district. Density of population per sq.km is 64 in Karbi Anglong as against 31 in North Cachar Hills.

The major tribes living in the Hill Areas of Assam, as already mentioned are the Karbis and Dimasa Kacharis. It is, therefore, considered relevant to furnish here brief ethnographic notes on the two tribes highlighting their life and culture.

The Karbis

The Karbis are Mongoloid group of people. Linguistically, they belong to the Tibeto-Burman family. They appear to be "an interesting tribe in the sense that though they belong to Assam-Burma group of the Tibeto-Burman linguistic family, they can neither be put under Bodo nor any other linguistic group. Grierson (1904) classified them as an intermediate group, between the Bodo and the Western Naga, on the basis of language. Again, some others want to suggest that Karbi language shows the mixture of Austric and Bodo languages, though they undoubtedly belong to the Tibeto-Burman linguistic family. According to some scholars, the Karbi language has some similarities with certain Naga dialects, on the one hand, and Lushai Kuki dialects, on the other" (Kar, 1994). Lyall (1971) opines, "........they should be classed rather with these tribes which form the connecting link between the Nagas and the Kuki-Chins, and that the preponderance of their affinities lies with the latter of these two races, especially those dwelling in the south of the Arakan Yoma range, where the Chin tends to merge into Burma of the Irrawady Valley." Taking into consideration, the ballads prevalent among the Karbis, it may be assumed that they belong to the Kuki-Chin sub-group.

While dealing with the original habitat and migration of the Karbis, Bordoloi (1985) comments, "The original home of the Karbis, like the other tribes of North East India, was the Western China near the Yang-tse-Kiang and the Howang-ho rivers. From these places they went down the courses of the Chindwin and the Irrawaty rivers and entered Burma and stayed there for some time. From Burma, they went down the courses of the Brahmaputra and entered Assam by the north-east route, through the Patkai Ranges the along with other Tibeto-Burman races before several centuries (B.C.)"

At present, the highest concentration of the Karbis is found in the Karbi Anglong district, although Karbi settlements are scattered over the districts of North Cachar Hills, Kamrup, Nagaon, Morigaon, Golaghat, Sonitpur and Lakhimpur, etc. Moreover, their settlements are known from the States of Nagaland, Manipur, Meghalaya and Arunachal Pradesh.

The total population of the Karbis is 1, 72,845 in Karbi Anglong and 4,349 in North Cachar Hills as per 1971 Census. They constitute 45.57%, 38.91% and 1.21% of the total population of Karbi Anglong, the Hill Areas of Assam and the State of Assam respectively. Their rate of literacy is 13.18% (Males 21.09%, Females 4.95%) against 26.02% of literacy among the Scheduled Tribes of Assam (Males 34.62%, Females 17.16%) as reflected in 1971 Census.

The Karbis generally establish their villages on hill slopes/ tops. However, the villages are observed in the plains also. Each village consisting of few households is usually named after the *Gaonbura* (Headman). Previously the people used to live in pile dwelling houses (*hemthengsong*) but, at present, they construct houses on the grounds (*hemlongle*).

The Karbis have five clans (*Kur*) viz., Teron, Inghi, Ingti, Terang and Timung. The clans are socially equal in status. Each clan is further divided into a number of sub-clans such as Ingti - 5, Teron - 6, Inghi - 30 and Timung - 30. The clans are exogamous and therefore, marriage between members of the same clan never takes place. Violation of this social norm (*Laisenam*) leads to excommunication from the society.

Monogamy is the usual practice among the people. Cross-cousin marriage (mother's brother's daughter) is highly preferred by them. Divorce and widow remarriage are permissible. Junior levirate i.e., marriage with the younger brother of the deceased husband is allowed in the society. Bride price and child marriage are absent. The most common method of acquiring a mate is marriage by negotiation.

The Karbis practice patriarchal family system and hence the father is the head of the family. Descent is traced through the male line only. Sons but not daughters inherit property after the death of the father. In absence of sons, the nearest male relatives of the deceased inherit the same. The daughters, however, receive mother's property, such as, ornaments, clothes and looms, etc.

The primary occupation of the Karbis is agriculture. *Jhum* is practised by them in the hilly areas while wet cultivation is carried out in the low-lying areas. Terrace cultivation is also undertaken by some households. They rear cattle, pigs and poultry, etc. Weaving, bamboo and cane works and sericulture are the cottage industries carried out by them mainly for domestic consumption. The economic condition of the people, however, is not satisfactory. Indebtedness, land alienation and *paikas* system, etc., have aggravated their economy.

Rongker and *Hachakekan* are the two main agricultural festivals celebrated by the people. The former is observed before the beginning of cultivation, while the latter is performed after the harvest.

The Karbi people appear to be indifferent towards health and hygiene. Tuberculosis and leprosy are the major diseases among them. They propitiate deities and apply indigenous drugs for curing patients. Now-a-days, scientific methods of treatment of diseases have been accepted by the people to a considerable extent.

The staple diet of the people is rice with vegetables, edible roots and tubers, etc. Pork, chicken and fish are their delicacies. They take meals in the morning and evening. Consumption of rice beer is very much favourite to them.

The Karbis have traditional dress and ornaments, dance and music. The women wear *Pini* (*mekhela*), *Wamkok* (belt) and *Jiso* (a piece of cloth taken over breasts), while men wear *Rikong* (loin cloth), *Choi* (shirt) and *Poho* (headgear) etc. The traditional ornaments used by the womenfolk include *Roi* (bracelet), *Lel* (string of beads), *Arnam* (ring), *No thengpi* (ear rings) and *Kadengchinro* (silver tube) etc. Now-a-days, the younger generations have the habit of wearing modern dresses and ornaments. The traditional musical instruments are *Pongsi* (flute), *Muri* (pipe), *Cheng* (drum) and *Kum* (one stringed fiddle) etc.

It may be pointed out here that the traditional institutions of the Karbis are Village Council (*Mei*), Bachelors' dormitory (*Farla / Jirkedam*) and Grain Bank (*Kerung Amei*), etc.

Hinduism has influenced the Karbis to a great extent, although traditional beliefs and practices are in vogue among them. They believe in the existence of Supreme God (*Arnam Kethe*) as well as a number of benevolent and malevolent deities. They do not have idol, temple or shrine. Moreover, they do not worship trees and animals. They believe in witchcraft and black magic. *Chojun* or *Swarag* is the important household religious festival among them. But the most important and expensive religious ceremony is the *Chomangkan* or death ceremony. It may be noted here that a section of the Karbis has converted to Christianity also.

The Karbis cremate the dead in the place allotted against each clan in the crematorium (*Thiri*).

The Dimasa Kacharis

Like other tribes of Assam, the Dimasa Kacharis are also of Mongoloid origin. They are included in the Bodo group of Assam-Burmese branch of the Tibeto-Burman linguistic family. At present, they live predominantly in the North Cachar Hill district. However, their settlements are scattered in Nagaon, Karbi Anglong and Cachar districts of the State. The literal meaning of the term Dimasa is the descendant or son of a big river. *Di* means water, *Ma* means big and *Sa* means son. This may refer to the Brahmaputra River or its tributary Dhansiri.

The Dimasa had their capital at Dimapur of present Nagaland, which was later on shifted to Maibang of North Cachar Hills and Khaspur of Cachar district respectively.

The total population of the Dimasas in the Hill Areas of Assam as per 1971 Census is 39,344, the males and females being 20,713 and 18,631 respectively. The rate of literacy among them is 18.84% (Males 27.36%, Females 9.36%) only as reflected in 1971 Census.

Generally, the people build their villages on hill slopes, located near a river or stream. Each village is surrounded by fencing, for the purpose of necessary protection. The thatched houses are constructed on the plinth of earth.

It is interesting to note that the Dimasas have 40 patrilineal clans (*Sengphong*) and 42 matrilineal clans (*Zulu*). The clans are exogamous and marriage between members of the same clan can never take place.

The people follow patriarchal family system. Father is the head of the family. The sons inherit the property after the death of father. The daughters inherit the maternal property, consisting of clothes, jewelry and looms, etc.

Monogamy is the usual practice among the people. Marriage by negotiation is the normal procedure. Bride price (*Kalti*) is prevalent among them. Widow remarriage and divorce are allowed in the society. Junior levirate is permissible.

Agriculture is the main source of livelihood of the people. Both *jhum* and wet cultivation are practised by them. Moreover, some of them carry out terrace cultivation. They possess livestock population. Weaving, bamboo and cane works and sericulture are carried out mainly for domestic consumption. On the whole, the Dimasas are not economically sound.

Rice is their staple food. Rice beer (*Zu*) is the favourite beverage. But they do not have the habit of drinking milk. Pork, fish and meat, etc., are delicacies.

The important traditional institutions of the Dimasas are Village Council (*Salis*), Bachelors' dormitory (*Nodrang*) and Youth Association (*Hangsuo*), etc.

It may be mentioned here that the harvesting festival (*Busu*) is celebrated by the people on a large scale. A well decorated gate (*Fangsla*) is also constructed before the celebration of the festival.

So far as the religion of the people is concerned, Majumdar (1980) opines, "The religious organisation of the Dimasas is also unique. There is a religious head for the whole community who is known as *gisia*. The whole Dimasa habitat is divided into 12 religious areas, known as *daikho* and each *daikho* has a religious head known as *janthai*. The traditional religious system of the Dimasas is very much on the decline. In A.D. 1813 the Dimasa king Krishnachandra accepted Brahmanical Hinduism and since then the process of Hinduisation has started among the Dimasas and a large number of Dimasas have now become Hindus."

The Dimasas cremate the dead preferably on the bank of a river or stream and the death ceremony is performed according to their customs.

The Study and its Methodology

The present study attempts, to bring into focus the prevailing socio-economic conditions of the tribal communities in the Hill Areas of Assam. Altogether 293 villages (218 in

Karbi Anglong and 75 in North Cachar Hills) were selected, for the study on the basis of 20.00% random sampling out of the total number of 1468 villages, having 50.00% or more tribal population in the Hill Areas of Assam as per 1971 Census. Household and village schedules were prepared for systematic collection of all relevant data. Although the field work was started from the month of December, 1988, it could be completed in the month of March, 1992 only due to various constraints.

Major Findings of the Study

Demographic Structure: The study reveals that out of the total number of 293 villages in the Hill Areas of Assam, the number of households is 9,260 and the total population is 53,475. In order to have an insight into the demographic structure, we have taken into consideration the distribution of villages by size of population, distribution of population according to age group and sex ratio in the surveyed villages.

While dealing with the distribution of the villages by the size of population, it has been found that out of 293 villages, 208 (70.99%) are in the category of up to 200 individuals. Again, 67 (22.87%) and 13 (4.44%) are in the range of 201-400 and 401-600 individuals respectively. Moreover, there are 5 (1.70%) villages in the category of above 600 individuals. This indicates that the villages under study are not thickly populated.

With regard to the distribution of population according to age group, it may be mentioned here that out of the total population of 53,475, the population numbering 22,875 (42.78%) is the highest in the age group 0 - 15 years. While the population numbering 1,501 (2.81%) is the lowest in the age group of 61 years and above. However, in the age groups of 16 - 30 years, 31- 45 years and 46 - 60 years, the population is found to be 15,755 (29.46%), 8,686 (16.24%) and 4,568 (8.71%) respectively. This shows that from the age group 0 - 15 years onwards, the percentages of population to the total population in the surveyed villages have decreased gradually.

The total population in 293 villages, as already noted, is 53,475 out of which the males are 28,029 and the females are 25, 446. The sex ratio of the total population is worked out to be 907, which are higher than that of the State as per 1971 Census (896). On the contrary, it is lower than that of the State as per 1991 Census (923). Mention may be made here that in 71 villages (24.23%), the females outnumber the males and in 11 villages (3.75%), the numbers of males and females are equal. The highest sex ratio is 1586, while the lowest one is 536.

Infrastructural Facilities: In the sphere of socio-economic development in any region, the infrastructural facilities and basic amenities are essential pre-requisites. The study is, therefore, oriented towards highlighting the prevailing facilities in and around the surveyed villages.

Transport and Communication: According to the field investigation, out of the total number of 293 villages, 208. (70.99%) villages are located within a radius of 0 - 5 km. from the nearest motorable road. Again, 46 (15.7%) and 24 (8.19%) villages are located in the range of 6 - 11 km. and 12 - 17 km. away from the motorable road respectively. Moreover, the people from as many as 15 villages (5.12%) have to move beyond 17 km., to reach the nearest motorable road. Thus, the provision of motorable roads does not appear to be satisfactory. Furthermore, the bus services are not regularly maintained by the concerned authorities for the benefit of the people.

So far as the railway facilities are concerned, it has been found that only 87(29.69%) villages are conveniently located in the range of 0 - 15 km. from the nearest railway station. The people of the remaining 206 (70.31%) villages have to cover a distance of more than 15 km. to arrive at the nearest railway station. In fact, due to distant location of the villages from the railway station, the people cannot derive much benefit.

Development Block H.Q.: In the Hill Areas of Assam, the

total number of Development Blocks is 15, out of which 11 are in Karbi Anglong and 4 in North Cachar Hills. As a matter of fact, the Development Blocks have to play the pivotal role in uplifting the socio-economic life of the tribal people, since the *Gaon Panchayat* system functioning in the plains districts of the State is not in existence in the two autonomous hill districts. The field investigation reveals that out of 293 villages, 154 (52.56%) villages are conveniently located at a distance of 0 - 15 km. from the respective Block headquarters while 139 (47.44%) villages are not suitably located since some of the villages are at a distance of more than 47 km. from the respective Block headquarters.

District Head Quarters: In respect of the location of the surveyed villages from the District H.Q., it may be said that out of 293 villages, the number of villages located in the broad range of 0 - 80 km. is 137 (46.76%) villages against 156 (53.24%) villages, situated at a distance of more than 80 km. from the District H.Q. This reveals the facts that most of the villages under study are inconveniently located from the District H.Q.

Civic and Educational Facilities: In order to understand the resourcefulness of a particular region, it is necessary to take into account the civic and educational facilities viz., post and telegraph, medicare and educational institutions, etc., in the region.

The study reveals that, out of 293 villages, 252 (86.00%) villages are located at a distance of 0 - 15 km. from the nearest post office, while 93 (31.74%) villages are located in the same range of distance, from the nearest telegraph office. However, 41 (14%) and 200 (68.26%) villages are more than 15 km. away from the post office and telegraph office respectively. From this analysis, it can be inferred that the people of the surveyed villages are in a better position to derive maximum benefit from the post office rather than the telegraph office.

The Hill Areas of Assam are provided with Medicare facilities viz., Civil Hospital, Rural Hospital, Primary Health Centre (PHC), Dispensary and Veterinary Dispensary, etc. one hundred fifty-two, (51.88%) out of 293 villages are situated at a distance of 0 - 15 km. from the nearest hospital, while 56 (19.11%) villages are located in the range of 16 km. - 30 km. from the hospital. But the people from 85 (29.01%) villages have to move more than 30 km. to reach the nearest hospital for the necessary treatment. In respect of PHC and dispensary, it is seen that 155 (52.9%) and 167 (57.00%) villages are lying at a distance of 0-10 km. from the nearest PHC and dispensary respectively. Again, 67 (22.87%) villages are situated in the same range of distance from the nearest dispensary. The number of villages located beyond 20 km. is 71 (24.23%) from the PHC and 67 (22.87%) from the dispensary. With regard to the veterinary facilities, it may be mentioned here that out of the total surveyed villages, 174 (59.39%) and 55 (18.77%) villages are located in the range of 0 - 15 km and 16 - 30 km. from the nearest veterinary institution respectively. The people from as many as 64 (21.84%) villages have to cover more than 30 km. to reach the nearest veterinary institution for the treatment of their livestock population. The field investigation further reveals that there are some private medical practitioners in and around the surveyed villages. Out of 293 villages, 116 (39.59%) and 62 (21.16%) villages are located at a distance of 0 km. - 5 km. and 6-10 km. from the private medical practitioner respectively. The number of villages located beyond 10 km. from the private medical practitioner is 115 (39.25%). It may be relevantly pointed out here that, although there is dearth of Medicare institutions to cover the entire population of the Hill Areas of Assam, most of the existing institutions lack adequate staff, medicine and scientific equipments, etc. Furthermore, some people try to cure the patients using indigenous drugs or worshipping various deities. They reach to the nearest Medicare institution only when they fail to cure the patients by the traditional method of treatment.

There are 223 Primary, 108 Middle, 81 High and 9 Higher Secondary Schools including 4 Colleges in and around the villages. The total number of students attending various educational institutions from 293 villages is 11,459 out of which the males are 6,517 (56.87%) and the females are 4,942 (43.13%). Again, out of 6,517 male students, 3,850 (59.07%), 1,341 (20.58%), 1,181 (18.12%), 123 (1.89%) and 22 (0.34%) are attending L.P., Middle English, High, Higher Secondary and College respectively. Similarly, out of 4,942 female students, the number of students reading in L.P., Middle English., High, Higher Secondary and College is found to be 3,162 (63.98%), 1,103 (22.32%), 648 (13.11%), 27 (0.55%) and 2 (0.04%) respectively. This analysis indicates that, after primary standard of education, most of the students give up further studies. Moreover, it is interesting to note that the percentage of attendance of female students in primary standard exceeds that of male students. On the contrary, the percentage of attendance of male students exceeds that of female students in the High School standard or above. The attitude of the students as well as the guardians towards modern education cannot be said to be satisfactory.

The main sources of drinking water for the people of the surveyed villages are well, natural spring, river, tap water, and pond and tube well. According to the field investigation, the people from 158 (53.92%) villages depend upon *katcha* or *pucca* well numbering 462. Again, the people from 84 (28.67%) villages fetch water from the natural spring. Moreover, the people from 72 (24.57%) villages use water from the nearby river. Tap water facilities have been provided to 64 (21.84%) villages only. The total number of ponds in 56 (16.72%) villages for the purpose of drinking water is found to be 205 in number. Tube wells numbering 263 have been installed in 49 (16.72%) villages, for the purpose of drinking water. It is to be noted here that most of the people do not adopt scientific treatment of water except the traditional method of filtration. As a result, the people are likely to suffer from water borne diseases. Suitable schemes should be executed by the Public Health Engineering Department for supply of drinking water to the people.

There are 71 market places (daily, bi-weekly and weekly), 88 fair price shops and 254 grocery and other shops within the surveyed villages. The people sell their produces viz., rice, maize, mustard, sesame, ginger, betel nut, betel leaf and vegetables, etc., in the nearby market. On the other hand, they purchase essential commodities such as cloth, sugar, salt, tea, *atta, dal,* fish, mustard oil, kerosene, *bidi,* tobacco, and cigarette and other stationery articles, etc., from the market places. So far as the distance of the surveyed villages from the market places is concerned, it is found that 154 (52.56%) villages are conveniently located in the range of 0 - 5 km. from the nearest market. There are, however, 73 (24.91%) villages located at a distance of 6 - 10 km. from the market. But the people from as many as 66 (22.53%) villages have to cover more than 10 km. to visit the nearest market.

The main objective, of the establishment of the Large Area Multipurpose Co-operative Societies (LAMPS) in the Hill Areas of Assam, is to supply essential commodities to the people at reasonable price. The field investigation reveals that out of 293 villages, 215 (73.38%) villages are located at a distance of 0 - 15 km., while the remaining 78 (26.62%) are located beyond 15 km. from the LAMPS. It is to be noted that although most of the people of the villages under study are in a position to derive benefits out of the LAMPS, the services of the co-operative societies in the Hill Areas of Assam are not satisfactory to the desired level. Most of them are incurring heavy losses due to high establishment cost, shortage in stocks, transportation cost, marginal profits on essential commodities, high amount of interest accrued to Government loan and malpractices among the staff, etc.

Banking facilities in the Hill Areas of Assam have geared up with the establishment of branches of commercial banks as well as rural bank. The branches of State Bank of India, Central Bank of India, United Commercial Bank, Bank of Baroda, Union Bank, Assam Co-operative Apex Bank and Langpi Dehangi Rural Bank, etc., have been rendering services to the customers. So far as the distance of the surveyed villages from the nearest bank is concerned, it is found that 215 (73.38%) and 41 (13.99%) villages are located at a distance of 0-15 km. and 16-30 km. from the nearest bank respectively. But there are 37 (12.63%) villages situated beyond 30 km. from the nearest bank. It may be mentioned here that most of the people do not have the habit of savings for future. Moreover, the people appear to be reluctant to avail financial assistance due to complicated procedures of the banking authorities.

Provision of electricity in the surveyed villages is far from satisfactory. Only 89 (30.38%) villages out of 293 villages have been covered by electricity. Most of the people use it for domestic consumption only. The number of households using electricity for agriculture and irrigation is very limited. Mention may be made here that in some villages, electricity is used for street lighting also.

There are 38 socio-cultural organisations with a total membership of 1,446 in the surveyed villages. The organisations have received Govt. aid amounting to Rs. 20,000/- in 1986-87 and Rs. 20,500/- in 1987-88. The main objectives of the socio-cultural organisations are to promote traditional songs and dances, games and sports, extend help and co-operation in the celebration of socio-religious festivals and ceremonies and perform development works in the villages, etc.

Economic Profile

According to 1991 Census, about 84.00% of the total population of the Hill Areas of Assam lives in rural areas. Agriculture including shifting cultivation *(jhum)* is the mainstay of the people. The economy of the region is absolutely agrarian. An attempt is being made here to highlight the prevailing economy of the people living in the surveyed villages on the basis of occupational structure, land-holding pattern and extent of income and expenditure, etc.

Occupational Structure

The field investigation reveals that out of the total households of 9,260 belonging to 293 villages, 8,226 (88.83%)

practise cultivation as primary occupation. The number of households engaged in service, business and daily wage as primary occupation is 614 (6.63%), 105 (1.13%) and 315 (3.40%) respectively. It is, therefore, seen that agriculture plays a significant role in the economy of the people.

Some households of the villages under study resort to secondary occupation also for supplementing their income. Thus, out of the total number of 1,338 households having secondary occupation, 439 (32.81%) have adopted cultivation while 221 (16.52%) have taken up service. The number of households engaged in business is found to be 224 (16.74%) only. As many as 454 (33.93%) households are in the habit of practising daily wage as secondary occupation.

In order to understand the position of workers and non-workers in the surveyed villages, the total population is classified into earners, earning dependents and non-earning dependents. The person whose annual income is more than the rest of the members of the household is included in the category 'earners'. Again, the persons between the broad age group 16 - 60 years except those included in the category 'earners' have been included in the category 'earning dependents'. The members of the age group 0 - 15 years and above 60 years are included in the category 'non-earning dependents'. According to field investigation, out of total population of 53,475 individuals, the number of earners is 9,260 (17.32%) while that of non-earning dependents is 19,839 (37.10%). There are also 24,376 non-earning dependents constituting 45.58% of the total population. In the surveyed villages, the percentage of earners appears to be less. But it is to be noted that in a tribal community, particularly practising *jhum* cultivation, the females and other adult members contribute significantly towards the maintenance of the families. Therefore, the total number of earners and earning dependents may be considered as the potential working force. It is found that the total workers constitute 29,099, the percentage being 54.42. On the contrary, the non-earning dependents or non-workers numbering 24,376 constitute 45.58% of the total population.

Land-Holding Pattern

To discuss the land-holding pattern not only in the surveyed villages but also in the Hill Areas of Assam as a whole, is a difficult task, since the quantity of land possessed by a household varies annually due to the practice of *jhum* cultivation. Moreover, land records from the cadastral survey, in respect of all villages, are still not available. Despite the aforesaid problems, an attempt is being made here to highlight the land-holding of various types in the surveyed villages, on the basis of verbal statements of the respondents.

Out of 1, 17,793 *bighas* of land possessed by 9,260 households of 293 villages, the area of land under *jhum*, wet and terrace cultivation is worked out to be 35,504 (30.14%), 59,524 (50.53%) and 2,659 (2.26%) *bighas* respectively. Homestead land covers 15,279 (12.97%) *bighas*. The total amount of land under fishery is a meager 741 (0.63%) *bighas* only. Horticultural land accounts for 2,532 (2.15%) *bighas*. The quantity of fallow land is 1,554 (1.32%) *bighas*. This reveals that despite implementation of various *jhum* control programmes in the Hill Areas of Assam, the people still resort to *jhum* cultivation for their livelihood. On the whole, the average land-holding per household and per capita land-holding in the villages are 12.72 *bigha* and 2.2 *bigha* respectively.

Area of Land, Yield and Value of Major Crops

The people generally grow mixed crops in a single plot of *jhum* land. Therefore, the area of land utilised for each type of crop under *jhum* is difficult to take into account. That is why, the approximate production and value of the major crops from *jhum* cultivation have been mentioned here. Out of 35,504 *bighas* of land brought under *jhum* cultivation, the amount of paddy, wheat and maize obtained by them is 63,960 quintals, 278 quintals and 7,867 quintals respectively. The approximate value of paddy, wheat and maize is Rs. 159.82 lakh, Rs. 1.27 lakh and Rs. 17.30 lakh respectively. The yield of pulses is 1,410 quintals, the value of which is Rs. 7.25 lakh. In respect of oil seeds, the amount of production is 12,394 quintals, the approximate value being Rs. 73.86 lakh. Again, the people obtain 765 quintals of fibers for which they receive an amount of Rs. 6.84 lakh. In case of ginger, the total production is 2,902 quintals and the value stands at Rs. 16.29 lakh. Moreover, the approximate amount received by the people from vegetables is Rs. 29.94 lakh. Thus, it is seen that the people of the surveyed villages practise cultivation of various types of crops in the *jhum* fields and the production of paddy is the highest followed by oil seeds.

So far as settled cultivation is concerned, it has been found that the total area of land brought under paddy cultivation is 53,569 *bighas*. The total yield is 1, 67,746 quintals, the value of which is to the tune of Rs. 419.16 lakh. Wheat is cultivated in 168 *bighas* which produce 364 quintals, worth Rs. 1.66 lakh. The people derive an amount of Rs. 2.56 lakh against 1,173 quintals of maize obtained from 452 *bighas* of land. Pulses are cultivated in 711 *bighas*. The quantity of the produce is 134 quintals, the value of which is Rs. 7.04 lakh. The people also carry out cultivation of varieties of oil seeds in 3,768 *bighas*. The yield is 10,486 quintals and the value is Rs. 62.80 lakh. From the cultivation of fibers in 498 *bighas*, the people obtain 1,004 quintals and the value of which is Rs. 9.00 lakh. The cultivation of ginger in 32 *bighas* yields 381 quintals and the value of the produce is Rs. 2.24 lakh. From the cultivation of sugarcane in 397 *bighas* and vegetables in 3,619 *bighas*, the people derive Rs. 2.25 lakh and Rs. 9.82 lakh respectively. The value of horticultural products grown in 2,532 *bighas* of land is Rs. 16.75 lakh. This analysis reveals that the people practise various types of crops under settled cultivation for earning their livelihood. However, it is to be noted that most of the people do not use high yielding varieties of crops, chemical fertilizers and pesticides, etc. Moreover, proper irrigation facilities are also lacking.

Paddy under terrace cultivation has also been practised by some households of the villages under study. It has been found that the people derive an amount of Rs. 23.93 lakh for 9,575 quintals of terrace paddy produced in 2,659 *bighas* of land. On the whole, the amount of production of paddy per *bigha* is 1.80 quintal in *jhum,* 3.13 quintal in wet cultivation and 3.60 quintal in terrace cultivation.

Fishery

Due to the nature and topography of the Hill Areas of Assam, suitable land for pisciculture is very limited. As already noted, the total area of land under fishery in the surveyed villages is 741 *bighas* only. There are altogether 585 fisheries comprising 484 tanks, 29 *beels,* 43 natural fisheries and 29 channels. The people normally use the production of fish for their consumption. However, they sell the surplus products in the nearby markets. The amount of income generated from fishery is worked out to be Rs. 11.47 lakh. It may be mentioned here that the people have also received financial assistance to the tune of Rs.1.16 lakh from the Government for the development of pisciculture.

Cottage Industry

Weaving, bamboo and cane works and sericulture are the important cottage industries, prevalent among the people of the surveyed villages. The womenfolk weave various types of clothes with artistic design in their loin looms or fly shuttle looms. The number of households engaged in weaving is found to be 5,992 (64.71%). Again, 2,910 (31.43%) households carry out bamboo and cane works at leisurely hours. These include various types of baskets, bamboo mats, *murha* and fishing traps, etc. Moreover, the number of households engaged in sericulture activities is 1,371, the percentage being 14.81. Silkworms are reared by them and *eri chadars* are prepared out of the cocoons. Sometimes cocoons are sold in the local market also. It is to be noted that these cottage industries cannot improve the economic condition of the people, unless these are taken on commercial level by implementing suitable schemes by the Government. However, the amount of income derived by the people from cottage industries is to the tune of Rs. 23.01 lakh.

Livestock

The livestock population plays an important role in the economy of the tribal people. The field investigation reveals that the people possess animals and birds such as bullocks, cows, buffaloes, pigs and poultry, etc. It is interesting to note that in North Cachar Hills, the buffaloes are left in semi wild state which causes wanton destruction. The total livestock population is found to be 1, 94,520, out of which the number of poultry is the highest i.e. 1, 12,242 (57.70%), while the number of sheep is the lowest i.e. 375 (0.19%) only. Pigs with 29, 567 numbers and ducks with 13306 numbers constitute 15.20% and 6.84% of the total livestock respectively. There are 10,724 (5.51%) bullocks, 6,669 (3.43%) cows and 9,606 (4.94%) buffaloes. The number of goats and pigeons is 10,540 (5.42%) and 1,491 (0.77%) respectively. Thus, the people of the surveyed villages appear to be interested in rearing different kinds of animals and birds for their benefit. The annual income of the people from livestock stands at Rs. 269.73 lakh.

Household Properties

In a tradition bound tribal community, particularly practising *jhum* cultivation, important household properties are not generally observed. However, with the passage of time, the lifestyle of the people has undergone changes. Therefore, it has been found that there are 2,343 bicycles, 3,460 radios, 4,033 watches, 519 tape recorders, 109 televisions, 1,588 guns, 94 vehicles, 351 bullock carts and 7,331 ploughs, etc., in the surveyed villages.

It is also seen that the traditional housing pattern in the villages has undergone changes. There are 92 R.C.C. buildings, 422 *pucca* Assam type houses, 1,810 *kutcha* Assam type houses, 1,647 pile-dwelling houses and 12,300 thatched houses in the villages under study. This reveals that a tendency has developed among the people to possess important household properties.

Annual Income and Expenditure

It is indeed a difficult task to discuss the annual income and expenditure of the families, since they do not possess any written record. However, an attempt is being made here to present the pattern of income and expenditure, based on the verbal statements of the respondents.

'Land' is the primary source of income for the people, because they derived 55.30% of the total income from land alone. This means that agriculture plays the dominant role in the economy of the people. The next source of income is 'Livestock' which constitutes 18.04% of the total income. The third source is 'Paid employment including daily wage' which accounts for 16.04% of the total income. Moreover, the people derive 8.42%, 1.46% and 0.73% of the total income from 'Trade and Commerce', 'Cottage Industry' and 'Fishery' respectively. Thus, the average gross annual income of a household is Rs. 17,002.48 and per capita annual income is Rs. 2,944.24 only.

The major head of expenditure of the families is 'food' which constitutes 56.58% of the total expenses. In 'dress and ornaments' the people spend 7.53%. On the other hand, they utilise 5.74% and 5.04% of the total expenditure in 'education' and 'health' respectively. The amount of expenditure is found to be 4.66% in 'beverage, tobacco and betel nut', 4.54'% in 'kerosene, toilet and utensil', 3.65% in 'festivals and ceremonies' and 3.42% in 'traveling and transport'. In case of 'residential building and furniture' the amount of expenditure is worked out to be 2.13%. The people spend 1.86% in 'radio, watch, bicycle and television' and 2.00% in 'amusement'. Furthermore, they spend 2.85% of the total expenses under the head 'miscellaneous' which includes expenditure in relation to fishery, cottage industry, livestock and land revenue, etc. On the whole, the average annual expenditure of a household is Rs. 14,755.94 and the per capita expenditure is Rs. 2,555.21.

This reveals that the average household has a marginal surplus budget of Rs. 2,246.54 only. Per capita surplus is Rs. 389.03 per annum. It may, therefore, be said that the economy of the people is at subsistence level.

Indebtedness

The field investigation revels that out of 9,260 households, 958 (10.35%) household are in debts. The indebted households take loans for various reasons viz., self employment, livestock, fishery and horticulture, etc. The sources of taking loans are banks, DRDA, village people, *Mahajans* and Shopkeepers, etc.

The total amount of loan obtained by 958 households is Rs. 25.57 lakh out of which Rs. 19.06 lakh are availed by 336 (35.07%) households from banks, DRDA, etc., at nominal rate of interest. The amount of Rs. 6.51 lakh is availed by 622 (64.93%) households from the other sources viz., village people, *Mahajans* and Shopkeepers, etc., against exorbitant rate of interest. The average debt per household is Rs. 276.00 and the average debt per indebted household is Rs. 2,669.00.

Conclusion

The Scheduled Tribes living in the Hill Areas of Assam are lagging far behind in every sphere, although several decades of India's attainment of independence have already elapsed. The economy of the people is still at subsistence level. The Karbi Anglong Autonomous Council, Diphu and the North Cachar Hills Autonomous Council, Haflong have endeavoured to uplift the masses through various plans and programmes but the pace of development is not up to the desired level. It is, therefore, felt necessary to undertake some ambitious schemes by the two Councils so that fruits of development percolate down to the common people. For this purpose the following suggestions have been incorporated for necessary consideration by the concerned authorities.

Mass awareness should be generated among the people for scientific methods of cultivation adopting high yielding varieties of crops, chemical fertilisers and pesticides, etc. Proper irrigation facilities should be made available to them. The practice of *jhum* cultivation should be reduced to the minimum to avoid environmental hazards and the people may be motivated for the cultivation of coffee, rubber, tea, pineapple, orange, banana and citrus, etc., for maximum benefit.

Each village of the Hill Areas of Assam should be connected by all weather motorable roads so that communication could be maintained throughout the year. Although it is a gigantic task with involvement of crores of rupees, steps may be taken for phase-wise construction of the roads.

Existing Medicare institutions should be provided with sufficient staff, medicine and scientific equipments, etc. Adequate steps may be taken for further construction of such institutions, in the areas to attract the people towards modern methods of treatment of diseases.

Efforts should be made to check drop-out of students in the school level. The number of educational institutions may be increased to remove the darkness of illiteracy from the Hill Areas of Assam.

Drinking water, the elixir of life should be provided by the Public Health Engineering Department to the people, who use contaminated water from the river, stream, etc.

Since the agro-climatic factors for livestock development in the Hill areas of Assam are ideal and the people are also interested in rearing animals and birds, the Department of Animal Husbandry and Veterinary may motivate the people for rearing improved varieties of livestock in a scientific manner, to supplement their economy.

The Department of Fisheries, the District Industries Centre and the Department of Handloom and Textiles, should encourage the people to derive benefits out of the available schemes.

The 'sixty-forty' syndrome in the implementation of the welfare schemes by the Development Departments should be eradicated.

Co-operative Societies, Banks and other financial institutions should provide assistance to the illiterate persons on easy terms and conditions.

Cadastral survey may be completed at the earliest so that the people possess complete records of land and ownership right.

Of late, a new problem has arisen owing to infiltrators in the guise of agricultural labour. The Karbi Anglong Autonomous Council has had allotted lands to *jhumias* for wet cultivation but the *jhumia* Karbis have allowed immigrant settlers to cultivate their lands. Now the real tribal owners are facing a great problem to regain the lands and the immigrant settlers are also adamant not to return. This is happening in Howraghat areas. The very purpose of weaning away the tribal *jhumias* has been frustrated. The concerned authority should wake up to this sensitive situation.

Various tribal communities have been living in the Hill areas of Assam with peaceful co-existence, maintaining their traditional cultures and ethos since remote past. Under no circumstances, the cultural identity of the ethnic groups should be allowed to be eroded by endogenous or exogenous forces. Development activities should be initiated without affecting the core of the culture. This is more applicable particularly in case of tribal groups under the Sixth Schedule areas. Sizeable funds have been spent during the Five Year Plans (Hill Plan) and in order to cater to the special needs of the hill people, the Autonomous Councils have been empowered to chalk out need based schemes. Yet people's aspirations have not been fulfilled. The need of the hour is a purposeful evaluation and constant monitoring of the schemes implemented by various Development Departments.

REFERENCES

Bordoloi, B.N., 1985, "The Karbis – Their Origin and Migration". *Bulletin of the Tribal Research Institute, Assam, Guwahati* 1, 3: pp. 55-64.

Kar, R.K., 1994, "The Tribes of North East India: An Overview", In Sarthak Sengupta (Ed): *Tribes of North East India*. pp. 1-20, Gyan Publishing House, New Delhi.

Lyall, C., 1971, *The Mikirs*. United Publishers, Guwahati.

Majumdar, D.N., 1980, "North East India – A Profile". In T.C. Sharma and D.N. Majumdar (Eds): *Eastern Himalayas*, pp. 23-62. Cosmo Publications. New Delhi.

12

Socio-economic Life of the Dimasa Kacharis

—Sultana Hazarika

The Dimasa Kacharis are one of the earliest known autochthones of Assam. They build up a kingdom in the upper Brahmaputra valley in or about 12th century. Thereafter, in the 16th century, they migrated to Surma valley being pushed by the Ahoms and they continued to rule there till the middle of the 19th century.

The Dimasa kings were great builders and patrons of learning and literature. The remains of Kachomaripathar, Dimapur, Maibong, and Khaspur still bears testimony to their attainments in sculpture, architecture and engineering skill which show something unique in the Indo-Mongoloid culture.

The Dimasas were also expert warriors and good cultivators, fair knowledge or irrigation technique of cultivation as well as domestication of animals. They were also expert in rearing of silk worms and also spinning and weaving of multi-coloured clothes which are said to be important contribution of the Indo-Mongoloids to the Indian civilisation. The Dimasas are historically known to us after the advent of the Ahoms in the early part of 13th century A.D. In the absence of the script, the Dimasas used Assamese and Bengali languages. They were rich in folk literature, folktales, folklores, ballads, idioms etc. The legends referring to their kingdom and early history were used to be recited by village singers till the recent times. Tradition and custom taught them proper behaviour and folktales imparted to them the lessons of morality and ethics.

The Socio-economic Aspects

Religious faith and Ceremonies: The Dimasas believed in one Supreme Being of the universe. They worshipped the natural deities like trees, serpents etc. They believed every natural phenomenon has spirit or God. They worshipped *Madais* or *Bangla Raja* as deity of earthquake and *Arikhidima*, a Divine bird of whom they believed to be the descendants. They even sacrifices to the rivers like Kopili and Dvijen or Jamuna. The Dimasas also worshipped a female deity called *Ranachandi* who is believed to be the wife of Siva. *Longmailoi* which is identified as Goddess of wealth was worshipped by them.

Community worship took place at an interval of 3–4 years at *Madaikho* or temple located in certain fixed place, where completely black goat were sacrificed in addition to buffaloes, pigs, fowls, pigeons, eggs etc. These sacrifices were called *Misingba*. At the time of natural disaster like famine, the community worship was held. On the previous day of sowing seeds, the villagers performed the ceremony called *Hajagerba* to please deities inhabiting the jungles for getting food crops without any infection of pests. During weeding they observed the ceremony of *Maislaigerba* i.e. the worship of the Goddess paddy for luxuriant production. During *Busu* festival they worshipped *Brai Sibrai*, the Lord of corns and *Gamadi*, the Goddess of rain and wind, to get blessings for surplus production. The Dimasas in the family level perform *Madaima daimba* for the welfare of a particular individual in the family concerned. A religious ceremony called *Muli linga* is performed by issueless spouses to have children by sacrifices some fishes to the Gods.

The Dimasas believe that the evil spirit or *Sagim nijik* (witches) were responsible for the diseases like dysentery, diarrhea, leprosy, black fever, cholera etc., and they offer sacrifices of fowl, tortoise for the remedies.

In marriage, the bride price called *Kalti* was prevalent which was observed only in token form. Marriage is approached by offering one kilogram of salt to the boy's guardian and the acceptance of the packet meant giving consent to the proposal. This custom is known as *Sandidangba Singba*, the ceremony of giving salt. In the second step, the boy's father offer four small *Laothai* full of rice beer. This custom is called *Laothai Langba*. The formal visit was repeated three times during which some discussions regarding fixation of date, bride price etc. took place. Marriage was solemnised within one month. Before wedding procession started the bridegroom's father perform *Mayofangarba*, the worship of all deities by sacrificing an egg, for safe journey and to drive away the evil spirit. Entering the village the groom's father sacrifices a pig for prosperous life of the couple. The flesh of the pig was roasted and eaten by the party with rice beer provided by the bride's father at his house. After taking blessings from elderly persons, the bride was taken as daughter-in-law by uttering some *mantras*. Afterwards, a party was given to the guests with rice, meat and rice beer.

Diet and Food habit: Like other tribes of north eastern region, rice is the staple food of the Dimasas. They prepare vegetables like brinjal, gourd, pumpkin, pulses, lemon, some kind of jams, and herbs etc. A sticky type of rice called *Bara* is used to make various kinds of cakes (*pitha*) during festive time. They ate flesh of almost all kinds of animals except dogs, cat, monkeys etc. Birds like hen, pigeon, ducks and all kinds of fishes, white ants were their delicacy. Pork and eggs are preferred for festival and buffalo meat for funeral fests. *Zu* or rice beer was their favourite drink. It was an indispensable item in the entertainments and ceremonies which were served in bamboo pipes and metal vessels along with fried eggs, boiled rice and roasted chicken. They believed that *Zu* is good for health.

Economic life: Agriculture was the main occupation and basis of their economy. They practised both dry and wet cultivation, following both transplantation and broadcast method. They also practised *Jhum* (shifting) cultivation. In North Cachar hills, the lands were not suitable for *jhuming* due to rocky hills, so the Dimasas used hoe for cultivation. If lands were available, they practised wet cultivation also. In Karbi Anglong district, the Dimasas practised both shifting and wet cultivation and those living in the plains of Cachar practised wet cultivation with the help of plough. Dimasas know the technique of irrigation since very early time, though the agricultural activities were regulated by seasonal cycle.

They raised three crops in a year – (i) The *Aus* (*Ahu*) or early crop, (ii) the *Amon* (*Sali*) and (iii) *Asra* or *Bao*. Of these *Sali* was the largest grown crop.

They also cultivated other crops like maize, millet, sesame, sugarcane, pulses, *kalaimah,* linseed castor, mustard and vegetable like pumpkin, gourd, brinjal, chilly, ginger etc.; cotton, jute, hemp and tobacco were also cultivated. Particularly, cotton was their most important cash crop. Fruits like pineapple, orange were cultivated on the slopes of the hills. Bamboo grooves found surrounded within the boundary of their homestead and the fruits like mango, guava, and jackfruit along with betel nut were very common.

Towards the later part of Dimasa rule, some agricultural corporate bodies of voluntary membership were formed called *Khels* (unit) which brought the uncultivated lands under cultivation. Some associations were also formed for leasing of fisheries, catching of elephants etc. These also include Hindus, Muslims, Nagas, Bengalis, Kukis etc along with the Dimasas.

Live Stock: Pigs, buffaloes, cows, goats, and birds were used for consumptions and for sacrifices in socio-religious ceremonies and festivals. The hill Dimasas of North Cachar kept *Mithang* or *Methone,* dogs, pigs, cats and even deer and birds like ducks, pigeons, fowls etc. but not cows. The *Saraniya* section (those who were hinduised) kept fowls but not pigs. They kept ponies and elephants for trading.

Fishing and Hunting: Fishing is practised with different techniques. Various kinds of indigenous fishing gears made up of bamboo and metal were used like *labber* or pointed iron rods for piercing big fishes ; *Nakhulu* for fishing trap, net etc. Particularly, females were engaged and expert in fishing and males were in hunting. They hunted wild animals like *mirimsa* (wild deer), *Moso* or *Sarpohu* and *metna* or hill cow etc. and birds. The Dimasas used to catch wild elephants, *miyung* and *goray* or horses. The wild elephants were caught by hunting system called *Kheda*.

Cottage industries: *Eri* or *endi* (*Attacus ricini*), *Muga* (*Anthera assamensis*), cotton clothes etc., were their cottage industries. These were practised only by the women along with the art of dying and embroidery by using different wild herbs known to them.

The Dimasa man-folks were expert in basketry. They made different types of necessary household articles like mats, baskets, fishing traps from bamboo and cane. *Khailem*, a basket with layers for keeping valuable articles; *Yamsa Naonaslao*, a decorated bamboo mat to be used on special occasions, *Dikhankara*, a basket for carrying firewood on back, *Longkhai*, a basket for carrying paddy, *Samtho-remin* a wooden paddy husker with husking stick, *Shangkon*, a bamboo fan, *Rangdon* and *Mairong photho* for weighing rice and paddy, *Do-katlai* a weighing scale etc. were some important household articles made by them. *Laothai* a kind of pot made by dried gourd for storing water and rice beer was used. When a handle was fixed, it called *Daimai*. *Laothaisa* was another kind of gourd pot used in offering rice beer in religious and social functions. In addition to those carpentry, black-smithy, iron-smithy, gold washing, gold smithy and salt making were their important industries. It seems that Sonowal, Thengal and Tiruwal Kacharis were workers of gold, silver and iron respectively. The gold washers of Ahom kingdom belonged to the Kacharis. Gold was extracted out from the rivers like Subansiri, Dikrong, Lohit, Dihing, Seese Tengapani etc. Not only gold, there were mines of iron near the hill side of Jaidam and Tengapani and

Gharghar River. Silver, copper and salt were also produced. Making of images from pure gold, during the reigns of Dimasa king, like Bikramadityapha showed that gold was found extensively within the Dimasa kingdom.

Amusements: Besides fishing and hunting the Dimasas were engaged in dancing, singing and playing on musical instruments. Some of the instruments were *Muri*, a long wooden bamboo pipe, flutes like *Suphin* and *Muri-wathisa* etc. made of bamboo. *Khram* or drum and a kind of string instruments called *Khram-dubang* made of weeds. The flute players entertained the villagers every evening accompanied by drummers.

Bisu or *Busu* was the most important social festival celebrated after the harvest, when they took the first autumnal rice. The feast organised on this occasion was accompanied by merry making, dancing and singing. Another festival *Hangseow* is continued for seven days. The village headman prayed to Siva by singing devotional songs seeking more production of grains.

Some popular games like *Panthaomalo khabala i.e.,* jackfruit thief game, *Balibathang* a game similar to *Kabadi, Ramannibaiba* or pushing the bamboo pole on two sides by two players etc were played by the Dimasa people.

Trade and Commerce: During the reign of Dimasa king, external trade with Tripura, Manipur, Burma, Bengal, Syllhet and Dacca were carried out by land and water routes. The articles for trade and commerce were generally food staff, forest products, animals, and mineral products, silk and salt etc.

Wild elephants were captured and sold after proper training. There were two varieties of elephant viz. *Kumeriah* and *Mirgia. Doasla* or *Nasib* was a cross-breed between the above two classes. These were sold at high rates.

Timber and some valuable woods like sandal along with cane, ivory, cotton, silk etc. were exported to Bengal. The timbers were exported by water route from river Surma to

Bengal. The timbers sold in Cachar were classified into three, i.e. Gundah, Dum and Kari, used for posts, beams and boats. Considerable quantities of dried fishes, betel nut, *tezpata* (*Malabathrum*) were exported to Manipur.

Buffaloes and ponies were brought from Manipur and Burma for selling at the annual *Mela* at Silchar. It was visited by traders from Sylhet and Dacca. From Dimapur articles of pottery, weaving clothes etc. were supplied to Golaghat and Rangpur in the Ahom kingdom. In the vicinity of Dimasa border towards Kopilimukh at Rangrung, that is within Tripura kingdom, a market is held where Dimasa, Manipuri, Kuki and Tripuri traders met. The Dimasa carried goats, birds, dry fishes, rice, salt, oil, molasses, tobacco etc. Manipuri brought *Chak Chaki*, a kind of metal dish, *Khesh Kapur*, a cotton cloth etc. Tripuris carried brass, salt, oil, dried fishes. Kukis sold bison, ivory, black peeper, betel nut, and leaf, paddy, cotton, gourd, ginger, melon, brinjal etc. to the market. But it is to be noted that before the Burmese invasion trading in edible products were not encouraged in the society. During Burmese invasion, they started to sell these commodities to the Burmese soldiers in their camp and so the system of brisk trade in food staffs started in the Dimasa kingdom. They also practised an intermediary trade in iron weapons and implements with Zemi, Liangmei, and Rengma Nagas. Some other articles like shawls, spears, ivory armlets, brass utensils were also exchanged between Dimasas and Nagas. To carry out this trade, the transportation through rivers like Dhansiri, Langting, Mahur, Dayang and Kopili were used as chief channels.

13

Marriage Among the Dimasas

— ***Birinchi Kumar Medhi* and *Arifur Zaman***

The prehistoric past of Assam is still a matter of conjecture, in the absence of adequate authentic information. Whatever might be the case of the prehistoric times, it is a known fact that, from early distant past, Assam was like a highway connecting the rest of India with South East Asia, through which passed peoples of diverse ethnic groups, who had different cultural entities and spoke various languages. Most of them not only left behind cultural remnants in this land, but also contributed towards the ethnic composition of the peoples (Das, 1967). Assam is the abode of a good number of tribes, most of which live in the plain areas of the State. Numerically, the Bodo occupy the first position among the tribes of Assam. Their identity is not uniform as an ethnic group. Different names are used to designate the Bodos of different origins and history.

The Dimasa Kacharis belong to the Bodo group of people which, besides the Dimasas, includes the Bodo Kacharis, Rabhas, Lalungs, Tipperahs, Meches, Koches, Chutias, and the Morans (Bordoloi, 1984). They live in the hills as well as in the plains of Assam. North Cachar hill district is the principal habitat of the tribe; they are also found in small groups in Karbi Anglong and Silchar and Karimganj districts of Assam. The Dimasas living in the Barak Valley for generations are known as Barmans.

The word Dimasa literally means 'the son of the big river' —*di* means water, *ma* means big and *sa* means son or descendant. It is worthwhile to mention here that Brahmaputra is the biggest river of Assam. The Dimasas may consider themselves as the offspring of the Brahmaputra River. However, different scholars opine differently on the origin of the term Dimasa. Linguistically they belong to the Tibeto-Burman group. The Dimasas are sometimes referred to as Dimasa Kacharis. The present chapter directs its effort to elicit out some aspects of the marriage system of the Dimasas.

Cultural Universe

Basically, the Dimasas are hill dwellers. They establish their villages on the hill slopes. In such a village a cluster of pile dwellings arranged in linear pattern is seen.

The Dimasas, living in the plain areas, construct their houses on earthen plinths. Agriculture is their mainstay. In the hill slopes, they practise shifting cultivation and produce varieties of crops and vegetables in a single plot of land. In the plains they principally earn their livelihood through settled cultivation. Both in hills as well as in plains, paddy is the main crop of the Dimasas.

They domesticate a few animals and birds like buffalo, goat, pig, duck, fowl, etc. The buffaloes are let loose in the nearby forests and only in the time of necessity they are taken to the respective residences. Besides the animals and birds, they domesticate an insect known as *endi* (*Philosomia ricini*). The Dimasa women weave warm clothes from the yarn extracted from the cocoons of *Philosomia ricini*. The art of spinning, dyeing, weaving and sericulture has long been known to the Dimasa women. According to Hagzer (1974), due to the domesticated pigs, most of the Dimasa villages remain dirty. However, the Dimasas of Barak Valley do not domesticate fowls and pigs.

It has been already stated that the Dimasa women are expert in weaving. A girl who does not know the art of weaving can hardly be tied in marriage in the society. The Dimasa man folks are adept in bamboo, and cane-work; they make different kinds of baskets for different purposes, the durability and strength of which are notable.

The Dimasas are animists by religion and believe in a good number of benevolent and malevolent deities. Almost all the Dimasa festivals are indispensably related to their principal occupation, i.e., agriculture. *Rajini gabra* and *Harini gabra* are their main festivals, which are annually performed before the starting of agricultural activities for the year. In those festivals. the main gate in the entrance of the village is closed and the village headman (*kunang*) propitiates the relevant deities for safety and prosperity of man, domesticated animal, property and crop. During the celebration of the said festivals, if any alien enters the village, the entire festival is abandoned and it has to be performed again in another day of that year. *Basu* is their harvesting festival, in which the village entrance is adorned with a meticulously constructed gate.

Marriage Regulations

There is no definition which adequately covers all types of human marriage. It is an institution of society, which can have very different implications in different cultures. Broadly speaking, however, marriage may be defined as 'a socially sanctioned relationship, involving two or more people of the opposite sex, whose relationship is expected to endure beyond the time required for gestation and the birth of children. The marriage is not co-extensive with sex life and excludes relationship with prostitutes or any other sexual relationship which is viewed as casual and not sanctioned by custom, law or church' (Mitchell, 1970). Marriage is an integral culture complex of each society and is the preferred medium to establish the family. Beals and Hoijer (1953) write, 'It seems, marriage is, everywhere, a set of cultural patterns to sanction parenthood and to provide a stable background for the care and rearing of children. It is, in effect, the major mechanism to insure the continuation of the family and other groupings based on 'kinship'.

Though marriage is a common feature of every society, whereas, the norms, values and rituals related to it are different in different societies. 'All societies have faced the problem of reconciling the need of controlling sex, with that of giving it adequate expression, and all have solved it by some combination of cultural taboos, permissions and injunctions' (Murdock, 1965). The Dimasas also have a pristine complicated set of taboos, preferences and prohibitions, integral to marriage.

The Dimasa tribe is divided into a number of male and female clans; the male clans are known as *sengphong* and the female clan as *zuluk*. Among them, the daughters of a family are included into the mother's clan, while the sons get membership of the father's clan. Presence of male and female clans provides conspicuous dimensions to the social structure of the Dimasas. The clans are strictly exogamous and a person is tabooed to marry in his father's and mother's clan. However, a boy can marry from the clan of father's mother. If the rule of clan exogamy is not violated, cross-cousin marriage is permitted. 'All societies provide, in their cultures, some means of regulating marriage in respect of consanguine relationships, already in existence, presumably so that the marriages of members of family groupings will disturb inter-familial harmony and cooperation as little as possible. Such devices are known as incest regulation, that is, the forbidding of marriage between designated categories of consanguine kin, or, less often, the requirement that marriage may be contracted only between members of certain kin groupings' (Beals and Hoijer, 1953). The Dimasas rigidly follow the rule of clan exogamy and breach of this taboo leads to ex-communication. There is traditional stricture in the Dimasa society not to marry outside the tribe. A person, who violates this rule, has no place in the society.

Monogamy is the preferred type of marriage among the Dimasas, although polygyny is also not restricted. Polygyny is a rare case in the Dimasa society, however. They practise both junior levirate and junior sororate types of marriages.

Child marriage is not known and widow marriage is not prohibited among them. Divorce, which is rather rare in the Dimasa society, can be obtained only through the approval of village head man and the village elders. Generally, due to incompatibility between the spouses, conjugal infidelity, unfaithfulness, etc. divorce may take place with due permission of the head man and elders of the village. Divorced woman is allowed to marry again if the rule of exogamy is not violated.

Marriage, by negotiation, is the norm of marriage among the Dimasas. Before finalising a marriage, based on negotiation, consent of the boy and the girl is always taken into consideration. Marriage by elopement is also not uncommon among them. A couple, living as husband and wife after elopement, is accepted by the society, only after a formal marriage held later at a convenient date.

Marriage Negotiation

Marriage by negotiation, is associated with elaborate rituals among the Dimasas. First step of it is known as *sandidang singba.* In this step of the ritual, the boy's father along with some of his male kins visit the girl's house informing ahead about their venture. The party carries about one kilogram salt making a bundle in plantain leaves tied with seven cotton threads. Both the parties talk about the boy and the girl and possibility of marriage in riddle like language. An example of such conversation will give an idea about the frolic loving Dimasas:

Boy's party : We come here crossing seven hills and seven rivers.

Girl's party : Why have you come from such a distance? What is your intention?

Boy's party : What do describe? Broadcasting of brinjal seeds should be followed by transplantation of saplings; likewise after broadcasting of chili seeds also it is

> necessary to transplant seedlings. If we give birth to sons and daughters, boys should be tied with wives; girls should be given to husbands. We have searched in good number of households. Where will we go? If we think throughout the day, we locate your house. If we think the whole night, then also we find your house. Somebody tells us that here is a girl, who is grown-up, in your lap.

The girl's party replies that their girl does not know any household work; they also do not have the economic strength to perform a marriage. After saying so also if they accept the packet of salt, it means the acceptance of the proposal. Refusal of acceptance, the same means the rejection of the proposal.

After a few days of *Sandidang singba,* the second step of negotiation is performed, which is known as *Laothai langba.* In this ritual, country liquor (*ju*) in four small gourd containers, locally known as *laothai,* has to be taken by the boy's party to the girl's house. From the gourd containers, i.e., *laothai,* the ritual acquired its name as *laothai langba.* Along with a few male co-villagers, the boy's father goes to the girl's house. They offer the country liquor to the girl's father, if the girl's father is dead, the containers full of rice beer are offered to the eldest male member of the girl's household. The party is warmly received by a group of male and female co-villagers in the girl's house. Both the parties discuss about performance of intended marriage and fix another date for further discussion. The assembled people are entertained with a feast by the girl's family. On the fixed date, the boy's party again visits the girl's house for the third time. This time the party carried rice-beer only in two gourd containers. A group, consisting of girl's kins and co-villagers, receives the boy's party. Both the parties discuss about the bride-price *(kalti).* It is customary among the Dimasas to pay bride-price in marriage. The date of marriage is also fixed in that sitting.

The marriage is generally performed, within a month, from the second step of negotiation.

Marriage Ceremony

Before the day of marriage, a few adult persons from the boy's side, visit the bride's house and enquire about their condition. This visit is known as *gulum gasa,* where the boy's party enquires about the physical and mental conditions of the girl's kin. If in her family, somebody is seriously ill, or if the family is suffering from some kind of natural calamity, then the marriage is postponed. If everything is alright in the girl's family, the boy's party goes to the girl's house in the morning of the marriage day. Prior to the venture, the groom's father appeases the deities by sacrificing a fowl's egg, which is known as *mayofa garba.* They take a pig along with them and the groom's father sacrifices it at the entrance of the bride's village to propitiate the benevolent spirits. This ritual is known as *mido garba.* Generally, the bride is not taken out of the house at the time of marriage. However, it is customary among the Dimasas to ritually tie the bride to the groom before the mid day. The groom's father goes inside the bride's house and offers the bride-price in her hand. This ritual is known as *yaopara.*

In the courtyard of the bride's house, the bride's and the groom's parties sit in two directions making two conspicuous groups. Senior primary kins of the groom sit close to him, while the senior primary kins of the bride, sit in the front row of the bride's group. The groom bows down to all the seniors of both the parties starting from his parents. Then the bride's father announces that from that day onward his daughter will be the family member of the groom's family. This ritual is known as *yaopaba.* After that the groom is taken inside the bride's house. The groom is tabooed to meet the bride on that day. On the next day only, he is allowed to meet the bride in the innermost cooking place of the house.

On the day of marriage, the groom's party leaves the bride's village. The lone groom has to stay for a few days in the bride's house. Spending a few days at the bride's house, the groom returns to his village with his wife and her few kins. The occasion is known as *firasah*. On the way, the couple propitiates the deities seeking their blessings. This ritual is known as *maiyaofargaba*. A feast is arranged in the groom's house to mark the occasion. After relishing the feast, the bride's kins return to their natal village.

Concluding Remarks

'Every kind of human grouping comes into being, and is maintained, through a process of recruitment by which various persons become its members. In every human family, the majority of the members are recruited into it by being born into it. But before children can be born, some women (in patrilocal societies, men in matrilocal societies) must be recruited into it. A family comes into being through such a communication of spouses. Marriage is the socially recognised from such recruitment through communication' (Majumdar and Madan, 1997). In brief, marriage is the institution which admits men and women to family life. It is more or less, a stable relationship, in which one or more men and one or more women are socially permitted to have children, implying the right to sexual relations.

The principal motive to perform marriage is common to all societies, but the integral traits of marriage vary from society to society. The Dimasas also have a pristine system of marriage, which is somewhat complicated due to the presence of bilineal descent. Marriage by negotiation is the preferred practice among the Dimasas, which is performed only with the consent of the boy and the girl. The Dimasas parents never compel their offspring's to marry against their will. Marriage is the mentionable occasion, among them where all people of bride's and groom's societies, irrespective of age and sex, enjoy a few days by drinking rice beer, relishing feasts, chatting and merry-making.

The Dimasas invariably perform marriages in the months of *Aghon* (November-December), *Puh* (December-January) and

Magh (January-February). It has been already stated that the mainstay of the Dimasas is agriculture, and after harvesting paddy in the month of *Aghon* only they get leisure to perform marriage ceremony. They believe three particular days of the week are inauspicious and carefully avoid Thursday, Saturday and Sunday for the celebration of marriage. Rice beer is an indispensable ingredient of the Dimasa marriage, where plenty of it is consumed by the attendees irrespective of sex and age. The bride's and the groom's societies are united through a marriage to establish a family of procreation.

According to Hagzer (1974), the Dimasa females are more laborious than their male counterpart. A girl performs a good number of household and agricultural duties, and therefore, she is considered as an asset of the family. Parting of a girl through marriage is, therefore, has to be compensated through bride price by the boy's family. Bride price varies from Rs. 200 to Rs. 500 according to economic status of the boy's family. Residence, after marriage, is patrilocal among them; however, if both the parties agree, a son-in-law can live as a member of his father-in-law's family. This system is known as *minihawaba*.

After the bride enters the groom's house, the principal events of a marriage come to an end. Within a few days after marriage, the newly wedded girl is transformed to a common house wife. She becomes the part and parcel of the husband's household and works for that family in the house and agricultural field, instead of doing work in her family of orientation.

REFERENCES

Beals, R.L. and H. Hoijer., 1953, *An Introduction to Anthropology*. Macmillan Publishing Co, New York.

Bordoloi, B.N., 1984, *The Dimasa Kacharis of Assam*. Tribal Research Institute, Guwahati, Assam.

Das, B. M., 1967, "A Note on the Races of Assam". *Kamrupa*, Souvenir XII Session of All India Science Teachers' Association. Guwahati.

Hagzer, N., 1974, *Dimasa*. Asom Sahitya Sabha, Chandrakanta Handique Bhawan, Jorhat, Assam.

Majumdar, D.N. and T.N. Madan., 1997, *An Introduction of Social Anthropology*. Mayoor Paperbacks, Noida.

Mitchell, G. D., 1970, *A Dictionary of Sociology*. Routdledge and Kegan Paul, London.

Murdock, G. P., 1965, *Social Anthropology*, Collier-Macmillan-Canada Ltd. Toronto.

14

The Dynamics of Death—The Social Dimensions of Funeral Traditions of Karbis

— *Upala Barua*

Death rituals are as old as the civilisation itself. Archaeologists have discovered burial grounds of Neanderthal man, dating back to 60,000 years BC with animal antlers on the body and flower fragments next to the corpse indicating some types of ritual and gifts of remembrance. Every culture and civilisation attends to the proper care of their dead. An analysis of the stage of life cycle presents three common features, (1) some types of funeral rites, rituals, and ceremonies, (2) a sacred place for the dead and (3) The memorials in the name of the dead.

Funeral infers the post death activities, performed by a family, that may include any type of meaningful ceremony to commemorate the life of the deceased. There are controversies leading to the basic objectives of funerals. A seven-point list is prepared by Rosted (2002), which indicates that:

- A funeral helps confirm the reality and finality of death.
- Provides a climate of mourning and the expression of grief.
- Allows the sorrows of one to become the sorrows of all.
- Is the only time when love is given and not expected in return.

- Is a vehicle for the community to pay its respects.
- Encourages the affirmation of religious faith.
- Is a declaration that a life has been lived, as well as a sociological statement that a death has occurred.

For Gluckmann (1937), mortuary customs impose on the survivors, not only certain modes of behaviour but also the simulation of certain emotions, which may or may not be felt. Radcliff Brown, while talking about mortuary customs, makes it clear that, the mortuary customs as modes of social behaviour are concerned not with the dead man's own individual personality or his personal relations with his survivors. They deal with his social personality, the ideal position which he occupied in the society. Following Tylor, those who regard the contents of the rites and beliefs and observances as the primary phenomena of ancestor worship, necessarily, seek to interpret it as a product of eschatological ideas and of doctrines about the souls and spirits. Others follow Malinowski (1925) and seek an explanation in the need for emotional reassurance against the loss and against the dread of annihilation.

The mortuary practices of the Karbis—a tribe of Assam living in Karbi Anglong district—are very widely known today, because of the elaborate performances. Survey and analysis show that—mortuary practices, in other Karbi locations—especially in plains—vary significantly. There are variations, in respect of the rites and rituals, performed by the Karbis living in plains. A burial of this community takes place in discrete cemeteries. The present chapter is an attempt to record the mortuary practices of the Karbis living in plains.

To record a complete account of their rites, necessitated witnessing of many funeral rites, in several villages as the custom differs at the death of different persons, depending upon age, sex, and social standing. To obtain their explanations and superstitions, long discussions were carried on with the village elders. This is not an easy task, as they do not like to talk about their dead all the time.

Concept of Death

Death is looked upon as a mysterious event by the Karbis and its suddenness always creates fear unto the living. The cause of death is an important indicator, which determines the nature of death rituals to be performed. This is always left to be decided by the religious priest – *Kathar* and consultation is also done with the administrative head *Bangthai*; but the final decision is of *Kathar*'s. From their elaborate mortuary rituals, coupled with the formal erection of megaliths in the name of the deceased establishes their belief that the death is a process, by which the soul get shifted from its mundane state to the other world of the dead. Thus, for the Karbis, the death is a transition of the soul of the dead and goes to the other spirit, a world where its ancestors or relatives reside. For them the death is not the end of a person's existence. The spirit of the deceased will continue to influence the lives of his living relatives with blessings or curses depending on how he was treated by the living.

Their concept of death is closely associated with Hindu concept where *Baikuntha* (the abode of Lord Vishnu) and the *Narak* (the hell) have also found a place as an abode of death. The traditional *Jom Recho* or the *Jom Raja* is regarded as the lord of spirits who rules the *Jom Arong* – his abode beneath the ground where the dead spirits reside. The entry of the deceased's soul to the *Joma's* place is subject to the detailed performance of the rituals by the relatives of the deceased. Unless these rituals satisfy the *Jom*, the entry is prohibited and the soul has to wander around. It is because of this belief that the Karbis are very careful in the performance of the death rituals.

Like in any other society, the Karbis also differentiate death according to the nature of its occurrence. Two broad categories are: (i) natural death and (ii) unnatural death. Natural death is looked upon as a normal and good sign, while unnatural death is regarded as an omen. It is believed that such death occurs to a sinful person and such death is mated to the person according to the sins committed by the person during his lifetime. Deaths due to suicide, epidemic, accidents etc are regarded as unnatural deaths. They have separate provisions for dealing with such unnatural deaths, which are not usually elaborate.

The unnatural death is looked upon as bad death and is looked upon as an ominous sign for the family of the deceased. The body, in such cases, is taken to a separate cemetery, not the community cemetery, and left there to get decomposed. The bereaved families are supposed to perform some additional rites, over and above what is prescribed for normal death, so as to get rid of impending danger.

Concept of Soul

The Karbi concept of soul is somewhat similar to that of the Hindus. They differentiate body from soul; believe on a life of the soul after death and rebirth. At any stage of its life, the soul is believed to have bearings on its family, especially at the initial stage of its migration from the body. The family members perform various rites to make it free from various types of evil spirits that may come on its way to its heavenly abode. This belief in the world of spirits rests on the actual fact that a dead person continues to affect society (Brown, 1922); the soul is considered as a sacred entity and assumed as having supernatural power. Sometimes, the soul is also invited to solve some earthly problems. The soul, after death, migrates to its predetermined abode and later takes rebirth. Rebirth is again subject to successful performance of the death rituals, and more importantly, the *shraddha* ceremony. The soul may take rebirth in any form and usually believed to come back to its society, while the Hill Karbis believe, that it takes rebirth in its own family.

Erection of Megaliths etc. and Journeys of Soul

The traditional belief is that the soul during its lifetime visits its family and society on different occasions. A separate place, outside the village, is kept reserved as resting place or transit camp of the soul. The place is called *silputa* (i.e., a place where memorial stones are erected). Here, the families erect, permanent monoliths or megaliths in memory of the dead and on the pedestal of each megalith or monolith, place a flat stone for resting of the soul during it's to and fro journey. It is the place where they provide food and other items that were loved by the departed annually.

Pre Crematory Preparation of the Body

For a full understanding of the mortuary customs of a community, we require to examine the detailed information, regarding the prescribed rules of behaviour. Information on this point has been recorded by various writers on the hill Karbis, but information about the plains Karbis is scanty. Despite the fact that, this account is based on the observed data in various plains of the Karbi villages, I would suggest that a more detailed studies could be profitably be made.

The death of a person is first confirmed by the *Baidya* (medicine man) or the *Kabiraj* of the village or very often the elders. Once it is confirmed, the formal announcement is made and then all relatives are informed of the death and if possible pay their respects to the dead. The essence of the funeral that is to follow is that it brings together all the kins. People, especially, the village elders assemble in the deceased's house. Then arrangement is made to bring out the body of the person died. Like in case of the Hindus, the Karbis also consider basil leave (*Ocimum sanctum*) very sacred. Water purified with sacred basil leaves is used to clean a place outside the residence, where the body will be kept till it is ready for the last journey to the cemetery. A bamboo cot is spread in the specific place and thereafter the body is brought out. The corpse is also purified with the sacred basil water and then clothed with a fresh *dhoti* if it is a man or otherwise a *mekhala*. Usually body is not kept in that position for long. But if in case, some important relatives are supposed to arrive to give the final respect to the diseased, the body is kept for some time. Necessary food, etc., is served to the deceased during this period along with the *Har* (the country liquor). The relative of the deceased may offer him or her food articles that the deceased loved during his lifetime. This offering of the food article is done using the left hand perhaps to differentiate giving to a living being and to a dead one.

Outside the house, the young males prepare a corpse carrier. The items are one tough bamboo and a roughly woven bamboo mat commonly called the *dhari*. The corpse is then tied to the bamboo firmly so that it does not get lose on its way to cemetery. The Karbis in plains are identified by their *khel* system. Each village has its own *khel* to which usually every villager is a member. Some villagers, however, may be members of *khels* of their original village or some may leave their village *khel* due to dispute and take membership of *khels* of a nearby village. Such things happen in minor proportion. All administrative and judiciary power of the village rests with the *khel*. The deceased cannot be taken to cremation if he/she does not belong to the *khel* of the village. One representative of the *khel* to which he/she belong, shall have to come to the village and allow it to be taken to *thiri* (cemetery). At this stage, the deceased is also offered with betel nut and betel leaf.

The Cremation

In the meantime, the cremation ground is prepared by some village people. Usually, the elders take the lead in preparing the pyre. The system of preparing the pyre is, more or less, similar to that of the Hindus. It is prepared in North –South direction.

The sons and the young boys of the village than pull up the corpse and make seven rounds around the house and in each round, the corpse is made to touch the wall of the main house to give him/her the last touch of his house where he lived during his life time. In some cases the number of rounds is reduced to three. The body is then taken to the cemetery. The villagers also follow the corpse along with the *Kathar* (priest) who conducts the cremation. There is no bar for the female members to attend the cemetery. On reaching the cemetery, the body is again purified with sacred basil water and then it is placed on the ground after making three rounds around the pyre in east-west direction. Thereafter, the corpse is put up on the pyre. Usually, the body is put in the pyre in the north-south direction and then firewood is placed upon it, in nine strata. Then the pyre is lit up by the family members and other neighbours.

After the cremation is over, people leave the place leaving one aged person behind. But before they reach their village they lit up a fire and jump across it. They believe that, in case any ghost takes shelter in someone's body that would burn up in the fire while jumping across it. The aged person, who was left behind, would then take a thorny branch of tree and draw a line on the ground along the boundary of the pyre chanting a *mantra*. This is the barrier put up between the living and the deceased. This line is not to be crossed by any man – the person beyond that line is no longer a man but becomes a *Debota* (deity).

Post Cremation Rituals

The family of the deceased would take only boiled rice and salt till the third day of the occurrence of death. In certain cases, the number of days is extended to five or seven depending on the wishes of the family. But whatever may be the days, it is usually odd numbered days. Karbi death rites are completely a community affair, right from the cremation to observing *Shraddha*. After the lapse of the period of three, five or seven days, as opted by the family, people of the village gather in the deceased's house on the next day. They bring with them various items like fish, chicken, etc., and start cooking. Among the items prepared, one curry with fish and alkali (*khar*) is a must; that is why the observance is called *Khar Mach*. After preparation of the items, they put all the items in a dish with left hand and place it in one corner of the compound inviting the departed soul to have the food. This is what they call *pinda dan*. The words come from Hindu rites of offering *pindas* to the departed soul – it is similar like the Hinduised practice of offering food to the deceased on the day of *Matshya Sparsha* (touching of fish), although the Hindus perform it after the *shraddha* ceremony. The observation of *Khar-Mach* enables the family of the deceased to come back to normal life. After offering the food to the deceased, all the family members take the food together. The Karbis living in towns perform this ceremony as *Daha* (i.e. rites performed on the tenth day) almost like the Hindus.

Performing *sraddha* is the final death ritual. The belief is that until and unless *sraddha* is performed, the spirit of the deceased could not get a place to reside. There is no hard and fast rule that provides for performing the *sraddha* on a particular day; but it should preferably be within the year of the death. The day for *sraddha* is fixed according to the ability of the family. Although a major part of the cost of performing *sraddha* is borne by the villagers, yet there are certain obligations from the part of the deceased's family also which may be burdensome. This is one reason why the society does not impose a fix date for performing the *sraddha*. The observance, of *sraddha* ceremony among the Hill Karbis, is a far more an elaborate affair, which they call *Chamangkan*. Among the plain Karbis, however, it is simple but they have preserved the ritual of erecting megaliths on the day of *sraddha*.

The *sraddha* is considered as a costly affair, mainly because, its observance requires at least one pig – not small, but a fully grown pig. A pig of such size costs around Rs 2000 to Rs 3000 according to its availability. Spending such a huge amount of cash is not a simple matter. Most of the Karbi villagers are of lower middle-income earning people. In fact, they are simply at the subsistence level of living. The family when decides about the day of *sraddha*, informs and invites the *Kathar* and the *Burha Bangthai* (the administrative head of the village) about the date. The *Bangthai* then engages the *Hariya* (messenger) to inform the villagers about the *sraddha*. The distant relatives of the family are also informed accordingly.

Erection of Megaliths

On the day before the *sraddha* - a young group of people along with the *Kathar* (priest) go to the nearby hills with a pot full of *Harlung* (Karbi rice beer considered as a sacred item) and some coins to find out a pair of typical stones (*Long-dang*) required to erect as monolith and the resting spot. It is a triangular shaped elongated stone with the top getting smaller although not pointed and apparently appears to be flat. Another type of round flat stone is selected so as to make sitting arrangement with it for the soul to take rest. After selection of the stones, these are worshipped offering beer and coin and saying that "......Mr X (the name of the person) has died and for him we will be taking you to *long ae*. Kindly help us taking you there without difficulty". After the ritual, they leave the spot. On the day of *sraddha*, early in the morning, the same group along with others go to the hill and bring the stone already selected. They carry the stone on a carriage made of branches of *Modar* tree (*Erythrinu stricla*) and sugarcane. The stones are brought to a place called *long ae*. This is the place where they erect the stone monuments in memory of the deceased. There are variations in the name of the place. As the stones are called *long dang*, the place name also has the Assamese version – *longdang-guri*.

The elongated stone is then erected straight on the specified ground in the *Long-ae* and this is considered as representing the deceased. If the deceased was a male, the stone is dressed in male attire with a *Paguri* (turban) on the top while a female is dressed in female attire. At the bottom of it, the flat round stone is put up over three small stones like a three legged table. Here the *pinda* (the offerings to a deceased) is offered. Pig and other offerings brought for the ceremony is sacrificed here and the meat and blood is cooked without spices in bamboo cylinders, specially prepared for the ceremony, is offered to the deceased.

The *Shraddha* Ceremony

While this group is working on erecting megaliths, the other i.e. in the family front, the *Kathar* comes in the morning to the residence of the deceased and first purify the residence and then all family members. There is a specific procedure laid down for this purpose. While purifying, apart from basil (*Tulsi)* leaves of two other plants are also used; one of which is called *kuchia kata* and the other is *harha kata*. Another important plant used in the process is known as *Tibung* or *thubong* – a sugar cane like plant (*Phragmatis sara = Khagori* or common reed) found in the jungle. Three *thubongs* are tied in one – with *tangal* (thick bamboo filament or twine); the *sesuks* (the waste of bamboos) produced in the process are not to be wasted but kept separately for use. On the body of the *thubongs* on each joint, the *harha kata* and *kuchia katas* are tied. Then these *thubongs* are placed on one bank of the stream and on the other bank, bamboos prepared specifically for this purpose are fixed in such a way that the top, of both bamboo and *thubong,* touches each other and the structure appears like a gate over the stream. A small round basket of bamboo is than made and hanged from the middle of the joining point of the gate-like structure and the *sesuks* (bamboo waste) and an egg is placed within it. This is the holy egg and is considered as soul.

Next is the purification stage. Each of the members of the family are now to cross the gate-like structure across the stream and on the direction to which the water flows. The *Kathar,* standing on the other side of the gate chants *mantras.* Each member throws the *kuchia kata* behind him or her as he or she crosses the gate. On the other side, a fire is lighted where some aromatic items (*dhuna = Canarium bengalense*) are given and each of the members after crossing the gate take the warmth of the fire on their faces with their hands. Now it is turn of the *Kathar* to examine whether the members are actually purified or not. It is determined through divination. A bamboo cylinder (*chunga*) is prepared and *harha kata* and *kuchia kata* are put inside it. The *chunga* is then cut across, so as to make it in two equal parts. Thereafter, the egg which was put inside the pot is brought back and cut into two pieces with a special knife by the *Kathar*. Then it is checked whether the divisions are symmetrical. Then the two parts of the bamboo cylinder, held in such a way as if it is one piece and suddenly released to the ground. If, of the two parts, one fell showing the face on top and the other giving the back on top, then the purification is taken as complete. Otherwise, the whole exercise is repeated. This is done up to three times. If even after three times, the bamboo parts do fell on the ground showing incomplete purification, then it is taken as incomplete purification. However, the process is not repeated any further.

Each Karbi villagers have a strong and stout post supporting the roof in their kitchen, which is called – *Nang-pe* or popularly known as *mudha khuta*. It is considered as sacred post and so is the kitchen. For them it is the place where *devatas* (deities) reside. The *Kathar* after the *suddhhi* (purification), come to the kitchen and scatter the specially prepared *Pitha Guri* (rice powder) mixed with water on the *Nang-pe* and in all doors of the house. On this day, all the villagers used to bring something for the *shraddha* according to their mite. The pig and other animals sacrificed in the *Long-ae*, (*silputa*) is later brought to the deceased's house. The meat is prepared with the *Damabru* leave.

While the preparation for the *shraddha* feast is going on, the *Kathar* alone or sometimes with another person goes to a silent place nearby to perform the rite called *Jiuli Mata* (inviting the soul). He lights a lamp and calls for the soul of the deceased requesting him/ her to come. He catches an insect there symbolising it as the soul of the deceased and bring it to the house of the deceased and place it on the *Nang-pe-* saying that "I have placed you here. From now onward you will live here". The *Kathar* leaves the insects there and it is believed that from then onwards the soul lives in that place. The Karbis, therefore, believe the kitchens as the most sacred place. After this establishment of the soul, a small portion of all the items cooked are taken to the *long-ae* and all the relatives gift an amount on the platform of the megalith with the left hand and thereafter return home. The *Kathar* chants *mantra* only after completion of the rite feast. Thus *shraddha* is complete.

The problem of life and death happens to be the most burning questions that the mankind has faced since ages. It was not completely in people's consciousness that a person was alive, had lived and then suddenly was no more since he had died. People always like to prolong the existence of a person. The result of this desire is the belief in the spirit – the second life of the soul. It is a type of consolation, because there is no doubt about the physical death. The concept of soul still has not improved much than what Tylor (1871) observed more than a century back *i.e.* the soul is a subtle, immaterial human form, somewhat like steam, air, or a shadow in its nature; it forms the reason for life and thought in that being which it animates.

For the Karbis mortuary practices as discussed above is more an emotional satisfaction than any significant sociological understanding. Belief in spirit is the central theme of the practices. This spirit is figured in their ritual beliefs and practices. Two other things are also made the subject of this ritual. Firstly, there is his body, which must be disposed of in some way. Secondly, there is what Radcliff-Brown and Forde (1950) calls his social personality: "The sum of characteristics by which he has an effect upon the social life and therefore on the social sentiments of others. ...... A person occupies a definite position in society, has a certain share in the social life, and is one of the supports of the network of social relations." He goes on to say that "death constitutes a partial destruction of the social cohesion, the normal social life is disorganised, and the social equilibrium is disturbed. After the death, the society has to organise itself a new and reach a new condition of equilibrium."

REFERENCES

Barua, U., 1994, "Karbi Xokolor Mahapaxan Parampora" (in Assames) *Srimayee,* Special Puja Issue, 1994.

Durkheim, E. 1915. *The Elementary Forms of the Religious Life* (English translation), The Free Press, London.

Firth, R. 1955. *The Fate of the Soul,* Cambridge.

Gluckman, M. 1937. "Mortuary Customs and the Belief in Survival After Death Among the South-Eastern Bantu", *Bantu Studies,* 11, 2 :.117-136.

Malinowski, B., 1954, *Magic, Science and Religion, and Other Essays.* (Reprint) Doubleday. New York.

Radcliff Brown, A.R. and D. Forde., 1950, "Kinship and Marriage among the Ashanti". In A. R. Radcliff- Brown and D. Forde (Eds) : *African Systems of Kinship and Marriage.*

Radcliff Brown, A.R. 1922. *The Andaman Islanders,* The Free Press Glencoe, Cambridge.

Tylor, E. B. 1871. *Primitive Culture,* Vol - II.

15

Somatometric Characters of the Deoris of Assam

— Sarthak Sengupta and *Gitimallika Gogoi*

The Deori is a Scheduled Tribe inhabiting the plain districts of upper Assam. Ethnically, they are affiliated to the Tibeto-Mongoloid tribal group. They were considered as the priestly section and one of the major sub-divisions of the Chutiya (Gait, 1976), a numerically dominant Mongoloid community of Assam. The original habitat of Deori was in Lohit district of Arunachal Pradesh, on the bank of the river Kundil and also in Sadiya, Assam. At present they are mainly found in Lakhimpur, Dhemaji, Dibrugarh, Sibsagar, Jorhat and Shonitpur districts of Assam. According to 2001 Census, their total population was 41,161. There are three sub-divisions or territorial groups of the Deori: the Tengaponiya, the Borgonya, and the Dibongiya. The name of each sub-division owes its origin from a particular river of their original homeland. They are bilingual.

The present chapter is an attempt to find out intra-group differences, in respect of few somatometric characters among three territorial sub-groups of Deori tribe of Assam. Morphological distance, with regard to somatometric characters, was also examined.

Material and Method

The somatometric measurements were taken on 256 adult males (Tengaponiya = 77, Borgonya = 81, Dibongiya = 98) and 272 adult females (Tengaponiya = 79, Borgonya = 90,

Dibongiya = 103). Fifteen absolute linear, curvilinear and ponderal measurements were considered for the present study. Seven indices were calculated from the above measurements. No preference whatsoever was given for the selection of individuals for measurements. The only restriction was, that we avoid measuring more than one individual from the same family, to make the data more representative and to have a bit wide coverage. Persons below the age of 20 years were also excluded for obvious reasons. Crippled or individuals above 55 years of age were also not considered for the measurements. An effort had been made to take into consideration those methods and techniques of measurements suggested by the International Biological Programme, given in Weiner and Lourie (1981) and Sen (1994).

To look at inter-group difference, Hotelling's T^2 test (1953), Sanghvi's T^2 method (1953) were applied. Only the absolute measurements have been included, because indices are on the basis of measurements. Rao (1948) has already pointed out that there is no theoretical justification for treating an index as separate character, in addition to the absolute measurements, from which it is calculated.

Results and Discussions

With regard to stature, the Tengaponiya Deori males are the tallest, whereas the Dibongiya Deori males are the shortest. The mean values of stature shows that only the Tengaponiya male fall in the above medium category, while the Borgonya and Dibongiya Deori male belong to the class medium. The Dibongiya male stands significantly apart from both Tengaponiya and Borgonya males, among whom not much variation is observed. On the other hand, the Borgonya females are the tallest and the females of Dibongiya Deori are the shortest. The mean values of stature, in both Dibongiya and Tengaponiya Deori females, falls in medium category and shows close affinity between each other, and both of them show significantly lower mean value than that of the Borgonya Deori.

The sitting height, of the Borgonya males having the highest mean value, differs significantly from Dibongiya. Similarly, the Borgonya Deori females also have the highest mean value in this regard and stand significantly apart from the Tengaponiya and Dibongiya Deori, who are close to each other in respect of this trait.

With regard to head length, irrespective of sex, different sub-samples of Deori are very similar to one another in having almost uniform mean values in them. The test of significance also does not reveal any significant variation among them. The head breadth in male Tengaponiya is seen to differ from the Borgonya and Dibongiya. In the case of the female, it is noted that the Borgonya and Dibongiya Deori, having lower mean value of head breadth, differ significantly from that of Tengaponiya. The intra-group differences with regard to cephalic index also, are found to be significant in the females, while in male the Tengaponiya only stands significantly apart from the Borgonya. The other values are not significant suggesting similarities among them.

The lowest mean value of head height is observed in the males of Borgonya Deori and thus they stand far apart from each of Tengaponiya and Dibongiya. The female sub-samples are similar to each other in having almost uniform mean values in them. With regard to length height index, except Borgonya X Dibongiya male, the variations, observed among different samples irrespective of sex, are not statistically significant. Similarly, significant differences exist between Borgonya X Dibongiya males, in respect of breadth height index too.

The variation, observed among different Deori sub-samples with regard to bizygomatic breadth, is not statistically significant. Morphological upper face of Borgonya males stand apart from each of Tengaponiya and Dibongiya. On the other hand, the female Tengaponiya showing the lowest mean also significantly differ from the Borgonya and Dibongiya. In both the sexes, the mean value, of morphological upper facial index of Dibongiya Deori, is relatively high in comparison to that in Borgonya and Tengaponiya. The Tengaponiya and Borgonya show a great deal of similarity in this regard. On the other hand, Dibongiya, showing the higher mean value, differs significantly from Tengaponiya and Borgonya. The mean values, of total facial height in all the male sub-samples, do not reveal any significant variation among them. On the contrary, in females, the Tengaponiya, having lower total facial height, differ significantly from Borgonya and Dibongiya. The difference between Borgonya and Dibongiya is also found to be statistically significant. The male Tengaponiya and Borgonya are almost similar to one another with regard to total facial index. However, barring them, all other comparisons turned out to be highly significant.

The mean values, of nasal height in the males of Tengaponiya, Borgonya and Dibongiya, reveal that they are statistically similar to each other. On the other hand, the Tengaponiya female, having the least mean value differs significantly from each of Borgonya and Dibongiya. As regard to mean nasal breadth the male Tengaponiya and Borgonya are similar to each other but striking statistical deviation from them is exhibited by Dibongiya. In females, the Tengaponiya differs from Borgonya and Dibongiya sub-samples, among whom non significant variation is observed. The male Dibongiya only differs from Borgonya male with regard to nasal index. On the other hand, all the female sub-samples of Deori differ from each other and exhibit a good deal of heterogeneity among them.

The Tengaponiya and Borgonya males are similar to one another with regard to girth of thorax, while the Dibongiya stands far apart from them. With regard to mean girth of bicep, it is noted in both the sexes, the Tengaponiya Deori differs significantly from each of Borgonya and Dibongiya. The mean girth of calf in each sex reveals statistically significant differences between Tengaponiya Deori and others. Statistical analysis of variation also records significant differences in horizontal circumference of head between male Tengaponiya X Dibongiya and female Tengaponiya X Borgonya only.

Table 15.1 : Anthropometric Characters of Deori Males

Characters (in cm)	*Tengaponiya (N=77)*			*Borgonya (N=81)*			*Dibongiya (N=98)*		
	Mean +	*S.E*	*S.D*	*Mean +*	*S.E*	*S.D*	*Mean +*	*S.E*	*S.D*
1	*2*	*3*	*4*	*5*	*6*	*7*	*8*	*9*	*10*
Stature	167.29	0.60	5.60	166.53	0.58	5.26	164.22	0.64	6.33
Sitting height	88.04	0.80	3.06	88.38	0.37	3.39	87.14	0.38	3.80
Head length	18.30	0.07	0.65	18.14	0.05	0.51	18.09	0.07	0.78
Head breadth	14.81	0.07	0.62	14.34	0.07	0.69	14.49	0.06	0.56
Head height	13.49	0.13	1.17	13.14	0.10	0.91	13.43	0.07	0.73
Upper facial height	8.27	0.08	0.77	9.04	0.06	8.22	8.28	0.04	0.43
Total facial height	12.68	0.10	0.95	12.60	0.06	0.59	12.62	0.07	0.64
Bizygomatic breadth	13.57	0.08	0.77	13.16	0.06	0.57	12.73	0.07	0.70
Nasal height	6.12	0.06	0.61	6.05	0.03	0.35	6.07	0.03	0.34
Nasal breadth	3.75	0.03	0.31	3.71	0.02	0.25	3.62	0.03	0.29
Girth of thorax	91.22	0.55	4.90	92.61	0.56	5.07	89.51	0.53	5.29
Girth of upper arm	26.29	0.20	1.83	25.71	0.18	1.69	24.42	0.19	1.93
Girth of calf	34.64	0.22	1.98	34.37	0.22	2.00	33.83	0.25	2.43

1	2	3	4	5	6	7	8	9	10
Hor.circum. head	55.97	0.20	1.84	55.49	0.14	1.27	55.26	0.17	1.66
Weight	58.55	0.86	7.63	57.21	0.72	6.53	54.12	0.73	7.14
INDICES									
Cephalic	80.72	0.49	4.34	78.95	0.39	3.53	80.00	0.42	4.13
Length height	73.98	0.78	6.84	72.39	0.58	5.23	74.09	0.42	4.17
Breadth height	91.36	0.84	7.40	91.70	0.72	6.41	92.74	0.54	5.36
Upper facial	65.28	0.32	2.79	64.53	0.31	2.79	65.59	0.29	2.91
Total facial	93.75	0.95	8.32	95.84	0.61	5.43	99.38	0.68	6.71
Nasal	62.05	1.14	9.98	61.45	0.52	4.69	59.74	0.48	4.73
Body Mass	21.00	0.30	2.30	20.60	0.20	1.90	20.00	0.21	2.10

Table 15.2: Anthropometric Characters of Deori Females

Characters (in cm)	*Tengaponiya (N=77)*			*Borgonya (N=81)*			*Dibongiya (N=98)*		
	Mean +	*S.E*	*S.D*	*Mean +*	*S.E*	*S.D*	*Mean +*	*S.E*	*S.D*
1	2	3	4	5	6	7	8	9	10
Stature	154.41	0.52	4.58	156.21	0.50	4.81	153.28	0.58	5.87
Sitting height	81.69	0.52	4.63	83.24	0.26	2.51	82.01	0.27	2.75
Head length	17.51	0.07	0.64	17.50	0.06	0.61	17.44	0.06	0.59
Head breadth	14.27	0.07	0.59	13.77	0.06	0.49	13.92	0.06	0.64
Head height	13.04	0.11	0.99	12.93	0.08	0.86	12.88	0.07	0.68
Upper facial height	7.46	0.09	0.83	7.89	0.05	0.51	7.99	0.04	0.44
Total facial height	11.68	0.09	0.84	12.30	0.07	0.68	12.09	0.06	0.59
Bizygomatic breadth	13.77	0.06	0.53	12.90	0.05	0.50	12.29	0.06	0.59
Nasal height	5.51	0.08	0.67	5.85	0.03	0.35	5.89	0.03	0.31
Nasal breadth	3.52	0.03	0.30	3.41	0.02	0.16	3.37	0.02	0.21
Girth of upper arm	25.14	0.24	2.16	24.13	0.15	1.47	23.80	0.19	1.90
Girth of calf	32.80	0.23	2.08	31.98	0.23	2.20	31.90	0.23	2.30
Hor. circum. head	54.99	0.15	1.35	54.49	0.14	1.40	54.06	0.35	1.63

1	2	3	4	5	6	7	8	9	10
Weight	50.22	0.71	6.27	48.90	0.45	4.31	47.50	0.64	6.60
INDICES									
Cephalic	81.62	0.49	4.41	78.49	0.46	4.45	79.76	0.43	4.41
Length height	74.50	0.66	5.96	74.09	0.51	4.94	73.91	0.39	4.00
Breadth height	91.45	0.86	7.73	93.86	0.62	5.94	92.84	0.57	5.81
Upper facial	63.93	0.49	4.37	63.90	0.39	3.74	66.06	0.24	2.40
Total facial	88.15	0.81	7.24	95.12	0.56	5.36	98.58	0.55	5.61
Nasal	64.59	1.13	10.13	58.57	0.43	4.08	57.38	0.46	4.62
Body Mass	20.95	0.29	2.63	20.05	0.16	1.61	20.20	0.23	2.30

Most of the adult males and females are lean. In each sex, Dibongiya being the lightest differs from the others. The other values are similar to each other. The mean values of body mass index of Dibongiya males is significantly lower than that of the others. On the other hand, the index is significantly higher in Tengaponiya female as compared to Borgonya and Dibongiya females.

Thus, on the basis of the above findings, perhaps it could be said that there exist considerable morphological variations amongst the three Deori sub-groups. The differences in the constitution of a Tengaponiya, Borgonya and Dibongiya are obvious, but at the same time the differences between them do not appear to be racial in nature.

Values for Morphological distance (Hotelling's T^2 test) clearly indicate that in both the sexes, the Borgonya Deori maintains almost similar distance from both Tengaponiya and Dibongiya, whereas the maximum morphological distance is observed between Tengaponiya and Dibongiya. Thus, a deviating tendency among the Dibongiya Deori from the other two sub-groups was noted.

In order to have a better understanding of the ethnic affinity of the Deori tribe of Assam with other neighbouring populations having Mongoloid ethnic affiliation, we have performed univariate students t test and calculated Morphological distance (T^2) as suggested by Sanghvi (1953). The data available on Mongoloid populations from Assam are given in Table 15.3. Inter-group homogeneity test as set out in Table 15.4 reveals that there is considerable variation among these groups. Though geographic proximity of the Sonowal, Jharua, Thengal, Moran, Mishing, Ahom and Khamiyang population to the Deoris of upper Assam leads one to expect some sort of biological interrelationship, but all these population groups, who mostly concentrated in the Districts of upper Assam, appear to be quite different from the Deori tribe. The Chutiya, another cognate group which consider Deoris as their priestly section and one of the major

Table 15.3: Test of Significance : Anthropometric Characters

Characters	*Male*			*Female*		
	T x B	*T x D*	*B x D*	*T x B*	*T x D*	*B x D*
Stature	0.59	3.24*	2.71*	2.49*	1.45	3.82*
Sitting height	1.55	0.00	2.58*	2.66*	0.54	3.28*
Head length	1.86	1.62	0.00	0.11	0.76	0.71
Head breadth	4.65*	3.36*	1.62	5.43*	4.02*	1.53
Head height	2.13*	0.41	2.37*	0.81	1.23	0.47
Upper facial height	7.70*	0.11	10.54*	4.17*	5.38*	1.56
Total facial height	0.69	0.49	0.21	5.44*	3.79*	2.28*
Byzygomatic breadth	4.10*	7.90*	4.66*	11.14*	17.45*	7.81*
Nasal height	0.75	0.45	0.47	3.98*	4.45*	0.94
Nasal breadth	0.83	2.83*	2.50*	3.05*	4.16*	1.42
Girth of thorax	1.77	2.11*	3.89*			
Girth of upper arm	2.04*	6.67*	1.41	3.56*	4.37*	1.36
Girth of calf	0.86	2.43*	1.62	2.52*	2.76*	0.24
Hor.circum.head	1.84	2.59*	1.04	2.43*	1.46	0.16
Weight	1.19	3.96*	3.05*	1.57	2.78*	1.71
INDICES						
Cephalic	2.83*	1.12	0.90	4.65*	2.82*	2.02*
Length height	1.64	0.12	2.37*	0.24	0.77	0.28
Breadth height	0.31	1.38	1.15	2.27*	1.35	1.21
Upper Facial	1.68	0.72	2.49*	0.05	3.90*	4.72*
Total facial	1.85	4.81*	3.87*	7.07*	10.65*	2.74*
Nasal	0.48	1.86	2.41*	4.97*	5.90*	1.89*
Body Mass	1.11	2.73*	2.06*	2.72*	2.03*	0.53

*Indicates significant at 5.0% level of probability

Table 15.4: Values of Morphological Distance* among the Deoris

	Tengaponiya	*Borgonya*	*Dibongiya*
Tengaponiya	-	63.27	106.13
Borgonya	84.88	-	52.58
Dibongiya	211.18	112.82	-

* Hotelling T^2 test

Table 15.5 : Anthropometric Characters: Deori and Other Population Groups

Characters (in cm)	Deori N=256 Mean	S.E.	S.D.	Chutia N=83 Mean	S.E.	S.D.	Moran N=100 Mean	S.E.	S.D.	Sonowal N=111 Mean	S.E.	S.D.
	(Present Study)			(Das et al, 1985)			(Das et al., 1985)			(Phookan,1974)		
Stature	165.77	0.61	9.74	164.11	0.55	5.01	162.97	0.62	6.20	163.46	0 58	6.11
Sitting height	87.80	0.50	7.98	84.13	0.36	3.28	84.59	0.33	3.30	83.99	0.37	3.90
Head length	18.19	0.06	0.96	18.38	0.07	0.64	18.80	0.06	0.60	18.61	0.06	0.65
Head breadth	14.54	0.07	1.12	14.68	0.07	0.64	14.46	0.05	0.50	14.98	0.05	0.53
Head height	13.36	0.10	1.59	13.63	0.18	1.64	13.55	0.13	1.30	13.28	0.12	1.21
Upper facial height	8.52	0.07	1.12	6.76	0.06	0.55	7.29	0 05	0.50	7.12	0.05	0.52
Total facial height	12.63	0.08	1.27	11.59	0.08	0.73	11.98	0.07	0.70	11.92	0.05	0.54
Max. bizyg..breadth	13.12	0.07	1.12	13.44	0.06	0.55	13.39	0.06	0.60	13.99	0.05	0.53
Hor. Cirum..head	55.54	0.17	2.71	55.16	0.21	1.91	55.81	0.15	1.50	55.15	0.15	1.53
Nasal height	6.07	0.04	0.79	5.04	0.05	0.45	5.39	0.04	0.40	5.38	0.03	0.32
Nasal breadth	3.69	0.03	0.47	3.78	0.03	0.27	3.80	0.03	0.30	4.00	0.02	0.26
INDICES												
Cephalic	79.89	0.43	6.88	80.36	0.41	3.73	77.76	0.39	3.90	80.13	0.37	3.95
Upper facial	65.16	0.30	4.80	50.24	0.48	4.37	54.46	0.47	4.70	50.58	0.35	3.73
Total facial	96.56	0.73	11.68	85.83	0.60	5.46	89.44	0.73	7.30	84.96	0.48	5.12
Length-height	73.52	0.57	9.12	74.05	0.90	8.19	72.73	0.68	6.80	70.77	0.60	6.36
Breadth-height	91.99	0.68	10.88	92.66	1.24	11.29	93.88	0.90	9.00	88.58	0.77	8.13
Nasal	60.97	0.69	11.04	75.59	0.90	8.19	70.62	0.55	5.50	75.62	0.61	6.46

Table 15.5 : Anthropometric Characters: Deori and Other Population Groups—(*Contd.*)

Characters (in cm)	*Jharua N=100*			*Thengal N=100*			*Mishing N=100*			*Sonowal N=111*		
	Mean	*S.E.*	*S.D.*	*Mean*	*S.E.*	*S.D.*	*Mean*	*S.E.*	*S.D.*	*Mean*	*S.E.*	*S.D.*
	(Phookan, 1974)			*(Phookan, 1974)*			*(Das et al., 1985)*			*(Das et al., 1985)*		
Stature	163.29	0.62	6.25	161.49	0.56	5.64	161.13	0.50	5.00	162.83	0.62	6.20
Sitting height	83.98	0.34	3.43	83.21	0.02	3.54	84.05	0.29	2.90	84.72	0.40	4.00
Head length	18.56	0.06	0.63	18.10	0.06	0.66	18.63	0.06	0.60	18.24	0.08	0.80
Head breadth	14.82	0.04	0.48	14.86	0.07	0.68	14.78	0.06	0.60	14.88	0.07	0.70
Head height	13.72	0.11	1.09	13.02	0.10	1.03	13.77	0.13	1.30	12.65	0.14	1.40
Upper facial height	7.27	0.05	0.55	6.92	0.04	0.44	7.19	0.05	0.50	8.98	0.05	0.50
Total facial height	12.04	0.07	0.73	11.62	0.06	0.63	11.97	0.06	0.60	11.46	0.06	0.60
Max. bizygo.breadth	13.74	0.04	0.44	13.69	0.04	0.44	13.65	0.06	0.60	13.65	0.05	0.50
Hor. cirum. head	54.83	0.14	1.45	53.93	0.14	1.42	55.94	0.15	1.50	55.45	0.18	1.80
Nasal height	5.40	0.03	0.35	5.73	0.04	0.37	5.28	0.04	0.40	5.27	0.04	0.40
Nasal breadth	3.79	0.03	0.27	3.70	0.02	0.25	3.69	0.02	0.20	3.78	0.03	0.30
INDICES												
Cephalic	79.92	0.39	3.96	82.24	0.44	4.38	79.70	0.31	3.10	81.71	0.45	4.50
Upper facial	52.88	0.40	4.00	50.41	0.35	3.47	51.91	0.46	4.60	50.94	0.32	3.20
Total facial	87.49	0.52	5.21	84.91	0.49	4.91	86.91	0.56	5.60	83.95	0.47	4.70
Length-height	71.59	0.64	6.43	72.09	0.57	5.78	70.99	0.57	5.70	69.05	0.73	7.30
Breadth-height	89.87	0.75	7.49	87.89	0.78	7.82	89.65	0.76	7.60	85.54	0.95	9.50
Nasal	70.57	0.68	6.78	70.67	0.71	7.07	73.21	0.76	7.60	71.67	0.64	6.40

Table 15.5. Anthropometric Characters: Deori and Other Population Groups—(*Contd.*)

Characters (in cm)	*Khamiyang N=85*			*Lalung N=100*			*Boro Kachari N=100*			*Rubha N=300*		
	Mean	*S.E.*	*S.D.*	*Mean*	*S.E.*	*S.D.*	*Mean*	*S.E.*	*S.D.*	*Mean*	*S.E.*	*S.D.*
	(Das & Bhagabati, 1963)			*(Das & Sharma, 1968)*			*(Das, 1960)*			*(Das, 1960)*		
Stature	159.90	0.44	4.05	162.37	0.59	5.98	163.05	0.59	5.94	161.25	0.57	9.87
Sitting height	84.90	0.25	2.30	85.33	0.30	3.03	85.49	0.32	3.24	84.36	0.31	5.36
Head length	18.72	0.04	0.36.	18.68	0.05	0.55	18.69	0.05	0.58	18.85	0.05	0.86
Head breadth	14.56	0.04	0.36	14.21	0.05	0.52	14.33	0.05	0.58	14.20	0.05	0.86
Head height	12.46	0.05	0.46	12.61	0.03	0.32	12.05	0.09	0.91	12.11	0.10	1.73
Upper facial height	6.81	0.03	0.27	6.88	0.05	0.45	6.79	0.04	0.45	6.61	0.05	0.86
Total facial height	11.73	0.05	0.46	11.37	0.06	0.61	11.43	0.06	0.62	11.20	0.05	0.86
Max. bizygo.breadth	13.71	0.03	0.27	13.31	0.06	0.56	13.70	0.04	0.46	13.50	0.04	0.69
Hor. cirum.head	54.91	0.09	0.82	54.20	0.14	1.39	54.08	0.18	1.82	53.56	0.12	2.07
Nasal height	4.98	0.02	0.18	4.96	0.04	0.38	5.00	0.03	0.37	4.76	0.04	0.69
Nasal breadth	3.84	0.02	0.18	3.79	0.03	0.29	3.84	0.02	0.27	3.83	0.03	0.52
INDICES												
Cephalic	78.48	0.26	2.39	76.19	0.33	3.31	76.74	0.31	3.10	55.40	0.28	4.84
Upper facial	49.55	0.62	5.71	50.29	0.55	5.52	49.64	0.35	3.50	48.73	0.35	6.06
Total facial	85.81	0.37	3.40	85.14	0.57	5.66	80.27	0.49	4.90	83.04	0.44	7.62
Length-height	67.02	0.82	7.55	67.54	0.64	6.43	64.38	0.49	4.93	64.45	0.51	8.83
Breadth-height	85.74	0.33	3.03	86.88	0.95	9.47	83.77	0.64	6.47	85.53	0.71	12.29
Nasal	77.26	0.52	4.73	75.92	0.82	8.23	76.99	0.71	7.10	81.52	0.73	12.64

Table 15.5. Anthropometric Characters: Deori and Other Population Groups—(*Contd.*)

Characters (in cm)	Dimasa N=100 (Phookan, 1974)			Karbi N=280 (Deb, 1979)		
	Mean	*S.E.*	*S.D.*	*Mean*	*S.E.*	*S.D.*
Stature	159.87	0.55	5.52	160.57	0.41	6.86
Sitting height	82.85	0.30	3.04	83.23	0.26	4.35
Head length	18.77	0.05	0.54	18.49	0.05	0.83
Head breadth	14.51	0.05	0.53	14.52	0.04	0.66
Head height	13.06	0.10	0.99	12.68	0.09	1.51
Upper facialheight	6.78	0.04	0.45	6.42	0.04	0.66
Total facial height	11.74	0.06	0.62	11.30	0.05	0.83
Max. bizygo. breadth	13.49	0.05	0.46	13.30	0.04	0.66
Hor. cirum.head	54.55	0.14	1.43	55.37	0.13	2.17
Nasal height	5.09	0.03	0.32	4.77	0.03	0.50
Nasal breadth	3.75	0.03	0.25	3.91	0.02	0.33
INDICES						
Cephalic	77.41	0.34	3.39	78.51	0.31	5.18
Upper facial	50.41	0.32	3.22	48.33	0.33	5.52
Total facial	86.92	0.52	5.23	85.08	0.45	7.52
Length-height	69.63	0.49	4.98	68.18	0.56	9.37
Breadth-height	89.88	0.71	7.09	86.78	0.69	11.54
Nasal	74.27	0.61	6.08	81.53	0.36	6.02

Table 15.6 : Anthropometric Characters : test of Significance

Characters	Deori compound with						
	Chutia	Moran	Sonowal	Jharua	Thengal	Mishing	Ahom
Stature	2.03*	3.23*	2.74*	2.85*	5.16*	5.88*	3.38*
Sitting height	5.58*	4.99*	5.73*	5.92*	8.69*	6.48*	4.81*
Head length	1.23	2.57*	4.95*	4.36*	1.06	5.18*	0.50
Head breadth	1.41	0.93	5.11*	3.47*	3.23*	2.60*	3.43*
Head height	0.74	1.15	0.51	1.12	2.40*	2.49*	4.12*
Upper facial height	19.08*	14.30*	17.92*	16.00*	22.19*	17.02*	5.34*
Total facial height	9.19*	6.11*	7.52*	5.55*	10.10*	6.60*	11.70*
Max. bizyg. breadth	3.47*	2.92*	10.11*	7.69*	7.07*	5.75*	6.16*
Hor. circum. head	1.40	1.19	1.72	3.22*	7.31*	1.76	0.36
Nasal height	14.71*	10.78*	13.80*	13.40*	6.01*	13.45*	14.15*
Nasal breadth	0.67	2.59*	8.61*	2.35*	0.27	-	2.12*
INDICES							
Cephalic	0.18	3.66*	0.42	0.05	3.81*	0.35	2.92*
Upper facial	25.76*	18.65*	31.63*	24.56*	32.00*	23.17*	32.42*
Total facial	11.27*	6.85*	13.27*	10.12*	13.25*	10.40*	14.52*
Length-height	0.48	0.89	3.32*	2.25*	1.77	3.12*	4.82*
Breadth-height	0.45	1.64	3.31*	2.09*	3.96*	2.31*	5.52*
Nasal	12.91*	10.90*	15.90*	9.91*	9.79*	11.80*	11.36*

*Indicates statistically significant at 5.0% level of probability.

Table 15.6: Anthropometric Characters : test of Significance—(*Contd.*)

Characters	*Deori compared with*					
	Khamiyang	*Lalung*	*Boro Kachari*	*Rabha*	*Dimasa*	*Karbi*
Stature	7.80*	4.00*	3.20*	5.42*	7.18*	7.07*
Sitting height	5.18*	4.23*	3.48*	5.45*	8.07*	8.11*
Head length	7.35*	6.27*	6.40*	0.58	7.42*	3.84*
Head breadth	0.24	3.83*	2.44*	3.95*	0.34	0.24
Head height	8.05*	7.18*	9.73*	8.84*	2.12*	5.05*
Upper facial height	22.47*	19.06*	23.99*	22.20*	24.13*	26.05*
Total facial height	9.54*	12.60*	12.00*	15.16*	8.90*	14.10*
Max. bizygo. breadth	7.75*	2.06*	7.19*	4.71*	4.30*	2.23*
Hor. Cirum. head	3.27*	6.08*	5.89*	9.51*	4.49*	0.79
Nasal height	24.38*	19.64*	21.40*	20.62*	19.60*	26.00*
Nasal breadth	4.16*	2.35*	4.16*	3.30*	1.41	6.11*
INDICES						
Cephalic	2.80*	6.82*	5.94*	8.75*	4.52*	2.60*
Upper facial	22.66*	23.73*	33.67*	34.71*	33.62*	37.74*
Total facial	13.13*	12.33*	18.52*	15.71*	10.75*	13.38*
Length-height	6.50*	6.97*	12.16*	11.75*	5.17*	6.68*
Breadth-height	8.26*	4.37*	8.80*	6.54*	2.14*	5.37*
Nasal	18.85*	13.01*	16.18*	20.42*	14.44*	26.41*

*Indicates statistically significant at 5.0% level of probability.

sub-divisions, also stand quite distantly apart from them. Population groups from Lower Assam like Boro Kachari, Rabha, Lalung, Karbi and Dimasa exhibit differences with much greater magnitude from the present Deori sample. Morphological distance also corroborates the observation made above.

Table 15. 7: Values of Morphological Distance: Deori and Other Population Groups

Populations compared	*Morphological Distance*	*Standardised Value**
Deori X Chutiya	4.75	7.25
Deori X Moran	3.80	5.80
Deori X Sonowal	5.24	8.00
Deori X Jharua	4.50	6.90
Deori X Thengal	4.85	7.40
Deori X Mishing	4.63	7.10
Deori X Ahom	3.88	5.90
Deori X Khamiyang	6.51	9.90
Deori X Lalung	6.11	9.30
Deori X Boro Kachari	6.55	10.00
Deori X Rabha	6.26	9.60
Deori X Dimasa	5.78	8.80
Deori X Karbi	5.95	9.10

*values are standardised to the maximum value in the series (in this case T = 6.55) which is taken as 10.

REFERENCES

Gait, E., 1976., *History of Assam.* (Revised edition). Thacker Spink and Co. Calcutta.

Hotelling, H., 1953. "Analysis of a Complex Statistical Variable into Principal Components". *Journal of Educational Psychology*, 216. p. 417.

Rao, C.R., 1948 , "The Utilisation of Multiple Measurements in Problems of Biological Classification". *Journal of Royal Statistical Society*. Series – (Methodological) 10 2. p. 181.

Sanghvi, L.D., 1953, "Comparison of Genetical and Morphological Methods for a Study of Biological Difference". *American Journal of Physical Anthropology*. 11 : pp. 385-404.

Sen, T., 1994, A *Guide to Anthropometry*. The World Press Pvt. Ltd., Calcutta.

Weiner, J.S. and J.A. Lourie., 1981, *Practical Human Biology*. Academic Press, London.

Index

C

D